TIMELINE HAWAI'I

Other Books by the Authors

Daniel Harrington
Hanalei: A Kaua'i River Town

Bennett Hymer
Honolulu Stories: Two Centuries of Writing (co-editor)
Big Island Journey: An Illustrated Narrative of the Island of Hawai'i (photo editor)
Hawai'i Looking Back: An Illustrated History of the Islands (co-author)

TIMELINE HAWAI'I
An Illustrated Chronological History
of the Islands

HONOLULU
Star Advertiser
THE PULSE OF PARADISE >>>staradvertiser.com

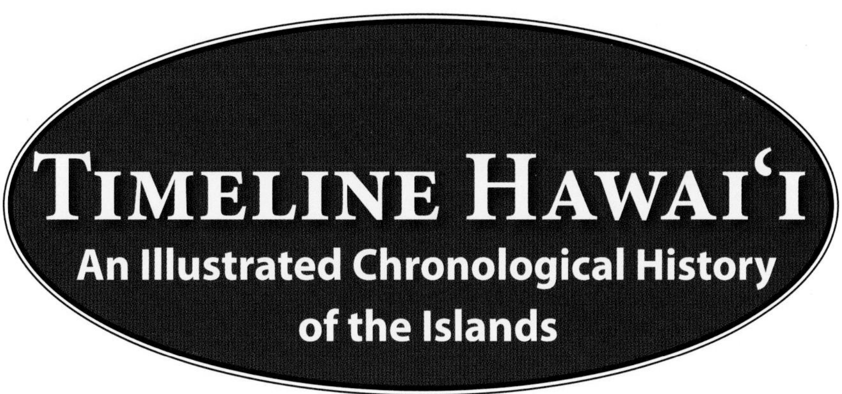

Daniel Harrington

with

Bennett Hymer, editor

Mutual Publishing

DEDICATED TO:

Thomas E. and Nancy J. Harrington
with Aloha

ISBN: 978-1939487-00-1
Library of Congress Control Number: 2013947529
Design by Jane Gillespie

First Printing, November 2013

Mutual Publishing, LLC
1215 Center Street, Suite 210
Honolulu, Hawai'i 96816
Ph: (808) 732-1709 / Fax: (808) 734-4094
e-mail: info@mutualpublishing.com
www.mutualpublishing.com

Printed in China

HISTORIC PERIODS

Colonization

A.D. 300 (±200)—600

Initial arrival and colonization of the Hawaiian archipelago by Polynesians, most likely from the Marquesas Islands about 2,500 miles to the southeast. Relatively little is known about the culture, social customs, and rituals of this time period.

Developmental

A.D. 600—1100

Evolution of food production and acquisition strategies; utilization of plentiful native and Polynesian-introduced resources, including plants, birds, shellfish, and fish (including large game fish); the population reaches an estimated 20,000 people, moving beyond the windward valleys into arid leeward valleys and coastal areas; a unique Hawaiian culture begins to develop.

Expansion

A.D. 1100—1650

Major increase in population; increased agriculture; the first true loko iʻa (fishponds) and the aquaculture techniques used to manage them; development of ahupuaʻa system (natural watershed land divisions extending from the mountains to the sea) with land divisions under the control of sub-chiefs responsible to a paramount chief; and other significant changes in social and political structures.

Protohistoric

A.D. 1650—1778

Further increases in food production, including irrigation in lower valleys; continuing social and political changes with independent chiefdoms competing for rule; changes in architecture of heiau (sacred places of worship), including increasingly large luakini heiau where human sacrifices occur.

Modern

A.D. 1778—Present

Western goods and weapons bring dramatic changes in traditional ways of living; the Hawaiian monarchy is overthrown in 1893; the Hawaiian Islands are annexed to the United States in 1898; sugar becomes the driving force of the economy through the first half of the 1900s; the Islands are increasingly utilized by the U.S. as a strategic military location, and become the 50th state in 1959; tourism grows to eight million annual visitors by 2012.

MAJOR POLITICAL PERIODS

1795—1893	Kingdom of Hawaiʻi
1893—1894	Provisional Government
1894—1900	Republic of Hawaiʻi
1900—1959	Territory of Hawaiʻi
1959—Present	Statehood

TABLE OF CONTENTS

20TH CENTURY 95

21ST CENTURY 161

MINI TIMELINES 171

The *Honolulu Star-Bulletin* traces its roots to the Feb. 1, 1882 founding of the *Evening Bulletin* by J. W. Robertson and Company. In 1912, it merged with the *Hawaiian Star* to become the *Honolulu Star-Bulletin.*

FOREWORD

We at the *Honolulu Star-Advertiser* have been an important part of Hawai'i's history. Both our founding newspapers began publishing as dramatic events were taking place in modern Hawaiian history. In 1856, the *Pacific Commercial Advertiser* started as a weekly newspaper, became a daily in 1882 and was later known as the *Honolulu Advertiser.* In 1913, the *Honolulu Star-Bulletin* was formed when the *Evening Bulletin* merged with the *Hawaiian Star.*

We appreciate the importance of imagery in recording or telling history. In 1989, the *Honolulu Advertiser* published *Hawaii 1959-1989, The First Thirty Years of Statehood,* and in 2009 the *Honolulu Star-Bulletin* celebrated the 50th anniversary of statehood with *Hawai'i 50: Five Decades of Photography.*

Timeline Hawai'i is our latest effort to commemorate Hawai'i's history. Through imagery and chronology this volume tells the island story in pointing out key events and people along with the just highly interesting. It utilizes newspaper headlines and photos from our archives particularly for the recent decades (along with images from Hawai'i's wonderful public archives and private collections).

Our island history is important. Besides telling the story of what happened it is a map for the future, a way to see what may be ahead. Most every issue today that the paper covers has antecedents in the past.

Please enjoy these pages, which can be thumbed through starting and ending at any page or read continuously. You will appreciate Hawai'i even more having a sense of its history. We at the *Star-Advertiser* appreciate being able to continue the storytelling.

— Dennis Francis,
President and Publisher, *Honolulu Star-Advertiser*

STATEHOO
House
Bill to
Honolulu Star-Bulletin
Statehood Extra
Special Radio, Phone Lines Flash News
Sirens, Bells Herald Statehood Arrival
First Class Citizens Now

Fasi Wins Honolulu Mayoralt
FINAL The Honolulu Advertise
It Looks Like Ni
Election in a Nutshell
Contest Tight for President
Statewide Voting
Fasi
In Mc
Demo Support Reaffirmed; Isle Turnout Sets Record

STARADVERTISER.COM
Aloha Friday
MOSTLY SUNNY
THE PULSE of PARADISE
Star-Advertiser
Merrie Monarch 50TH
A GRACEFUL NEW MISS ALOHA HULA
Late-night spots blamed for Ala Moana crime surge
KEEAUMOKU-AREA STABBINGS
Korean combat likely, defense expert says
Kim Jong Un likely "is going to have to start shooting" as the peninsula's tensions escalate

PREFACE

History comes from the memories of those who were there—what they said and wrote down and what photos they took—and keeping this history alive helps us gain a deeper sense of our own past. We are all leafs of a tree, and learning our trunk and roots is a worthy effort. To study history is to study ourselves, seeking to understand the past in order to illuminate the present with a light that also helps us see into the future.

This book covers Hawai'i's rich history and culture from ancient times to the present day by looking at the chronology of its major events and history makers. This book strived to capture the essence of the progression of the changing tides of time over the centuries, and show the events to inspire further pursuit of reading and studying of the many topics covered.

Histories are difficult, even ones that only chronologize major events. There is the constant fact checking, to prevent mixing up events, and persons especially with simliar names. For Hawaiian history, it is easy to lose the Island perspective and important cultural significances particularly for the pre-twentieth century period. When it's covering the modern era and most recent decades, there is not yet a defined collective wisdom indicating what should be considered of lasting importance versus temporary significance.

The project began in 2007 and quickly overtaxed the scope with the staggering amount of information involved and the blending of photos with text. Everything was there but what to finally exclude, or include so as to have the right flow was challenging.

Hawaiian words in this book conform to proper Hawaiian spellings, including diacritical marks. However, to preserve the authenticity of quotes, all directly cited material is presented as originally written.

ACKNOWLEDGMENTS

Many of Mutual Publishing's staff helped on this project as it made its arduous six-year journey to completion. First and foremost, special thanks to Jane Gillespie, Mutual Publishing's production director who guided the melding of text and illustrative material and then some. And to Kate Kincaid, former administrative research assistant who helped edit and input corrections and changes to the many drafts and rewrites. Earlier in the project, Mardee Melton, Jeremy Colvin, and Matthew Martin assisted. Neil Dukas was so kind to share his knowledge of Hawai'i's early military history. Megan Kakimoto assisted with the text on the Hawaiian monarchs.

And of course, deep gratitude to the curators and archivists of collections of historical imagery who keep Hawai'i's illustrated history alive—The Hawai'i Historical Society, the Ray Jerome Baker Room at the Bishop Museum, Hawai'i State Archives, Lyman House Museum, and Hawaiian Mission Children's Society. We never came across a vintage photo we didn't like.

Thanks also to Gay Wong who endured the fallout of the labor pains of finishing this book, and to all other staff members at Mutual Publishing who never became skeptical when we said that the *Timeline* would one day be finished.

INTRODUCTION—OVERVIEW OF HAWAIIAN HISTORY

This timeline covers the major events and persons of Hawaiian history—a history that actually began many millions of years ago nearly 20,000 feet beneath the ocean's surface when magma from deep in the Earth erupted onto the Pacific sea floor to form an undersea volcano which after thousands of centuries of growth, rose above the sea to become an island.

The human side of Hawai'i's story begins with the Polynesians when ambitious sailors in voyaging canoes ventured far from the Southeast Asian Continent to inhabit hundreds of Pacific islands, eventually discovering the Hawaiian Islands, the most remote archipelago on Earth.

By the time British Captain James Cook established Western contact in 1778, the Hawaiians had developed an amazingly rich, unique, and complex culture. Western weapons quickly played a key role in resolving conflicts between Island chiefs, particularly by the rising warrior Kamehameha, who had visited Cook's ship in 1778, and eventually established his rule over all the Islands.

The post-contact era that began with Cook's arrival saw Western explorers, traders, missionaries and military ships coming to the Islands. Hawaiians began their accelerated transition to the modern age with new materials, peoples, values, and standards that changed the traditional Hawaiian way of life abruptly.

Traditional Hawaiian religious beliefs were also eroding, a process that began when Kamehameha II, after Kamehameha I's death on May 8, 1819, ate with the dowager queens Keōpuōlani and Ka'ahumanu, leading to the complete overturning of the kapu system, the glue that held the ancient order together.

By the late 1800s the plantation economy with its major political and economic changes was American owned and influenced with virtually all aspects of life under the control of the "Big Five" sugar companies. In 1893, Hawai'i's sugar plantation owners and American businessmen helped overthrow the Hawaiian monarchy using the backing of American troops aboard the U.S.S. *Boston* ashore in Honolulu. To avoid bloodshed, Queen Lili'uokalani yielded not to the Provisional Government that followed but to the United States government.

U.S. President Cleveland denounced the overthrow and ordered the queen's power restored, but he was succeeded by President McKinley who favored Hawai'i's annexation. When the Spanish-American War spread to the Philippines in 1898, the Islands became strategically important as a coaling base for the United States fleet, and Hawai'i was annexed to the United States as the Territory of Hawai'i.

The rise of sugar had led to the mass immigration of plantation workers from China, Japan, the Philippines, Portugal, Korea, Spain, and Puerto Rico. Their descendants and the intermarriage that occurred between them became the basis of the Islands' "melting pot" culture. Sugar dominated Hawai'i's economy through the first half of the 1900s with lesser contributions from pineapple and tourism. Then, on December 7, 1941, the Japanese attacked Pearl Harbor entering the United States into World War II, and the Islands would change forever. Afterwards, a new political movement was led by returning veterans, particularly Hawai'i's second generation Japanese-Americans, who began the Democratic Revolution of 1954 favoring statehood, labor benefits, land reform, and equality in education.

In 1959, Hawai'i was officially admitted as the 50th state and the start of commercial jet service began to fuel a growing tourism industry. At the time of Statehood, 240,000 tourists were arriving each year, a number that would quadruple in the next decade and then keep growing.

Recent decades have seen a resurgence in traditional Hawaiian cultural knowledge and practices, infusing the Native Hawaiians with a renewed spirit and pride in ancient traditions. Increasing cultural awareness also brought renewed efforts toward resolution of Hawaiian sovereignty issues. In 1993, President Clinton signed a Joint Resolution of Congress (Public Law 103-150), that apologized to Native Hawaiians *"for the overthrow of the Kingdom of Hawaii"* on January 17, 1893. Currently pending in Congress is the Native Hawaiian Reorganization Act (the Akaka Bill), which seeks to provide federal recognition to Native Hawaiians.

Today, Hawai'i is an international destination whose urban centers face the problems of cities and towns everywhere—how to grow without spoiling the present beauty and protecting the environment, and the way of life everyone loves so much.

Ancient Times

ANCIENT TIMES

In the Beginning

"In very ancient times of darkness in the land of Hawai'i Nei, Kāne and Kanaloa arrived at this archipelago called from long ago Hawai'i Nui Kuauli. At that hill called by that ancient name, Kaukamōlī, they established Hōlani Kauhale and the Pae [rows of] Manu'u a Kāne. These people, Pae Manu'u a Kāne, were 'aumākua, called perhaps at this time guardian angels of men."

—Stephen L. Desha, *Kamehameha and his Warrior Kekūhaupi'o*

Kāne rules water and earth; he is the giver of life, and god of all living creatures. Lono is the god of agriculture and fertility, bringing rains, abundant harvests and peace. In the rocks and forests there is Kū, founder and architect, a benevolent god but also a war god. Deep in the ocean is Kanaloa, ruler of the dead and the banished gods.

Along with the four primary gods, there are many lesser gods. One of the most prominent is Pele, the goddess of fire and volcanoes, a creator and also a destroyer. The wife of Kū is Hina, mother of the god Māui who pulled the Hawaiian Islands up from the ocean. Hina's sister is Laka, the goddess of hula.

Origins of the Hawaiian-Emperor Chain

Each of the Hawaiian Islands was born on the seafloor of the Pacific Ocean at the site of the Hawaiian magmatic "hot spot," a stationary plume of magma (molten lava) rising up from deep in the Earth and erupting onto the seafloor to form volcanic islands. For the past 80 million years, this hot spot has created at least 107 volcanoes that now span over the Pacific seafloor for more than 3,100 miles to form the Hawaiian-Emperor Chain, with the Hawaiian Islands at the southwest end.

The Hawaiian Islands are continually carried northwest by the movement of Earth's crust. The southeast coast of Hawai'i Island (the most recently formed island at less than one-half million years old), is currently above one edge of the erupting hot spot plume of lava. The other edge of the magmatic hot spot is located about 18 miles off the southeast coast of the Hawai'i Island, where the newest undersea volcano is forming.

This newest volcano, called Lō'ihi Seamount, is about 3,116 feet below the ocean's surface and rises up more than 9,000 feet from the seafloor. The erupting summit of Lō'ihi should rise above the water between 50,000 to 200,000 years from now to become the next Hawaiian Island.

From 1983 to the present, Kīlauea Volcano on Hawai'i Island has erupted almost continuously, increasing the island's size by more than 370 acres. In 1984, Kīlauea Volcano fountains of lava erupted to heights of more than 1,500 feet.

The Hawaiian Archipelago

The Hawaiian archipelago includes the eight main islands as well as the Northwestern Hawaiian Islands, extending in a line from southeast to northwest for about 1,523 miles. Slicing through the Tropic of Cancer, the Hawaiian Islands extend from Hawai'i Island at about 19° north latitude, to Kure Island at 28.5° north latitude, and from 154° to 179° west longitude.

Ages of the Islands

Island	Age (in millions of years)
Kaua'i	5.1
Ni'ihau	4.9
O'ahu	2.6-3.7
Maui	1.32-.75
Lāna'i	1.28
Kaho'olawe	1.03
Moloka'i	1.76-1.9
Hawai'i	.4-.43

c.4,000 B.C.—Beginning of seafaring migrations from Southeast Asia to South Pacific islands.

c.1,500 B.C.—The Lapita, an ancient Pacific Ocean people, migrate eastward from the Bismarck Archipelago, a group of volcanic islands off the east coast of New Guinea. Their eastward expansion continues an early migration into the Western Pacific from Southeast Asia, and eventually gives rise to the Polynesians.

The Lapita culture, which was known for its distinctive and colorful earthenware pottery, was found through Melanesia to Samoa, Fiji, and Tonga, where many characteristics of Polynesian culture evolved during the first millennium. By the time Hawai'i was settled the use of pottery was replaced by stone adzes and other crafts.

c.1000 B.C.-900 B.C.—Western Polynesia (including Tonga and Samoa) is first settled, and becomes the homeland of the Polynesians who develop a Proto-Polynesian language that produced at least 36 documented Polynesian languages.

c.500 B.C.–A .D. 900— Western Polynesians migrate north, east, and southwest, and settle Eastern Polynesia, including the Marquesas, Society Islands, Austral Islands, Cook Islands, and eventually New Zealand, Easter Island, and the Hawaiian Islands.

c.300–500 A.D.—Polynesian voyagers reach the Hawaiian Islands, probably from the Marquesas Islands, 2,500 miles to the southeast of Hawai'i. By 1200 A.D. these ancient voyagers settle nearly every habitable island in over ten million square miles of the Pacific Ocean.

c.1100—A Tahitian kahuna (high priest), Pā'ao, arrives in Hawai'i to start a high priest line known as kahuna nui. He introduces the war god Kūkā'ilimoku and constructs luakini heiau (temples of human sacrifice). Pā'ao returns to Tahiti and brings back a chief named Pili, who rules Hawai'i Island and sires the royal line of a 700-year dynasty culminating with the Kamehamehas.

c.1200—A second major wave of immigrants from Tahiti conquer and dominate the earlier Marquesan settlers.

c.1250— As contact with southern Polynesia ceases and Hawaiians no longer complete long-distance, open-ocean voyages, a unique Hawaiian culture continues to evolve.

c.1555—Spanish navigator Juan Gaetano (Gaytan) documents an island group at the latitude of the Hawaiian Islands, but records an incorrect longitude. Gaetano names the island group Islas de Mesa ("Table Islands") or Los Majos ("The Tableland"). The Hawaiian Islands are located a few hundred miles from the routes used by Spanish ships traveling between the Far East and Latin America during this time period.

c.1580–c.1600—Līloa, the ruling chief of Hawai'i Island, has a relatively peaceful reign.

c.1600—Hawai'i Island chief 'Umi-a-Liloa ('Umi) marries Pi'ikea, the daughter of the Maui ruler, Pi'ilani. Lono-a-Pi'ilani, the eldest son of Pi'ilani, becomes ruler of Maui after his father dies, but then is defeated by his younger brother Kiha-a-Pi'ilani due to the assistance of his brother-in-law 'Umi-a-Līloa, who continues to rule the Hāna district. Kiha-a-Pi'ilani builds a road know as alaloa that circles the island.

c.1620—The legendary *Konaliloa* wrecks at Ke'ei near Kealakekua Bay on Hawai'i Island according to Thrum's 1882 chronology listing the marine casualties of the Hawaiian Islands. Some sources claim that the wreck occurred up to one century earlier. The vessel's captain and his sister barely make it to shore where they are cared for by the local inhabitants.

c.1620–c.1640—Keali'iokaloa, the son of 'Umi-a-Līloa ('Umi), is not a popular ruler of Hawai'i Island. His son Kuka'ilani is defeated by Keawenui-a-'Umi (Keawenui), another son of 'Umi-a-Līloa, who becomes the ruling chief of Hawai'i Island.

Previous spread: Ki'i pōhaku, or petroglyphs, are found on the Big Island, most on pāhoehoe lava, whose smooth and porous rock makes for an ideal carving surface. They were often located near or at trail junctions, or in areas considered to have mana, or divine power. The practice of making petroglyphs was brought by the first Polynesians. With no form of writing as we know it, the ancient Hawaiians used petroglyphs as forms of communication with their gods and spirits, religious observances, to commemorate important events, to indicate places of concentrated mana, and in some instances, even for mundane purposes. Whatever their purpose, ki'i pōhaku hold a certain ancient and inexplicable power over the beholder. [P.F. Kwiatkowski]

ANCIENT HAWAIIANS

The ancient Polynesians were master navigators who for thousands of years sailed their double-hulled voyaging canoes long distances to inhabit hundreds of Pacific islands. They finally discovered the Hawaiian Islands, an isolated island group of less than 6,500 square miles in the middle of the vast 70 million square mile Pacific Ocean.

These seafarers navigated the oceans guided only by clues provided by nature—the positions and movements of the sun, the moon, the stars, constellations, the prevailing winds and seas, and the flight patterns of birds. They likely began their west-to-east journeys when westerly winds replaced the prevailing easterly trade winds so if they failed to find land, they could wait for the trade winds to return and carry them home. To determine the direction toward Hawaiʻi they relied on the star that Westerners call Polaris or the North Star. Their word for this was Hōkūpaʻa, meaning Fixed Star, because it is located due north and appears "fixed" in the sky.

They also relied on their knowledge of the daily feeding and seasonal flight cycles of birds. Migratory birds such as the Pacific golden plover and the ruddy turnstone winter on central Pacific islands and then in April or May head back to their arctic breeding grounds. Sighting them revealed that somewhere to the north or northeast there was land.

Also helpful were the flight directions of pelagic (oceanic) birds, including petrels, shearwaters and albatrosses. Pelagic birds spend most of their time over the ocean seeking fish, squid, and crustaceans and then return to land during the nesting season.

Non-pelagic birds such as boobies, terns and tropicbirds all feed over the sea by day but return each night to their land homes. Seeing them at dusk meant land was nearby. During their open ocean journeys, the navigators also looked for birds congregating over feeding areas to reveal locations where fishing would be productive.

The voyagers brought to the islands pigs, chickens, dogs, and more than two dozen species of plants which they used for food and to make clothing and tools along with indigenous plants. Almost all plant parts were used—the bark, leaves, stems, flowers, seeds, wood, sap (resin), flower pollen, and flower bracts.

Plants were also used to make lei, dyes, scents, containers, tools, weapons, musical instruments, canoes, dwellings, and even sacred places of worship. Woven from vines were a great variety of twined baskets considered the finest in all of ancient Polynesia, as well as sleeping mats.

One of the most important plants brought to the Islands was kalo (taro), which was pounded into poi. A staple of the Hawaiian diet, taro was cultivated extensively in lowland areas in rock-terraced fields networked with irrigation channels.

The taro patches complemented the Hawaiians' extremely productive and well-stocked saltwater fishponds. The Hawaiians were the only Polynesian culture to construct and maintain shoreline saltwater fishponds where mullet and milkfish entered through sluice gates, to be raised and eaten when needed. Fish were also caught from the coral reefs and deeper ocean waters, along with honu (turtles) and other edible sea life.

Along the shoreline and in the shallow ocean waters limu (seaweed) was gathered that provided essential vitamins and minerals as well as a spicy flavoring. It was often mixed with sea salt, another natural resource gathered from coastal ponds. Some varieties of limu had spiritual and ceremonial uses—limu kala was worn as a lei to bring healing, and used in ho'oponopono, an ancient cultural process for offering and receiving forgiveness.

The sticky sap of the *pisonia umbellifera* was used to catch native forest birds whose colorful plumage was woven into elaborate and magnificently crafted

Opposite page: In this engraving from a drawing by Webber, a ceremonial canoe containing priests and possibly a feather-covered image of an akua is paddled across Kealakekua Bay. The paddlers and priests wear masked helmets fashioned from gourds, foliage and tapa strips. The purpose of this ritual or its relation to the presence of Captain Cook in the bay was unknown to the British at that time. Two centuries later, the symbolic events surrounding first contact still remain an elusive mystery to outsiders attempting to understand the ancient mind. [Hawai'i State Archives]

Right: The ancient Hawaiian religion, with its heiau, or shrines, priests, and chiefly support, died out after the breaking of the kapu, or taboo, system in 1819 and the unconnected arrival of the missionaries in the same year. But the gods and spirits that were close to the native heart survived, particularly away from Western and missionary eyes. Fishermen still left offerings at fishing shrines. Families still told stories of their 'aumākua, or ancestral spirits, appearing as animals such as sharks or owls. People still worshipped Pele and left offerings at Halema'uma'u crater, and Pele herself was reported to be seen from time to time, appearing as an old woman walking on the side of the road, or as a young and beautiful woman glimpsed in passing. Still today there are stories of encounters with Pele. [*Pele, Goddess of Hawai'i's Volcanoes*/Herb Kawainui Kāne]

The Legend of Pele

Pele, the legendary goddess of fire and volcanoes, is the daughter of Wākea, the Sky Father, and Papa (Haumea), the Earth Mother. Pele is a creator of mountains and islands, including the Hawaiian Islands. She is also a destroyer and a burner of lands. Pele is able to assume different forms, and said to be akua kino lau "...because of her ability to change into a child, a beautiful maiden, a plain matron, or a very old woman" ('Ōlelo No'eau).

According to legend, Pele protects her sacred fires today in Halema'uma'u Crater at the summit of Kīlauea Volcano on Hawai'i Island. Halema'uma'u means "House surrounded by the 'ama'u fern," referring to the ferns that surround the volcanic crater. These ferns are said to be the embodiment of the demi-god Kamapua'a, who pursued Pele's love but was rejected. The battle between Pele and her sister continues today on Hawai'i Island's southeast coast where the lava meets the sea in fiery explosions.

In ancient Hawai'i, the fruiting branches of the native 'ōhelo were thrown into Kīlauea Volcano as an offering to Pele. Another plant considered sacred to the goddess of fire and volcanoes was 'ōhi'a lehua. Pele is said to be found everywhere that fire comes up through the earth to light the sky. Wherever the ground is hot and steam hisses up from cracks in the earth, wherever the incandescent glow of molten rock and the smell of sulfur fill the air, and wherever lava erupts in fiery fountains into the sky, "...'ae aia la 'o Pele"—"...there is Pele."

feathered capes, cloaks, and crested helmets. Hawaiian featherwork was found nowhere else in Polynesia.

The early Polynesians also created many artistically decorated bowls and containers, even developing an innovative method of carrying the containers using a continuous unknotted cord. They also crafted large bottle gourds as well the double-gourd drum and coconut knee drums.

The Hawaiian culture that evolved in the Islands differed from the rest of Polynesia, Melanesia, and Micronesia. Part of the uniqueness can be attributed to the abundant variety of the Islands' unique natural resources and part to the Islands' isolation as further Polynesian migration to Hawai'i ended about 1600. The Hawaiian language that evolved to this day is considered among the most fluid and melodic of any language known.

Hawaiian surfing was also unique. While wave riding was likely first done in the Society Islands, it was in Hawai'i that surfing flourished. The first surfboards carved from coral tree, breadfruit tree, and koa trees were up to 18 feet long and weighed as much as 175 pounds.

Ancient Hawai'i's social structure was based on fairly rigid castes, but with a system of communal sharing of the natural resources according to wedge-shaped land divisions known as ahupua'a. The ahupua'a were defined by natural boundaries of mountain ridges and ocean bays and extended from the high valley to the sea including the offshore coral reefs. Within them could be found all the resources necessary to sustain life.

When Captain Cook and his crew established Western contact in 1778, they found a friendly, self-sufficient and productive people with a culture as highly developed as many found in feudal Europe.

This engraving of a heiau at Hōnaunau, Hawai'i Island was drawn by ship artist Robert Dampier in 1824. The structure is guarded by the images of many gods and was built to contain the bones of King Keawe and his relatives. Not all heiau were imposing stone structures. After the kapu was abolished in 1819 and Christianity arrived in 1820, the old religion was abandoned and heiau, modest or massive, were no longer attended to or maintained (at least publicly), serving only as reminders of the past. Today there are nearly 150 heiau sites on Hawai'i Island, most of which are only stone mound remnants of once-imposing structures that have endured natural forces, animal contact, and unwitting human theft. [Hawai'i State Archives]

Kapu

When the Tahitian high priest Pā'ao arrived in the Islands circa A.D.1200, he initiated a new social order. The highest class was to be the mō'ī (king, queen) and his/her 'aha kuhina (chiefs and advisers). Next were the ali'i (royalty), kāhuna (priests and experts in a given profession), maka'āinana (commoners, mostly farmers), and lastly the kauā (or kauwā) outcasts. He also introduced the kānāwai, a strict system of laws and regulations that determined if something was kapu (sacred or forbidden). Commoners would prostrate themselves in the presence of the chiefs, who possessed mana (divine power).

The strict sanctions of the kapu system ensured the separation of the classes, and prescribed much of the daily lives of the islanders. Kapu breakers and defeated warriors were subject to immediate death unless they could reach a pu'uhonua, or place of refuge, where a priest could absolve them. One such place was Pu'uhonua o Hōnaunau on Hawai'i Island's South Kona coast, which had a 1,000-foot long, ten-foot-high stone wall.

Heiau

The ancient Hawaiians built many heiau (sacred places of worship), religious shrines and places of refuge whose structures included stone enclosures, platforms, and earthen terraces. Some heiau included an 'anu'u, or oracle tower, covered with white kapa barkcloth. Offerings and prayers were made to 'aumākua, personal or family gods and sacred guardians that were considered protectors.

When the Tahitian high priest Pā'ao arrived circa A.D. 1200 he constructed the first luakini (temple of human sacrifice) known as Waha'ula Heiau, located at Puna on Hawai'i Island honoring Kūkā'ilimoku, the god of war. He also introduced Pele, the goddess of fire and volcanoes.

Other types of heiau built throughout the Islands were to insure good fishing, rain, food crops, and treatment of the sick. Many heiau were dedicated to Lono, the god of agricultural fertility. Agricultural heiau were known as waihau or unu, where gifts such as pigs, bananas, or coconuts were offered. Fishermen often placed a kū'ula (fish god) atop a stone altar located near the coast, while bird catchers in the mountains would make their offerings at a ko'a (stone platform).

The site of a heiau was chosen by a kahuna (master architect) who valued a location for its mana, or spiritual power. Major heiau were usually constructed of lava rock walls built into a rectangular formation on the ground, or raised terrace platforms forming a more substantial structure. Structures built within heiau utilized wood of the native 'ōhi'a lehua and cordage woven from olonā. Pili grass was used for thatching. Ki'i (wooden carved figures representing gods) were carved from 'ōhi'a lehua and placed in and around the heiau.

Above, upper: "A View in Owhyee with one of the Priest's Houses" by William Ellis. This quaintly titled engraving shows a Hawaiian village still untouched by the outside world. "Owhyee" was one of several attempts to spell "Hawai'i" in English before the Hawaiian language was put in written form by the early missionaries. In old Hawai'i, people lived in small coastal villages (kauhale) near good fishing grounds or beside fertile land, where they grew taro and sweet potatoes, main staples of their diet. The better Hawaiian house (hale) was raised on a stone foundation platform, and the floor was covered with small smooth pebbles. The homes of commoners had earthen floors covered with dry grasses and lauhala mats. [Hawai'i State Archives]

Lower: Surfing was a favorite pastime in old Hawai'i and fascinated early visitors. Disparaged by the missionaries who saw the pastime as wasteful, it was revitalized in the early 20th century. [Baker-Van Dyke Collection]

Above: Many of the original sketches by early shipboard artists were later retouched by copyists who changed the body and facial appearance of the Hawaiians to conform to the European idea of beauty. In this engraving by Choris, the Hawaiian male dancers appear to be accurately depicted. They carry elaborately decorated feather-embellished gourd rattles, and wear dog-tooth anklets, which make distinctive rattling sounds as they perform. Bracelets of large boar tusks decorate their wrists, contributing to the visual impact of the arm movements. Some dancers are heavily tattooed—widespread in ancient Polynesia, and the Hawaiians developed very specialized designs. The dancers do not wear customary malo (men's loin cloths), but seem to be wearing intricately wrapped tapa cloth or even imported cotton cloth from a trading ship. In the background, the musicians accompany the dancers, beating gourd drums and tapping on coconut shells with a short stick. Hula was performed by both men and women. [Hawai'i State Archives]

Left: The Hawaiian ali'i, or chiefly class, always left a marked impression on early Western visitors who wrote about their royal bearing, magnificent feather capes and helmets, beautiful accouterments of rank, and the pageantry of their processions. This tattooed chief, drawn in 1819 by French artist Jacques Arago, proudly posed with his royal symbols of rank including the mahiole, or feather helmet, and 'ahu 'ula, or feather cape. The traditional tattoos, including squares on the chest and triangles on the left thigh and lower leg, were spiritual motifs indicating rank and genealogy. [Hawai'i State Archives]

In this watercolor by John Webber, the cliffs of Kealakekua, or "the paths of the gods," reach down to the sea and shelter a Hawaiian village. When Captain Cook visited here in January of 1779, the first significant encounter between the cultures of Hawai'i and Europe took place along this rugged, lava-strewn shoreline. His arrival corresponded to the Hawaiian religious celebration of the Makahiki, a period of several months between November and February when war was suspended and peace prevailed. Lono, the god of abundance, peace and agriculture, was honored with competitive games, hula performances, and feasting. Whether the Hawaiians viewed Captain Cook as a great chief or a divine being, they received him and his crew with an outpouring of hospitality. To the far right is a portion of Hikiau Heiau, where he participated in a Hawaiian religious ceremony, receiving a feathered cloak in recognition of his chiefly status. [Dixon Galleries, State Library of New South Wales, Sydney]

18TH CENTURY

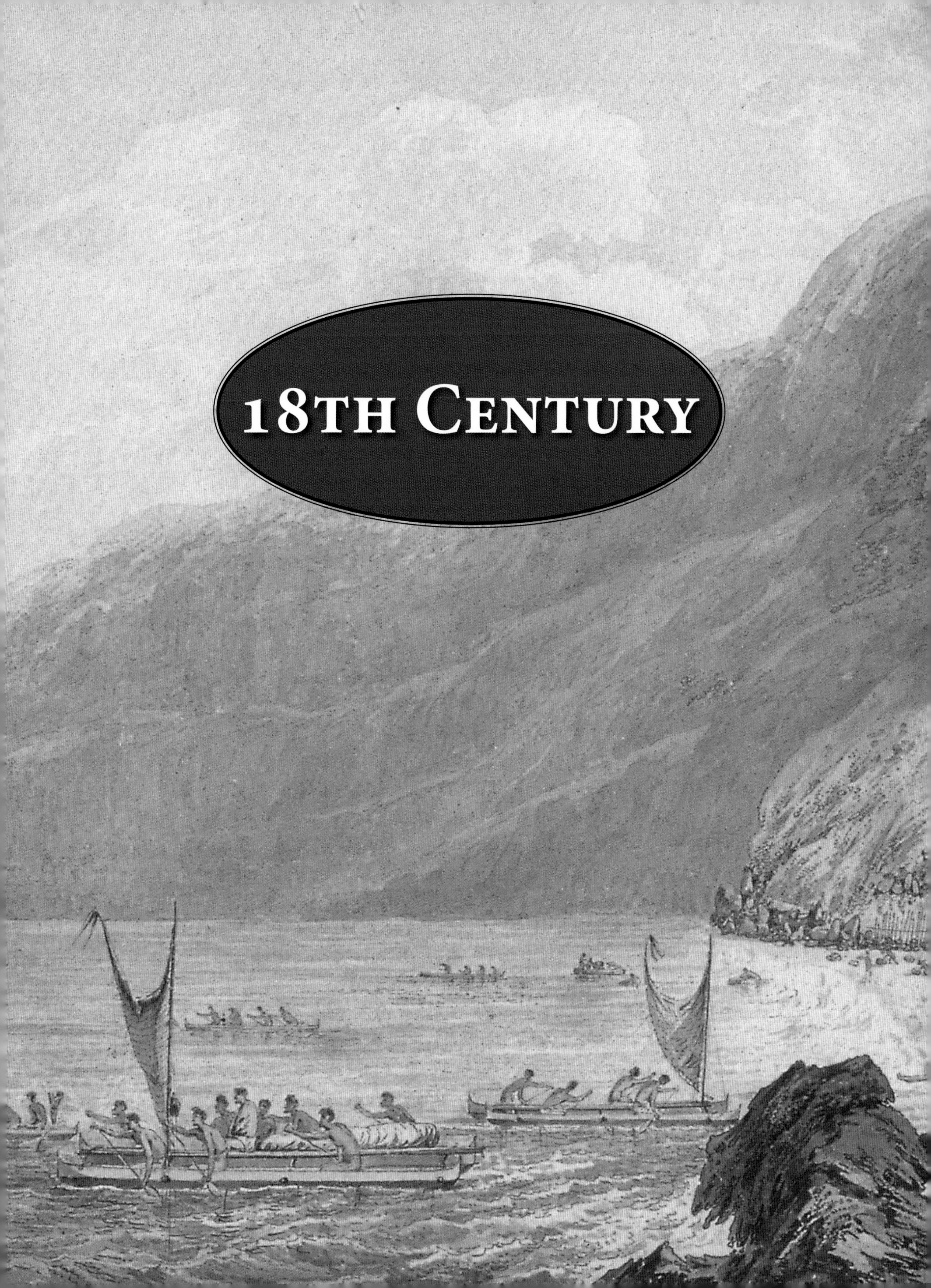

In this drawing by John Webber, the cliffs of Kealakekua, or "the paths of the gods," reach down to the sea and shelter a Hawaiian village. [Hawai'i State Archives]

c.1700—Lonoikamakahiki (Lono) is ruling chief of Hawai'i Island. Kanaloakua'ana, the grandson of 'Umi-a-Līloa, serves as Regent because Lono is so young. The warriors of Lono battle rebel chiefs on Kaua'i, O'ahu, and Moloka'i.

The forces of Alapa'iniu, the paramount chief of Hawai'i Island, attack the forces of Kekaulike on Maui. Kekaulike responds with a counterattack against Hawai'i Island. Kekaulike was the great grandfather of King Kamehameha I's sacred wife Keōpūolani.

1736—Warriors from the Hawai'i and Moloka'i islands, led by Alapa'inui, battle O'ahu's warriors at Kawela in south Moloka'i. Five days of fighting result in the defeat of O'ahu's forces and the death of O'ahu's chief Kapi'ioho-o-kalani ("The head curls of the royal chief"). Two years later, Alapa'inui's warriors invade Maui and again defeat the warriors of O'ahu.

c.1758—Birth of Pai'ea Kamehameha, the future King Kamehameha I, to Keōuakupuapāikalaninui [Keōuanui] and Keku'iapoiwa (II).

1775—The first major battle of the rising young warrior Kamehameha known as the Battle of Kalaeoka'īlio ("The cape of the dog") takes place at Kaupō, Maui where he rescues his mentor and war instructor Kekūhaupi'o.

1775— Kamehameha overturns the sacred Naha Stone on Hawai'i Island. A high priestess had said that if Kamehameha could move the nearly 4,000 pound royal birthstone he would conquer all of the Hawaiian Islands.

1778, January 18—The crews of Captain James Cook's two British ships, the HMS *Resolution* and HMS *Discovery,* become the first known Westerners to reach the Hawaiian Islands sighting O'ahu and Kaua'i. Cook goes ashore at Waimea, Kaua'i on January 20. They estimate the population of the Hawaiian Islands at about 400,000 (current estimates for that time vary from 300,000 to 800,000).

1778, February 2—During a trip to Ni'ihau, Captain Cook leaves ashore the first goats, a ram, and two ewes.

1778, November 26—Captain Cook begins charting the coasts of Hawai'i and Maui.

1778, November—The young chief Kamehameha goes aboard Cook's HMS *Resolution* anchored off Maui's east side near Hāna. He remains on board overnight, and the following day Kalani'ōpu'u, the Hawai'i Island ruler, visits the ship.

1779, February 14—Captain James Cook is killed during a violent encounter on the shore of Kealakekua Bay.

1781—In a battle known as Kaumupīka'o, Kahekili regains control of the eastern portion of Maui, including the fort at Hāna.

1782, April—Kalani'ōpu'u, ruler of Hawai'i Island dies and his oldest son Kīwala'ō becomes the island's new ruler. Kamehameha, his nephew, is given guardianship of the family's feathered war god, Kūkā'ilimoku. Slighted by Kīwala'ō's redivision of lands, Kamehameha unites with the chiefs of Kona and becomes their leader.

1782—The young Kamehameha leads his warriors to victory at the Battle of Moku'ōhai at Ke'ei, Kona, during which Kīwala'ō is killed.

1783—Maui's ruler Kahekili attack Kahahana's forces at Kaheiki on O'ahu and emerges victorious as the ruler of O'ahu.

1783—The warriors of Kamehameha battle the warriors of Keōuakū'ahu'ula and the twins Keawemauhili and Keōuape'e'ale at Pua'aloa near Pana'ewa (near Hilo). Kamehameha and Kekūhaupi'o lead the land forces while Ke'eaumoku leads the sea forces of 20,000 warriors and 800 canoes.

The fleet lands at Kawaihae during a storm known as Kaua'awa, and the battle becomes known as Kaua Kaua'awa ("Battle of the Bitter Rain"). Kamehameha's warriors are thwarted and retreat to Laupāhoehoe.

1784—The official account of Captain James Cook's third voyage includes

Ka'iana (1756?–1795) This prince of Kaua'i was more than six feet tall, and the first chief to travel to foreign lands. His high rank, fame in war, and knowledge of the use of foreign weapons gave him much prestige, and he was a valuable ally to Kamehameha for several years. When Ka'iana was suspected of having an affair with Queen Ka'ahumanu in 1793, Kamehameha became less friendly. During the invasion of O'ahu in 1795, Ka'iana and his brother Namakeha feared a plot and deserted to the side of Kahekili. He was killed fighting at Nu'uanu Pali in 1795. [Hawai'i State Archives]

La Pérouse's two ships, the *Astrolabe* and the *Boussole,* anchored off the village of Keone'ō'io. [Drawing by Blondela, Bishop Museum]

the first published chart of the Hawaiian Islands.

1785—Kamehameha marries Ka'ahumanu, the daughter of Ke'eaumoku Pāpa'iaheahe and Nāmāhana.

1785—Under the command of Captain James Hanna, an unnamed fur-trading brig on its way to China becomes the first trading ship to stop in the Islands.

1786—Kahekili rules Maui and O'ahu, and his half-brother, Kā'eokūlani rules Kaua'i and Ni'ihau. Western weapons are sought by the chiefs.

1786, May—The *Queen Charlotte* under Captain Dixon and the *King George* under Captain Portlock arrive at Kealakekua Bay from London. Dixon and Portlock become the first foreign captains to visit the Islands since Cook's death in 1779. The ships sail on to Waimea, Kaua'i, to scout ports for rest and provisioning for future fur trading vessels sailing to China from the Pacific Northwest.

1786, May 30—French explorer La Pérouse ceremoniously lands on Maui which Cook had sighted earlier on November 26, 1778.

1787, May 20—The fur-trading British ship *Imperial Eagle* arrives carrying Mrs. Frances Hornsby Trevor Barkley, the first European woman to come to the Islands. A Hawaiian woman hired as Barkley's maid becomes the first Hawaiian to sail from Hawai'i with Westerners. Surgeon's mate John MacKay becomes the first white resident of the Islands, settling on the Kona Coast.

1787, August 2—John Meares, a former British Navy lieutenant and a pioneer fur trader along America's Northwest Coast, arrives on the *Nootka.* When Meares leaves for Canton, China, he takes with him the chief Ka'iana, the half brother of the high chief Kahekili. Ka'iana becomes the first Hawaiian chief to travel to a foreign country. Ka'iana returns on the *Iphigenia* with Captain William Douglas in 1788 and later fights as an ally of Kamehamaha before being killed fighting against him in the Battle of Nu'uanu in 1795.

1788—The *Prince of Wales* and the *Princess Royal,* two trading vessels, spend three months in the Islands. Aboard the *Prince of Wales* is Scotsman Archibald Menzies, a naturalist, who later becomes the first Westerner to climb Mauna Loa.

1789, August—The *Columbia Rediviva,* an armed ship sailing out of Boston, arrives under the command of Robert Gray (1775-1806),

The Olowalu Massacre

Pioneering American trader Simon Metcalfe arrived in 1790 in command of the scow *Eleanora.* After the chief Ka'ōpūiki stole one of his skiffs, Metcalfe killed more than 100 Hawaiians as retribution. Off the coast of Hawai'i Island, Metcalfe also punished Chief Kame'eiamoku by whipping him. Kame'eiamoku attacked the *Fair American,* which was under the command of Metcalfe's 18-year-old son, Thomas, who was killed. Much of the young Metcalfe's crew was also killed in the attack with the exception of Isaac Davis, who was left tied to a canoe, half blind and nearly dead. Simon Metcalfe left his boatswain John Young onshore and sailed away from the Hawaiian Islands not knowing his son had been killed.

The *Fair American's* fortunes changed when it was taken over by Kamehameha, and Davis and Young became Kamehameha's supporters (and advisers), manning large guns from canoes during the invasion of the northern coast of Hawai'i Island as well as during a later attack on O'ahu.

John Young eventually became governor of several Hawaiian Islands and had estates on all the Islands. Isaac Davis eventually became a chief, married a relative of King Kamehameha I, became governor of O'ahu, and owned estates on O'ahu, Maui, Moloka'i, and Hawai'i. Young's granddaughter was Emma (1836-1885), the wife of Kamehameha IV.

Kamehameha led his war fleet to Maui with the intention of conquering the island. He stands aboard the *Fair American,* a Western-style ship, with his trusted advisors and friends Isaac Davis and John Young. [*Kamehameha on Fair American*/Herb Kawainui Kāne]

While Captain Cook met the peoples of Kaua'i and Hawai'i Island, he never visited the other Islands. On May 30, 1786, Admiral Jean-Francois de Galaup, Comte de La Pérouse, became the first European to step ashore on Maui. With his two ships—the *Astrolabe* and the *Boussole*—anchored off the village of Keone'ō'io, La Pérouse spent three hours on land with a small party of armed men. He was greeted graciously and ceremonially given two pigs. Declining to follow the European custom of claiming new lands for his country, La Pérouse simply left Maui with an abundance of food supplies, mats, feathers, shells, a cape, and a red helmet. [Hawai'i State Archives]

becoming the first American ship to visit the Islands and later the first American ship to circumnavigate the globe. Gray takes aboard a Kauaian named Opai, who becomes the first native Hawaiian to visit the United States. Opai returns to Hawai'i in 1791 on the vessel *Hope* under the command of Joseph Ingraham.

1790—Kamehameha lands his troops on Maui and is victorious over the Maui warriors of Kalanikūpule in a conflict that culminates at 'Īao Valley and becomes known as the Battle of Kepaniwai ("Battle of the Water Dam"). After the victory, the oracle Kapoukahi tells Kamehameha he will be victorious over all the Hawaiian Islands only if he builds a heiau at Kawaihae dedicated to his war god, Kūkā'ilimoku. The heiau is to be named Pu'ukoholā ("Whale hill").

1790—On Hawai'i Island, the chief Keōuakū'ahu'ula and his warriors head for Ka'ū after plundering Kamehameha's lands in Waipi'o, Kohala, and Waimea. As they pass over an area near Kīlauea Volcano, a chance eruption rains down ash and poisonous gases that burn and suffocate many of the warriors as well as men, women, and children traveling with the group.

1790—In what comes to be known as the Olowalu Massacre, pioneering American trader Simon Metcalfe kills more than 100 Hawaiians at Olowalu, Maui as retribution for the theft of a skiff.

1790—Haleakalā Volcano releases an estimated 22 square miles of lava, which flows to the sea where it cools and hardens to form the Cape Kīna'u Peninsula, changing the shape of the southwest Maui coastline and forming La Pérouse Bay.

1790—Hawai'i's sandalwood trade begins when it is discovered that the fragrant wood can be sold for a high price in Canton, China. Extensive sandalwood groves in the mountains of the Hawaiian Islands are harvested and shipped to a nearly insatiable Chinese market.

1791—Having already recaptured Moloka'i, Lāna'i, and Maui, Kahekili attacks Kamehameha's northern coastal lands on Hawai'i Island from Kohala to Waipi'o. Kahekili's forces meet Kamehameha's fleet off the northeast coast, and Kamehameha's counterattack becomes the first Hawaiian sea battle in which both sides are armed with foreign gunners and cannons. This battle becomes known as Kepūwaha'ula'ula ("War of the red mouthed cannon"). Neither side is victorious, and Kahekili and his army to return to O'ahu. His intentions of attacking the site of Kamehameha's construction of a heiau at Kawaihae are thwarted.

1791—Kamehameha completes the heiau at Kawaihae named Pu'ukoholā ("Whale hill") dedicated to his war god, Kūkā'ilimoku. He asks his rival Keōuakū'ahu'ula to attend the dedication. When he arrives he is killed along with many of his chiefs and sacrificed on the heiau altar atop the hill at Pu'ukoholā.

1791, October—The *Solide* becomes the first French trading ship to visit the Hawaiian Islands.

1792, March 5—British Captain George Vancouver arrives in command of the *Chatham* and the *Discovery*. He returns again in 1793 and 1794.

1793, February—The British trading ship *Butterworth* arrives under the command of William Brown. In December of 1794, it becomes the first foreign vessel to enter Honolulu Harbor.

1794, Summer—The death of Kahekili, ruler of Maui, O'ahu, Moloka'i, Lāna'i, Kaua'i, Ni'ihau, and Kaho'olawe, leads to war between his heirs. Kahekili leaves his domains to his half-brother, Kā'eokūlani, and his son Kalanikūpule, who become enemies.

1794, December 12—With foreign assistance, Kalanikūpule, the heir of Kahekili, defeats Kā'eokūlani, chief of Kaua'i, Maui, Lāna'i, and Moloka'i, near what is now called Pearl Harbor, resulting in the death of Kā'eokūlani. A victory salute after the battle is accidentally loaded with grapeshot, hitting the *Lady Washington* and killing its captain, John Kendrick, along with several of his officers.

1795, January 1—Kalanikūpule orders the killing of Captains Brown and Gardner of the English ships *Prince Lee Boo* and *Jackal* along with their crews in Honolulu Harbor. Kalanikūpule then loads war supplies onto the ships in preparation for an invasion of Kamehameha's O'ahu domains. The surviving members of the crews later force Kalanikūpule's warriors ashore, sail to Hawai'i Island, and give Kalanikūpule's war supplies to Kamehameha before leaving for China.

1795, January—After spending more than a decade preparing for war, Kamehameha is determined to defeat the forces of Kalanikūpule, the ruler of O'ahu. In preparation for the battle ahead Kamehameha builds many large war canoes.

1795, April—Kamehameha and his warrior army land in Waikīkī to invade O'ahu culminating in a battle at Nu'uanu Pali where many O'ahu warriors either decide to jump rather than be taken captive or are driven off the precipice meeting their deaths on the rocks hundreds of feet below. The Battle of Nu'uanu, Kamehameha's final major military conquest, gives him control of all of the Hawaiian Islands except for Kaua'i and Ni'ihau.

British naval commander George Vancouver was one of the most important early Westerners to come to the Island of Hawai'i. He had sailed with Cook, and was at Kealakekua when Cook was killed. He had met Kamehameha briefly then, and when he came back in the winters of 1793 and 1794, the two became friendly. Vancouver built Kamehameha a European-style ship, the *Brittania,* and as part of his mission to establish trade, he brought cattle and sheep. [Hawai'i State Archives]

George Vancouver Visits the Hawaiian Islands

British Captain George Vancouver (1757-1798) had served under Captain Cook on his second Pacific voyage, and was midshipman on Cook's third voyage when he first found the Hawaiian Islands. Vancouver returned to Hawai'i on March 5, 1792 in command of the *Chatham* and the *Discovery.*

Vancouver came to the Islands again in 1793 and 1794, meeting with many important Hawaiian chiefs. He introduced sheep, cattle, goats, and geese as well as a variety of seeds and plants including almond and orange trees as well as grapevines. Vancouver hoped that the food products would be raised and cultivated so the Hawaiians could later supply provisions for visiting British ships.

On February 25, 1794, Vancouver obtained an informal treaty of cession from Kamehameha. The two men were friends, and Kamehameha sought assurance that the Hawaiian Islands would be under British protection.

Kamehameha received a gift of a British flag (a Union Jack) from Vancouver, and flew the flag for the next 22 years at his compounds. It is uncertain what meaning Kamehameha attributed to the flag, since the British Parliament never ratified the apparent cession agreement with Vancouver. During Vancouver's 1794 visit, his carpenters helped Kamehameha construct the 36-foot *Britannia,* Hawai'i's first foreign-designed ship.

1795—Kamehameha marries 17-year-old Keōpūolani ("The gathering of the clouds of heaven"), who becomes his highest-ranking wife. They have three children: Liholiho (Kamehameha II), Kauikeaouli (Kamehameha III), and Nāhiʻenaʻena (Princess).

1796, April—Kamehameha's invasion fleet of 800 or more canoes and more than 8,000 soldiers sets sail for Kauaʻi. A storm swamps the canoes in the rough seas forcing the fleet to turn back.

1796, September—The last battle of Kamehameha I, known as Nāmakaehā's Rebellion, occurs in Hilo when his warriors defeat an uprising led by Nāmakaehā, the cousin of Kaʻiana, the half-brother of the high chief Kahekili. Nāmakaehā's forces are in control of Hilo when Kamehameha's forces arrive, and a battle ensues at Kaipaloa in south Hilo. Nāmakaehā is taken captive, and then offered as a sacrifice to Kamehameha's war god Kūkāʻilimoku at Piʻihonua heiau. Nāmakaehā's son, Ōpūkahaʻia, later becomes the first Christian convert.

1797—Kamehameha forgives a fisherman who 12 years earlier was punished for hitting him with a paddle, and legislates what comes to be known as Kānāwai Māmalahoe ("Law of the Splintered Paddle").

After Cook's Death, James King was put in command of the *Discovery* and ended up taking the expedition back to England. He was well liked by the Hawaiians and invited to stay. He finished the official account of the voyage, *Voyage to the Pacific Ocean,* as a collaboration with Cook. [Hawai'i State Archives]

CAPTAIN COOK ESTABLISHES WESTERN CONTACT

The Age of Discovery widened the borders of the Earth as vessels sailed from old Europe in search of a new world. Spanish, Dutch, English, and French ships cut innumerable lanes across the Earth's oceans. Yet for all their voyaging and for all their incursions into the region, no European ship had ever stumbled upon the Hawaiian Islands. Ferdinand Magellan came closest in 1522 as he skirted the Pacific on his way to the Philippines. It would take 256 more years before British Captain James Cook in 1778 finally established the first documented Western contact with the Hawaiian Islands.

The crews of Cook's two ships, the HMS *Resolution* and HMS *Discovery,* first sighted O'ahu and Kaua'i in the dawn hours of January 18, 1778. Weather and ocean conditions kept Cook's ships far offshore until the following day by which time they had also sighted the island of Ni'ihau. When Cook's ships approached Kaua'i's southeast coast on the afternoon of January 19, canoes paddled out to meet them. The Hawaiians traded fish and sweet potatoes for pieces of iron and brass, lowered down from the larger ships to the Hawaiians' canoes. So began Hawai'i's contact with Westerners.

Cook's ships remained offshore of Kaua'i's southeast coast. On the morning of January 20, Cook allowed a few Hawaiians to come on board before he continued on in search of safe anchorage. On the afternoon of January 20, 1778 Cook anchored his ships near the mouth of the Waimea River on Kaua'i's southwest coast. Cook and twelve armed marines boarded three small boats and went ashore for the first time.

As Cook and his men stepped onto land, hundreds of Hawaiians greeted them and offered various gifts including tapa (barkcloth), pua'a (pigs), and mai'a (bananas). Cook went ashore three times the next day, walking inland where he saw Hawaiian hale, heiau, and agricultural sites.

Cook's crew estimated the total population of the eight main Hawaiian Islands at 400,000, with 30,000 living on Kaua'i. Cook named the Islands "The Sandwich Islands" in honor of his patron, the First Lord of the Admiralty, the Earl of Sandwich.

Cook's return to the Hawaiian Islands the following year would end in bloodshed and presage centuries worth of misunderstand and mistrust between Hawaiians and other cultures who came to their Islands. After leaving the Hawaiian Islands, Cook had journeyed north in search of the elusive (and nonexistent) "Northwest Passage." On January 17, 1779, Cook sailed into Kealakekua Bay on Hawai'i Island to restock his ships and prepare for further exploration.

Unaware that he was visiting the Islands during the ancient Hawaiian harvest festival known as Makahiki, a period of several months when time is taken away from work for feasts, sports games, and other events in honor of Lono, the god of agricultural fertility, he arrived on Hawai'i Island and was greeted by processions and celebrations unlike any he had encountered previously. (Many historians state that Cook was received as the god Lono, fulfilling Hawaiian beliefs that Lono had long ago departed from Kealakekua Bay, promising to return.) Cook was brought to Hikiau Heiau, a temple where kāhuna put red kapa cloth on him and offered chants.

Cook left Kealakekua Bay on February 4, 1779 to survey the other Hawaiian Islands. When a foremast of the HMS *Resolution* broke, he returned to make repairs. As repairs were underway, one of the *Resolution*'s smaller boats was stolen. On February 14, Cook and a contingent of nine armed men went ashore, planning to detain and ransom the ruler of the island, Kalani'ōpu'u, for the boat's return. Meanwhile, members of Cook's crew had blockaded the harbor. When a canoe attempted to pass the blockade, the ship's crew fired, killing a chief. Learning that one of their chiefs had been killed, the Hawaiians gathered in a large crowd near shore just as Cook's group landed.

Captain Cook was honored for his accomplishments as a navigator and explorer. Strangely, for so famous a man, little is known of his personal life. His journals objectively comment on everything that he saw yet provide little inkling of the deepest thoughts and character of the man himself. [Hawai'i State Archives]

The first documented contact between Westerners and Native Hawaiians took place between 1778 and 1779, during Captain James Cook's visits to the Islands of Kaua'i and Hawai'i. Ship artist John Webber's extensive drawings are an important illustrative source of ancient Hawaiian artifacts and lifestyles. In this dramatic scene, Webber depicts the formal arrival of King Kalaniōpu'u to welcome Captain Cook on January 25, 1779, at Kealakekua Bay. Kalaniōpu'u leads two other large canoes filled with chiefs wearing rich feathered cloaks and helmets, and armed with spears and daggers. In the second canoe, the famed kāhuna, Kao'o, carries sacred images, or ki'i, displayed on red cloth. "Kalaniopuu, King of Owyhee bringing Presents to Captain Cook, ca. 1781-83," pen, ink wash, and watercolor. [Dixson Galleries, State Library of New South Wales, Sydney]

After coming ashore at Kealakekua, Captain Cook was taken in hand by kāhuna and escorted to Hikiau Heiau. An elaborate ceremony was performed, including the sacrifice of pigs and the offering of a feather cloak to Cook. At the time, his officers believed that their captain was being revered as the god Lono. Nineteenth-century American missionaries, such as Reverend Hiram Bingham, condemned Cook's apparent willingness to be so honored as a blasphemy that was punished by his later death. Some contemporary scholars and Native Hawaiians have challenged this view of Cook's "deification," arguing that this ceremony depicted by John Webber was to honor him as a great chief, not a god. [Hawai'i State Archives]

WITNESS TO HISTORY

A HAWAIIAN VIEWS THE LEGACY OF CAPTAIN COOK,

The seeds that he [Captain Cook] planted here have sprouted, grown, and become the parents of others that have caused the decrease of the native population of these islands. Such are gonorrhea, and other social disease; prostitution; the illusion of his being a god [which led to] worship of him; fleas and mosquitoes; epidemics. All of these things have led to changes in the air which we breathe; the coming of things which weaken the body; changes in plant life; changes in religion; changes in the art of healing, and changes in the laws by which the land is governed.

Samuel M. Kamakau, Feb. 16, 1867, *Ruling Chiefs of Hawaii*

On February 14, 1779, Captain James Cook was killed on the shores of Ka'awaloa at Kealakekua Bay on the island of Hawai'i. John Webber recorded this tragic scene, published in 1782 as an engraving, "The Death of Captain Cook." The unfortunate dispute arose over a stolen cutter, and the consequences were deeply regretted by both sides once their passions subsided. [Mitchell Library/State Library of New South Wales]

During a violent encounter on the shore, Cook and his men fired upon the Hawaiians. When Cook's men paused to reload they were attacked. Cook ordered his men to return to the ship, but it was too late. He was stabbed in the neck and killed. At least four others in the landing party were also killed. The survivors in Cook's group made an escape, retreating to the main ship and leaving behind their Captain and the other deceased crew members.

Hostilities escalated over the course of several days, and four marines and an unknown number of Hawaiians were killed. A stalemate existed over the return of Cook's remains, which had been taken inland. Eventually a procession of Hawaiians bearing white flags and beating drums returned Cook's remains wrapped in kapa (barkcloth) and covered by a feather cloak. Within the kapa, however, were only some of Cook's remains; the rest remained in the possession of native chiefs. Cook's hands and feet had been preserved with pa'akai (sea salt), with the rest of his flesh stripped from his bones and burned. Cook's crew held a naval burial service. The ship's cannons were fired in salute, and Cook's remains were lowered into Kealakekua Bay.

THE RISE OF KAMEHAMEHA

The man who would be known as King Kamehameha I, unifier of all the Hawaiian Islands, was born Pai'ea Kamehameha around the year 1758. His rise from warrior to ruler was marked by a number of great battles that shaped him as a strategist and a leader of men. A full reporting of Kamehameha I's campaign's would fill a number of volumes, following is a brief account of the battles that enabled his ascension.

Precipitated by the slaughter of his people at Kaupō, Maui by the warriors of Hawai'i Island ruler Kalani'ōpu'u in 1775, Maui Island ruler, Kahekili, raised an army to counter Kalani'ōpu'u's aggression. The ensuing clash has been passed down to history as The Battle of Kalaeoka'īlio ("The cape of the dog") and proved to be the first major test of the young warrior Kamehameha.

During the battle, Kalani'ōpu'u's warriors encountered a superior force and were compelled to flee. Despite the retreat, however, Kamehameha acquitted himself well, displaying both fierceness in battle and great loyalty for his fellow warriors, when he rescued his mentor Kekūhaupi'o from a surrounding group of Maui warriors. The surviving Hawai'i Island warriors returned home to regroup as Kalani'ōpu'u prepared to avenge his defeat by Kahekili. It is said that Kamehameha was displeased at having been ordered to attack the Kaupō people and complained to Kalani'ōpu'u, his uncle, that the assault was a cowardly act, unsupported by the god of war, and had engendered the defeat of the Hawai'i Island forces at the hands of Kahekili.

What Kalani'ōpu'u thought of his nephew's boldness has been lost to history, but the ruler did remember the warrior when, in 1780, he met with his chiefs to establish his successor. Kīwala'ō, Kalani'ōpu'u's oldest son, would assume the role of ruler upon his father's death. Kamehameha (Kalani'ōpu'u's nephew) would become chief of Kohala on land that was Kamehameha's by inheritance, and Kamehameha would be given guardianship of the family's feathered war god, Kūkā'ilimoku, along with the responsibility of caring for the heiau (sacred places of worship) associated with the war god.

Afterward, Kalani'ōpu'u captured an enemy chief of Puna named Imakakola for a human sacrifice ceremony to consolidate his chiefdom. Imakakola was taken to the luakini heiau (where human sacrifices are performed) at Kamā'oa called Pākini, which was built by Kalani'ōpu'u. When Kalani'ōpu'u's son Kīwala'ō initiated the sacrificial ceremony, Kamehameha boldly stepped in and finished the ritual, placing Imakakola on the altar. This action by Kamehameha caused controversy and led to a rift between Kīwala'ō and Kamehameha.

"Kamehameha's business agent John Young and a visiting foreign officer are in conversation with two guards beside one of the eighteen cannons that faced the bay. The thatched building in the distance at right is the king's retreat, the doorway concealed by a small guardhouse where Kamehameha could securely keep watch over the traffic in the bay as well as view his upland plantations. The heiau, built on a platform of rockwork, was dedicated to patron spirits of learning, the arts, and healing. The largest structure, the hale mana (house of power), required more than three hundred thousand ti leaves in the thatching. Ahu'ena heiau is now on the National Registry of Historic Places." Voyagers [*Ahu'ena Heiau*/Herb Kawainui Kāne]

Kalani'ōpu'u died in April of 1782, and Kīwala'ō brought the deceased ruler's bones to Hale-o-Keawe, the royal mausoleum at Pu'uhonua o Hōnaunau in Kona. Kīwala'ō then took his place as ruler of Hawai'i Island. The young ruler's first political act—the redistribution of the lands of Hawai'i Island—only served to exacerbate the ill-will between himself and his cousin, Kamehameha, and divided the loyalties of the island's chiefs.

Kīwalaʻō's redistribution took away from Kamehameha and the Kona chiefs lands that were formerly under their rule. This caused Kamehameha to unite with the chiefs of Kona, and he soon became their leader. The stage was now set for a battle for Hawaiʻi Island, one that would presage the ascendancy of a young warrior chief.

That battle, known as The Battle of Mokuʻōhai, was fought in 1782 at Keʻei, Kona. The young warrior Kamehameha led his warriors to victory, and the chief Kīwalaʻō was killed. When Kīwalaʻō died he was wearing an ʻahu ʻula (feathered cloak), which then became the property of Kamehameha. Afterward, Hawaiʻi Island was divided into three chiefdoms: Keawemauhili ruled Hilo and a portion of Puna and Hāmākua; Keōuakūʻahuʻula ruled Kaʻū and part of Puna; Kamehameha ruled Kona, Kohala, and northern Hāmākua.

Kamehameha then campaigned for nearly a decade to control the rest of Hawaiʻi Island. Kamehameha's two opponents were: Keōuakūʻahuʻula (Kīwalaʻō's younger brother and chief of Puna and Kaʻū) and Keawemauhili (Keōuakūʻahuʻula's uncle and Kalaniʻōpuʻu's brother). It was during this period that Kamehameha also began a military campaign to conquer other Hawaiian Islands.

In 1790, Kahekili was Hawaiʻi's most powerful aliʻi (chief), ruling Maui, Lānaʻi, and Molokaʻi. He was in alliance with his half-brother, Kāʻeokūlani, ruler of Kauaʻi, who seized Oʻahu by killing its chief and sacrificing him to his own war god, also killing lesser chiefs of Oʻahu and using their skeletons to construct a house of bones.

Fearing conquest of Hawaiʻi Island by Kāʻeokūlani and Kahekili, Kamehameha decided to strike first, and landed his troops on Maui to fight against Kalanikūkupule, son of Kahekili. Kamehameha considered it a good omen when the feathers of his war god Kūkāʻilimoku bristled.

Fighting between the two groups of warriors began in Wailuku, and then proceeded up into ʻĪao Valley where the precipitous cliffs at the head of the valley blocked escape. Kamehameha's forces had the advantage of superior western weapons (muskets) as well as

The Ahu'ena heiau at Kamakahonu, Kamehameha's royal compound in Kailua-Kona, in an early nineteenth century lithograph by Louis Choris titled *Temple on the Island of Hawai'i*, 1816. [Honolulu Academy of Arts]

Pu'ukoholā Heiau was built by Kamehameha as a gift for his war god Kūkā'ilimoku where he was honored with innumerable human sacrifices. Kamehameha was blessed with military strength and victory as a result of building the heiau. It was the last heiau to be built on the Island of Hawai'i. It was abandoned after the overthrow of the kapu in 1819. [*Kamehameha Building Pu'u Kohola Heiau*/Herb Kawainui Kāne]

Pu'ukoholā Heiau

After unsuccessful attempts to conquer Hawai'i Island in the 1780s, Kamehameha sent Ha'alo'u, the grandmother of the future Queen Ka'ahumanu, to O'ahu to request an oracle from Kapoukahi, a highly respected Kaua'i seer and kahuna (priest) who was in Waikīkī at the time. Kapoukahi answered that Kamehameha would be victorious over all the Islands only if he built a luakini heiau (where human sacrifices were performed) to his war god, Kūkā'ilimoku. The heiau was to be built at Kawaihae on Hawai'i Island and named Pu'ukoholā.

In the summer of 1791 Pu'ukoholā Heiau was completed. Kamehameha asked Keōua, chief of the Puna and Ka'ū districts, to attend the dedication, telling him that his presence was important between the rivals. Keōua and twenty-six of his chiefs and friends arrived in two large canoes at Kawaihae Bay. Greeting Keōua and his men were Kamehameha's war canoes arranged in a great crescent shape surrounding Kawaihae Bay to prevent Keōua's escape.

As they arrived at the shoreline Keōua and many in his party were killed (it is unknown whether Kamehameha ordered this attack). Their bodies were sacrificed on the altar of the luakini heiau atop the hill at Pu'ukoholā. With his rival dead, Kamehameha controlled Hawai'i Island.

a cannon manned by the foreigners John Young ('Olohana) and Isaac Davis ('Aikake).

Facing imminent defeat, Kahekili's son, Kalanikūpule, fled over a narrow mountain pass along with his high chiefs, and they sailed to O'ahu where Kahekili began war preparations. Kamehameha's troops returned to Hawai'i Island but Kamehameha sailed to Moloka'i to meet with his chiefs and advisers.

An early nineteenth century portrait of Kamehameha I may have been a copy of one of the two portraits known to have been sketched by the artist Louis Choris, who sailed with the explorer von Kotzebue. Kamehameha is shown wearing Western clothing. In daily life, he preferred the comfort of the traditional malo, or loincloth, but formal portraits called for Western formal wear. [Bishop Museum]

Following his victory at the Battle of Kepaniwai, Kamehameha sent Ha'alo'u (the grandmother of Ka'ahumanu) to O'ahu to consult with Kapoukahi, a highly respected kahuna (priest) of Kaua'i. Kapoukahi answered the request from Kamehameha for an oracle, telling Kamehameha that he would be victorious over all the Hawaiian Islands only if he built a heiau dedicated to his war god, Kūkā'ilimoku. This heiau was to be built at Kawaihae on Hawai'i Island, and named Pu'ukoholā ("Whale hill"). Kamehameha's royal architect Kapoukahi traveled from Kaua'i to assist Kamehameha in the construction and consecration of the massive heiau.

In the summer of 1791, with construction of Pu'ukoholā Heiau completed, Kamehameha asked Keōuakū'ahu'ula, chief of Hawai'i Island's Puna and Ka'ū districts, to attend the dedication of the heiau, telling Keōuakū'ula his presence was important if there was to be peace between the rivals. Keōuakū'ahu'ula and 26 of his chiefs and friends, including the highest chiefs of Ka'ū, arrived at Kawaihae Bay in two large canoes.Greeting Keōuakū'ahu'ula and his men were Kamehameha's war canoes arranged in a great crescent shape surrounding Kawaihae Bay to prevent Keōuakū'ahu'ula's escape.

As they arrived at the shoreline of Kawaihae Bay, Keōuakū'ahu'ula was killed along with many of his chiefs and other members of his group. The bodies of the killed chiefs were sacrificed on the altar of the luakini heiau atop the hill at Pu'ukoholā. With his rival dead, Kamehameha controlled Hawai'i Island.

Kamehameha's aspirations did not end with Hawai'i Island. In February of 1795, Kamehameha and his warrior army sailed from Kohala on Hawai'i Island to Lahaina, Maui to take on food and other provisions, and then sailed to Kaunakakai, Moloka'i where they prepared to invade O'ahu. In April of 1795 they set sail from Moloka'i to begin the invasion. It is estimated that Kamehameha's forces consisted of 960 canoes, 20 armed foreign ships, and troops totaling an estimated 16,000 soldiers, many trained in modern musketry.

The Pōhaku Naha (Naha Stone) today sits on the lawn of the Hilo Library. In ancient times this sacred rock was part of an important tradition as it was said that a newborn child who stayed quiet when placed on the stone was of royal blood if he/she remained quiet. In 1775 the young warrior Kamehameha moved this monumental rock after a high priestess predicted that whoever moved it would conquer all of the Hawaiian Islands. The prophecy was fulfilled in 1775 when Kamehameha became ruler of a united Hawaiin Kingdom. Also on the Hilo Library lawn is the Pinao Stone, which is said to have been a entrance pillar to Pinao, a heiau (sacred place of worship) that was also the former site of the Naha Stone. [Hawai'i State Archives]

"The wars were over and the Kingdom of Hawai'i firmly established. At Kamakahonu, his estate at Kailua Village in Kona, Kamehameha devoted his last years to ruling his kingdom as a benevolent and just monarch, encouraging prosperity, conducting business with foreigners, and educating his son Liholiho as his successor. [Here he is] wearing [a] simple kapa garment [while] in conversation with his son Liholiho. Beside him stands his prime minister, Kalanimoku. The prince's attendant, wearing a short yellow cape, is John Papa Ī'ī, who later became an important historian. The fish in the foreground represent the gifts brought daily to the court. Two ladies of the court are seated at the left. Kamehameha's residence was a complex of thatched structures around a tranquil cove at Kailua Bay. Across the cove stands 'Ahu'ena, his private temple." [*Kamehameha in Kona*/Herb Kawainui Kāne]

Also allied with Kamehameha were 16 foreigners, including several manning Kamehameha's cannons.

Kamehameha's warriors landed on O'ahu's southern shores from Waikīkī to Wai'alae, and then prepared to meet the forces of O'ahu's chief Kalanikūpule, an estimated 9,000 warriors arrayed throughout Pū'iwa and La'imi, and mauka (toward the mountains) all the way to Luakaha. Kamehameha's warriors who landed at Wai'alae marched over the plains of Kaimukī to Mō'ili'ili where they joined with the troops marching from Waikīkī. This united force then proceeded behind Pūowaina (now called Punchbowl Crater) to Nu'uanu where the warriors confronted the forces of the O'ahu ruler.

The first confrontations occurred at La'imi and Pū'iwa, and neither side gained a clear advantage. However, the O'ahu forces were gradually overpowered and retreated up into Nu'uanu Valley. Many of the fleeing warriors climbed the valley's sides while others retreated up to Nu'uanu Pali at the head of the valley.

Fleeing from Kamehameha's onslaught, some of Kalanikūpule's warriors escaped over the valley's ridges and others made it down the trail at the end of the pali (cliff). Those who didn't escape were confronted by Kamehameha's soldiers at the edge of the precipice at Nu'uanu Pali. Many of the O'ahu warriors were driven over the edge of the cliff at Nu'uanu Pali or jumped to avoid surrender, and met their death on the rocks hundreds of feet below.

Chief Kalanikūpule escaped from the battlefield and hid in the Ko'olau mountains. He was captured several months later in the upper Waipi'o-'Ewa area, then killed and presented to Kamehameha, who offered the body as a sacrifice to his war god.

The Battle of Nu'uanu was Kamehameha's final major military conquest; with his victory, Kamehameha gained control of all of the Hawaiian Islands except Kaua'i and Ni'ihau. In the wake of this conquest, Kamehameha established a system of governance for the Islands under his dominion, with himself as Mō'i, or king. The warrior's quest to consolidate his power and unify the Islands was, at last, complete.

The culminating battle of Kamehameha's thirteen-year struggle to unite the Islands was in 1795. The warrior chief's well prepared invasion force channeled the allied forces of O'ahu, Maui, and Kaua'i up Nu'uanu valley to face certain defeat atop a twelve-hundred-foot precipice. After the battle, only the Islands of Kaua'i and Ni'ihau remained beyond Kamehameha's immediate grasp. [*The Battle at Nu'uanu Pali* © 2009 Herb Kawainui Kāne]

Kānāwai Māmalahoe
Law of the Splintered Paddle

In 1797, Kamehameha forgave a fisherman who twelve years earlier had hit him with a paddle. The man was brought to King Kamehameha to be punished, but instead Kamehameha forgave the man, gave him land, and set him free.

He then passed what came to be known as Kānāwai Māmalahoe, or "Law of the Splintered Paddle," to protect weak people from injustices imposed by those who are stronger. It was the first law meant to protect commoners.

A Hawaiian saying states: "Aole i 'ena'ena ka imu i ka māmane me ka 'ūlei, i 'ena'ena i ka la'ola'o." ("The imu is not heated by māmane and 'ūlei wood alone, but also by the kindling."), which is explained to mean that a ruler, in order to be powerful, must have the loyalty of commoners as well as chiefs. [Pūku'i]

In 1853, Honolulu Harbor was a major port of call for whaling ships. The artist Paul Emmert sketched this wonderfully detailed view of the "lower roadstead" from near the lighthouse at the channel entrance. Nestled against the majestic Ko'olau Mountains with the distinctive "U-notch" of Nu'uanu Valley, and the ridge crest of the ancient crater Pūowaina, or Punchbowl, the town teemed with Hawaiians, foreign merchants and missionaries. The large three-story coral building to the left with with solid iron doors and shuttered windows was the old Custom House, built in 1843 at the foot of Nu'uanu on Queen Street. The two-story structure in the center was the popular Market House, built by the Hawaiian Kingdom in the 1850s. In the background rises the steeple of the Bethel Mission on Bethel and King Streets. From the 1830s on, this seaman's church ministered to the men who "went down to the sea in ships." [The Hawaiian Historical Society]

19TH CENTURY

1801—Hualālai Volcano on Hawai'i Island erupts above Ka'ūpūlehu at an elevation of about 5,750 feet, sending lava flows to the ocean. Kamehameha obeys the warning of a kāula (seer) that the volcano goddess Pele is angry and must be calmed with gifts. He first throws his offerings into the flowing lava, but when the eruption continues he cuts his own hair and throws it into the lava—an act that is symbolic of giving his own self to Pele—and the lava flow soon ceases.

1802—A Chinese man on Lāna'i becomes the first person in the Islands to process and refine sugarcane.

1803—Under the command of American trader William Shaler (c.1773-1833), the American brig *Lelia Byrd* brings the first horses to the Hawaiian Islands from California.

Henry 'Ōpūkaha'ia 1792–1818

In 1802, Kamehameha's armies killed the parents and baby brother of 'Ōpūkaha'ia, a ten-year old Hawaiian boy in Ka'ū. From then on, fear and sadness haunted the child. It was, he said, "better for me to go." In 1808, after hearing about the Christian God, 'Ōpūkaha'ia saled off on an American trading ship. Acknowledged as the first Hawaiian Christian, he studied at Andover Theological Seminary under a new name, Henry Obookiah. In 1816, the Congregational Church formed the American Board of Commissioners of Foreign Missions and opened a school in Connecticut where boys like Henry could learn how to bring the Christian word back home. 'Ōpūkaha'ia began translating the Bible into Hawaiian and prepared to retun to the Islands. But on February 17, 1818, he died of typhus fever. He left behind a journal that lamented that his native land was still steeped in paganism and ignorance. Published as Memoirs of Henry Obookiah and Supplement that same year, it quickly sold over 50,000 copies and inspired the formation of First Company of missionaries for Hawai'i. These New England Congregationalists pledged themselves to fulfill the young Hawaiian's dream. [Hawaiian Mission Children's Society]

A foal and a mare are unloaded at Kawaihae for John Young ('Olohana), and a mare and a stallion are landed at Lahaina for Kamehameha.

One foreigner who became a trusted friend and advisor to Kamehameha was the Englishman John Young, drawn in 1819 by Jacques Arago. In 1790, Young, or "Olohana" (from the command "all hands"), was taken captive by Kamehameha. Despite several failed attempts to escape, Young resigned himself to stay in the Islands, becoming an important military and political advisor. John Young was priviliged to be at the side of the great king when he died in 1819, having achieved the respected status of a chief among the people he served. [Hawai'i State Archives]

1804—Kamehameha continues planning to attack Kaua'i, but an epidemic of ma'i 'ōku'u (likely cholera), infects his warriors, killing thousands, including the high chiefs, Ke'eaumoku and Pāpa'iaheahe, and delaying for the second time a Kaua'i invasion. Kamehameha renews his attack plans, constructing with the help of foreigners a large armada of ships in Waikīkī.

1804, June 7—The first Russian ships arrive including the *Neva* under the command of Captain Urey Lisianski and the *Nadeshda,* under the command of Captain Adam Johann von Krusenstern. On a three-year around-the-world journey (1803-1806) their mission is to re-establish trade with China and Japan, and to find more fur trading opportunities. En route to China, the *Neva* runs aground on a shoal near Midway Atoll on October 15, 1805 (a nearby islet now bears the name Lisianski) and returns to the Islands in 1809.

1805—Hawai'i's population is estimated to be 264,160.

1808, September 8—Grace Kama'iku'i, daughter of Ka'ō'ana'eha and John Young, is born. She will go on to adopt her own niece, the future Queen Emma.

1809—ʻŌpūkahaʻia, son of Nāmakaehā, leaves Hawaiʻi on the *Triumph,* eventually reaching Connecticut where he becomes a Christian and takes the name Henry Obookiah. His death in Connecticut in 1818 inspires the first American Christian mission to the Hawaiian Islands.

1810—King Kaumualiʻi acknowledges the sovereignty of Kamehameha and agrees to place Kauaʻi and Niʻihau under his control. Kaumualiʻi is allowed to remain as Kauaʻi's vassal ruler, and Kamehameha declares the Hawaiian Islands to be one nation.

1810—Isaac Davis dies after apparently being poisoned for warning Kauaʻi's vassal ruler Kaumualiʻi of a plot against his life when he goes to Oʻahu to cede Kauaʻi to Kamehameha. His daughter, (Betty Davis) was the wife of Kaumualiʻi's son (Humehume).

1811—Juan Elliot d'Castro, Hawaiʻi's first trained foreign doctor, becomes Kamehameha's physician and secretary.

1812—Kamehameha returns to Hawaiʻi Island to live in Kailua-Kona.

1814, March 17—Kauikeaouli, Kamehameha III, is born at Keauhou, Kona.

1815—Russian representative Georg Anton Schäffer begins building a blockhouse near the Honolulu waterfront. After Schäffer is forced to leave, the Hawaiian monarchy rebuilds the fort known as Fort Kekuanohu using the original coral and adobe. Barracks and quarters are located inside the 340-foot by 300-foot structure having 12-foot-high walls and about 50 guns acquired from various visiting ships mounted on the parapets. In 1849, the French ransack the fort over a dispute about duties on imports and freedom of worship. The fort is later used as a police headquarters and prison before being demolished in 1857.

1815—John Palmer Parker arrives in Waimea on Hawaiʻi Island for Kamehameha to kill wild cattle whose meat and hides are to be sold to visiting ships. Parker later marries a Hawaiian princess and starts a cattle ranch now the second largest private ranch in the United States.

1816, May 21—After leaving Oʻahu, Schäffer entices Kauaʻi's vassal ruler Kaumualiʻi to sign a document placing Kauaʻi under the protection of the Russian Czar, and promises Kaumualiʻi independence from Kamehameha. Kaumualiʻi later renounces the treasonous agreement, and Schäffer is forced to leave the Islands.

Choris, a young Russian of German descent, accompanied Otto von Kotzebue on the voyage of the *Rurik* and made many sketches and watercolors in 1816, including several portraits from life of Kamehameha in his later years. [Hawaiʻi State Archives]

1816—Captain Otto von Kotzebue sails the Russian exploring ship *Rurick* to Kailua-Kona and befriends Kamehameha. The *Rurick*'s official artist, Louis (Ludwig) Choris, draws several watercolors and sketches of the Hawaiian Islands as well as portraits of Kamehameha, including the famous one of Kamehameha dressed in traditional Western sailor's clothes with blue pants, white shirt, red waistcoat, and a yellow silk necktie.

1817—Alexander Adams, the commander of Kamehameha's sandalwood trading fleet, sails the *Forester* (renamed *The Kaahumanu*) to China with a load of sandalwood but is refused entry into the harbor at Macao because the Hawaiian flag flown by the ship is not recognized. Adams is believed to be the person who first placed the Union Jack at the upper left corner of the Hawaiian flag.

1818, February 9—Kaʻoleioku, the son of Kamehameha I and Kanekapolei, dies. Kaʻoleioku was the grandfather of Bernice Pauahi and Ruth Keʻelikōlani.

1818, February 17—ʻŌpūkahaiʻa, a Hawaiian missionary also known as Henry Obookiah, dies in Connecticut.

1819, May 8—Kamehameha dies at his Kamakahonu ("Eye of the turtle") Kailua-Kona home. Ulumāheihei (Hoapili) is entrusted with hiding his bones.

MOMENT IN HISTORY

THE DEATH OF KAMEHAMEHA
MAY 8, 1819

As the great chief Kamehameha lay dying in Kailua-Kona on Hawai'i Island, his counselors, friends and family gathered in solemn attendance. The medical kāhuna agreed they could do nothing to prevent his death. One of them told Kamehameha, "You must place yourself in the hands of the god who alone has power over life and death." A human sacrifice to the great god Kūkā'ilimoku was suggested. Kamehameha prevented it by saying, "Men are sacred to the chief."

Born at Kohala, Hawai'i, some time between 1736 and 1758, Kamehameha was responsible for unifying the Islands under one leader. By 1795, through skilled warfare and astute negotiations, he controlled the islands of Hawai'i, Maui, Kaho'olawe, Lāna'i, Moloka'i and O'ahu. He tried to conquer Kaua'i and Ni'ihau, but two attempted invastions failed. By 1810 he convinced the great Kaua'i chief Kaumuali'i to submit to his supreme authority.

A fierce warrior in battle, Kamehameha proved to be a wise ruler in peace. He was devoted to the ancient ways and gods, and realized that the introduction of foreign influences would threaten the sovereignty of his people. To reflect the neutrality of his kingdom, he had a flag designed that cleverly incorporated elements of the British, American and French flags.

Kamehameha showed heightened concern for the stability of his country in the days preceding his death. Recognizing the youthful nature of his son Liholiho, destined to be Kamehameha II, he asked his favorite wife, the powerful Ka'ahumanu, to serve as kuhina nui, or regent. Among those also in attendance was his close friend and advisor John Young, the Englishman who assisted in the wars of unification.

On an evening in May 1819, according to historian Samuel M. Kamakau, Kamehameha was taken to the men's eating house and given a small mouthful of food and water. One of the chiefs asked Kamehameha to provide them with a last word.

"For what purpose?" he asked.

"As a saying for us," was the response.

"E oni wale no 'oukou i ku'u pono 'a'ole e pau." Endless is the good I have given you to enjoy.

Early the following morning the last breath left Kamehameha. As the great chief's memory was enshrined in the nation's heart, the islands he had united faced decades of upheaval and change.

1819, May 20—Kamehameha's 24-year-old son Liholiho takes the throne as Kamehameha II. Within months he eats food in public with the dowager queens Ka'ahumanu and Keōpūolani breaking the kapu (prohibition) against men and women eating together. This begins the erosion of traditional Hawaiian religious beliefs eventually leading to the complete overturning of the traditional kapu system.

1819, August 8—Louis de Freycinet, the French explorer, visits Hawai'i.

1819, Sept. 29—Two New England ships, the *Equator* and the *Balena,* become the first whaling ships to arrive, beginning Hawai'i's whaling era.

1819—Kekuaokalani, the son of Kamehameha's younger brother and the keeper of Kamehameha's war god Kūkā'ilimoku, rebels against Kamehameha II's abolishment of the eating kapu. His warriors fight Kamehameha II's forces at the Battle of Kuamo'o on Hawai'i Island. Kekuaokalani and his wife are killed, and the revolt is defeated. Another rebellion is later defeated in Hāmākua.

Kamehameha II 1797–1824

It is hard to imagine a greater contrast in characters than the one between young Liholiho (Kamehameha II) and his father, Kamehameha I. Where the great King had been firm, his son wavered; where the father held to Hawaiian traditions, the son ushered in an era of change.

Liholiho was twenty-two years old when he became King at Kailua-Kona on May 20, 1819. Hardly had he been sworn in before the gathered chieftains of his realm, than he demonstrated the deference to Ka'ahumanu that would to characterize his reign. Ka'ahumanu, his father's favored wife, confronted the new King in front of the assembled nobles and said that it had been his father's wish for her to share rulership of the land. Had anyone attempted such audacity in front of Kamehameha I, the culprit might well have been slain on the spot. Liholiho, offering no objection, split his power in half by accepting Ka'ahumanu as kuhina nui, a newly invented title meaning premier, but which implied the sharing of kingly power.

Above, upper left: During the reign of Kamehameha II (Liholiho), the ancient kapu system was overthrown, the American missionaries arrived, and the sandalwood trade flourished. Liholiho also led a stormy voyage to Kaua'i to bring back as his vassal Kaumuali'i, that island's king. [Hawai'i State Archives]

Upper right: Queen Kamāmalu, favorite wife of Kamehameha II, pictured during a 1824 trip to London where both died of measles within six days of each other.

Lower: Ka'ahumanu, the daughter of the Maui chief Ke'eaumoku, was Kamehameha I's favorite wife when this portrait was completed by Louis Choris in 1816. In 1793 when she was about sixteen years old, Captain George Vancouver described her as "one of the finest women we had yet seen on any of the islands." A bold and intelligent woman, she served as kuhina nui (premier) for Kamehameha II and as regent for Kamehameha III after the death of her husband. She played a leading role in the overthrow of the ancient kapu system. When the missionaries arrived in Hawai'i, they realized that efforts to convert a nation without the support of chiefs and chiefesses would be futile. King Kamehameha II had little interest in Christianity, as did his wife, Queen Kamāmalu. Attempts to proselytize often fell on deaf ears. Queen Ka'ahumanu originally rejected the religious zeal of Reverend Bingham, making the unofficial head of the mission bow and touch the tip of her finger in great deference Then in 1825, a nearly fatal illness, followed by a full recovery, led to her conversion—a spiritual transformation. [Hawai'i State Archives]

Opposite page: Kamehameha was possibly seventy years old when Choris drew this portrait in 1816. While his actual height and weight have been widely speculated, this lithograph depicts a white-haired gentleman with a muscular physique worthy of a warrior. [Bishop Museum]

In August of 1819, Captain Louis de Freycinet of the French warship *L'Uranie* sailed into the waters of Kawaihae, on the island of Hawai'i. There, he learned from John Young that Hawai'i's ancient religious system had just been overthrown and that the political situation for the new king, Kamehameha II, was very tenuous, as defenders of the old religion were mounting armed resistance. At Young's urging, a Catholic baptism was held for Chief Kalanimoku onboard the ship. Its chaplain officiated with the "utmost simplicity." In attendance were Ka'ahumanu, the queen regent; Boki, governor of O'ahu; and the interpreter Monsieur Jean Rives. Yet, even as the participants in this ceremony, as depicted by Jacques Arago, were being introduced to Catholicism, Protestant missionaries were preparing to sail from Boston to the Hawaiian Islands. [Bishop Museum]

Hanarourou (Honolulu) was a settlement of coral stone buildings dominated by the fort, the king's palace and surrounded by hundreds of grass houses, when Louis Choris, draftsman aboard the Russian exploratory vessel *Rurick,* sketched the village in the 1810s. Foreign vessels and the seaport trade were now making Honolulu a regular port of call as the king had moved from Waikīkī to the sheltered harbor. [Hawai'i State Archives]

The Sandalwood Trade

ʻIliahi, the Hawaiian name for the sandalwood tree, means "fiery surface" and refers to the tree's reddish blooms and new leaves. Ancient Hawaiians had many uses for the tree, including placing its powdered heartwood between layers of kapa barkcloth to impart the sweet fragrance to the cloth. A mixture added to kapa dyes was made by adding ʻiliahi to the oil of niu (coconut palm) heated with hot stones.

In 1790, ship captain John Kendrick (c.1740-1794) left two of his crew on the island of Kauaʻi to collect sandalwood. This was a prelude to the sandalwood trade, which began in 1791 when it was discovered that the fragrant wood could be sold for a high price in Canton, China. Extensive sandalwood groves in the mountains of the Hawaiian Islands were harvested and shipped to China where they valued the close-grained fine-smelling wood for making fine furniture, boxes, chests and carvings, as well as perfume and incense. The older trees were the most valued due to their increased fragrance (the scent increases with age).

In 1811, Jonathan and Nathan Winship arrived on the *O'Cain* and the *Albatross,* and took away a load of sandalwood. Kamehameha was pleased with his profits and granted the Winships and Captain William Heath Davis an exclusive ten-year contract for sales of sandalwood on all the Hawaiian Islands except Kauaʻi.

Between 1810 and 1820, sandalwood sold for about $125/ton, generating more than $3 million. The peak years of the sandalwood trade were from 1810 to 1840, a time that also saw a steadily increasing desire for Western goods in the Islands, and consequently a large debt incurred by the Hawaiian monarchy. By 1821, sandalwood exports totaled about 1,400 tons annually.

Chiefs forced makaʻāinana (commoners) to climb high in the mountains to cut down the tall trees. Carrying the wood down from the mountains was hard work, and intensive harvesting of sandalwood occurred at the expense of the loʻi kalo (taro patches) and other traditional agricultural food production and cultural practices. Sandalwood traders supplied the Hawaiians with furniture, clothes, liquor and other Western goods that increasingly eroded away at traditional native ways of living.

As the sandalwood forests of the Hawaiian Islands were logged at a rapid pace to meet China's growing market, the supply of the valued wood rapidly declined and was eventually exhausted. By 1840, nearly all of Hawaiʻi's large, marketable sandalwood trees had been cut down, ending the sandalwood trade with China. Though the large sandalwood groves of ancient times are gone, smaller trees remain. Currently only one of Hawaiʻi's four endemic (unique) sandalwood species is listed as endangered.

Three prominent chiefs drawn by Pellion. On the left is Keʻeaumoku the Second, brother of Queen Kaʻahumanu and one of the Kona chieftains who became governor of Maui under the assumed name "Cox." The tattooing on his right arm "... Tamaahmah Died May 8, 1819," was commonplace among those mourning their dead king. When Governor Cox died in March of 1824, his brother, high chief Kuakini, known as John Adams, Governor of Hawaiʻi and acting Governor of Oʻahu, reportedly had the body removed from the casket after the Christian funeral "to see whether the foreign God would know the difference." In the center of the picture is a "High Chief of Hawaiʻi" and on the right Keʻeaumoku's principal officer. 1819. [Hawaiʻi State Archives]

The early port of Honolulu—or "Honoruru" as it was sometimes pronounced—was a curious blend of architecture. Native grass-thatched homes stood next to Western-style frame houses, many brought from New England as prefabricated buildings. The introduction of cattle by Captain George Vancouver during the 1790s created a special problem: the animals often ate the pili grass roofs of native homes. Eventually stone walls were erected as protection from grazing herds that roamed freely. Honolulu had a natural harbor cut into the reef by freshwater streams[,] and was an ideal anchorage for large foreign vessels. The surrounding village grew quickly in the 1820s, where over four thousand Hawaiians and two hundred Westerners lived along the waterfront at what became known as Merchant Street and Nu'uanu Avenue. [Hawai'i State Archives]

The Breaking of the Kapu

Kamehameha's 24-year-old son Liholiho, took the throne as King Kamehameha II on May 20, 1819. Within months, the new king ate food in public with the dowager queens Ka'ahumanu and Keōpūolani, thus breaking the kapu (prohibition) against men and women eating together. This event was known as the 'Ai Noa (free eating).

When the defiant act brought no retribution from the gods, men and women eating together was no longer kapu, beginning a process that eroded away at traditional Hawaiian religious beliefs. It eventually led to the complete overturning of the traditional kapu system including the dismantling, abandoning, and burning of idols.

Kekuaokalani, the son of Kamehameha I's younger brother, Keli'imaika'i, rebelled against King Kamehameha II's abolishment of the eating kapu. He was the keeper of King Kamehameha I's renowned war god Kūkā'ilimoku, and was encouraged to revolt by revered kāhuna (high priests) including Kūāiwa and Holoialena.

In 1819, Kekuaokalani fought the forces of King Kamehameha II at the Battle of Kuamo'o on Hawai'i Island. Both sides were armed with Western weapons. Kalanimoku led Liholiho's forces, which were supported by canoe-mounted American swivel guns. Kekuaokalani was killed at Kuamo'o along with his wife Manono and the kahuna Kūāiwa. The last battles took place at Waimea, where the revolt was defeated. Another rebellion was later defeated in Hāmākua.

The Exploits of Georg Anton Schäffer

Georg Scheffer [Hawai'i State Archives]

Georg Anton (Egor Nikoloaevich) Schäffer (1779-1836) was a surgeon in the Russian army and had built hot air balloons in Moscow in 1812 to observe the movements of Napoleon's armies. In 1815, the Russian-American Company sent Schäffer to Hawai'i to retrieve or seek appropriate payment for the cargo of the *Behring,* which had wrecked off Kaua'i. When Schäffer arrived in late 1815, he cured King Kamehameha I of a feverish cold, and was given land on the Honolulu waterfront where he began building a blockhouse, which John Young persuaded King Kamehameha to halt the work lest the Russians become too influenced. (See 1815.)

With three Russian ships, Schäffer then traveled to Kaua'i where he befriended Kaua'i's vassal ruler, Kaumuali'i. On May 21, 1816, Schäffer enticed Kaumuali'i to sign a document putting Kaua'i under the protection of the Russian Czar. Schäffer proceeded to build Fort Elizabeth at Waimea, Kaua'i, naming the fort in honor of the consort of the Russian Emperor Alexander I. Fort Elizabeth overlooked Waimea Bay, and its guns were positioned to protect the anchorage's trading vessels. At Hanalei Schäffer built two more forts including Fort Alexander overlooking the mouth of the Hanalei River and Fort Barclay on Hanalei Bay.

Though Schäffer was overstepping his authority, he sought a trade monopoly for Russia of O'ahu's valuable sandalwood, and in return promised Kaumuali'i independence from King Kamehameha I and conquests of other Hawaiian Islands Kaumuali'i felt he had a hereditary right to rule because Kaumuali'i had ceded the island of Kaua'i to King Kamehameha I in 1810, so the agreement with Schäffer was considered treasonous. Nevertheless the Czar's flag flew over Kaua'i.

When Otto von Kotzebue visited the Hawaiian Islands in 1816 on the Russian Navy brig *Rurik,* he repudiated Schäffer's acts. In May of 1817, Kaumuali'i renounced his agreement with Schäffer, who was soon forced to leave. On July 7, 1817, Schäffer departed on the American vessel *Panther* headed for Macao. In 1821, he went to Brazil where he was made a nobleman by Emperor Dom Pedro I, under the title of Count von Frankenthal.

Parker Ranch

In 1815, John Palmer Parker arrived in Waimea, Hawai'i to kill wild cattle for King Kamehameha I. Kamehameha hired Parker to shoot the cattle, which had proliferated in Waimea due to a kapu (prohibition) placed upon them with the intention of letting the animals multiply after they were brought to the island by George Vancouver. The cattle were killed for their meat, which was salted and sold to visiting ships. The hides were also exported. Parker claimed to have shot well more than 1,000 cattle.

Parker later married a Hawaiian princess, the cousin of Kānekapōlei, the wife of the high chief Kalani'ōpu'u. Parker began acquiring grazing land and building up a herd of tame cattle, and he also built a sawmill. John Palmer Parker's son, John Palmer Parker II, continued to increase the size of Parker Ranch. In 1943, 30-year-old Richard Palmer Smart became the sole owner of Parker Ranch, the second largest private ranch in the United States at more than a half million acres.

A model of the Brig *Thaddeus* built by sailors of the Pacific Fleet Command at Pearl Harbor, O'ahu and presented to the Hawaiian Evangelical Association in Honolulu in 1934. It has been on display at Moku'aikaua Church since 1975. [LaRue Piercy]

Hiram Bingham, head of the first company of Protestant missionaries, was instrumental in Queen Ka'ahumanu's conversion to Christianity, and by extension, the entire Hawaiian nation's, after she pulled through an extensive illness. He and his wife were newlyweds when they posed for this portrait by Samuel F.B. Morse. They were introduced and married only weeks before the brig *Thaddeus* set sail in October 1819. [Hawai'i State Archives]

1820, March 31—The First Company of American missionaries arrives from Boston on the brig *Thaddeus,* under the command of Andrew Blanchard.

Physician Thomas Holman, a non-ordained missionary, and his wife Lucia arrived on the *Thaddeus* with the first group of Protestant missionaries. [Hawai'i State Archives]

1820, April 25—Hiram Bingham preaches his first sermon on and performes the first Christian marriage on August 11, 1822 when he marries Thomas Hopu to his bride Delia. Bingham preached and taught throughout the Islands for the next two decades. He was particularly influential among the ali'i. He helped develop the Hawaiian alphabet, assisted in the first translation of the Bible, and was the architect and first pastor of Kawaiaha'o Church. He also helped establish Punahou School for missionary and chiefs' children (originally called Kapunahou). The Binghams moved back to New England in 1840 due to Sybil's poor health. They had seven children.

1820, May 3—Missionaries Samuel Ruggles and Samuel Whitney arrive on Kaua'i with the son of Kaua'i's vassal ruler Kaumuali'i, Prince George Kaumuali'i (Humehume), who had been sent to the United States as a child. Kaumuali'i gives Ruggles and Whitney a residence and land to establish a mission station.

1820, July 16—Missionaries Elisha Loomis and Maria Loomis have a son, Levi Sartwell Loomis, the first Caucasian born in the Islands.

1821, July 21—Kamehameha II sails to Waimea, Kaua'i on the royal yacht *Ha'aheo o Hawai'i* (*Pride of Hawai'i)* to meet with Kaua'i's vassal ruler Kaumuali'i, who pledges his allegiance to the king and accepts his sovereignty. Kamehameha II completes a 42-day tour of Kaua'i and anchors in Waimea Bay on September 16, inviting Kaumuali'i to come aboard where he is taken to O'ahu as a prisoner. The powerful kuhina nui (premier) Ka'ahumanu, the former queen as wife of Kamehameha, later marries Kaumuali'i to ensure the monarchy's control over Kaua'i. Kaumuali'i passes away on O'ahu in 1824.

1821, September 15—A Hale Pule (Christian Meeting House) is dedicated at the future site of Kawaiha'o Church. The Hale Lā'au (Frame House), which serves as a missionary residence is also built.

1822, January 7—Missionary Elisha Loomis uses a second hand iron and mahogany Ramage press brought on the *Thaddeus* to complete the first printing in the Islands.

1822, January 25—Charles Reed Bishop, the future husband of Princess Bernice Pauahi is born in Glens Falls, NY. In 1889, he establishes the Bernice Pauahi Bishop Museum as a memorial to his wife.

1822, March 29—The colonial cutter *Mermaid* (a British sloop), arrives along with the *Prince Regent,* a 70-ton schooner built in New South Wales for Kamehameha fulfilling an earlier promise by

In the 1820s Kamehameha II and Kamehameha III lived in compounds which included traditional native houses as well as a prefabricated foreign house given to them by sandalwood merchants. This painting shows "A View of the King's Palace on Beretania Street and the southeastern part of Honolulu at O'ahu, May 1826." The first location of the royal compound was toward the rear of the village, near the home of the British Consul, which was called "Beretannia" or Britain, a name later affixed to the road through the area (now as Beretania Street). As chiefs became Christianized later in the decade, they moved closer to Kawaiaha'o, where the American Protestant mission was located. In 1845 the first 'Iolani Palace was completed near King and Richards Streets. [Hawai'i State Archives]

George Vancouver. The two ships carry a delegation of the London Missionary Society, including British missionary William Ellis, who had been living in Tahiti. Ellis spends four months on O'ahu communicating well with native Hawaiians in their language. His many notes, providing one of the most complete records of early Hawaiian life, later becomes a book.

1822, August 11—Missionary Hiram Bingham performs the first Christian marriage in the Islands by marrying the missionary youth Thomas Hopu to his bride Delia.

1823—William Ellis returns to the Islands and tours Hawai'i Island with three American missionaries searching for mission sites. In

In 1823 Kamehameha II and Queen Kamāmalu with an entourage of nobles sailed for England, where they were royally entertained and attended a performance at London's Drury Lane Theatre. John William Gear lithograph, 1824. [Hawai'i State Archives]

1825 he publishes *A Narrative of an 1823 Tour Through Hawaii* and in 1830 *Polynesian Researches, During a Residence of Nearly Six Years in the South Sea Islands,* containing extensive descriptions of Hawaiian history and culture.

1823, April 27—The *Thames,* under the command of Reuben Clasby, arrives with the Second Company of American missionaries.

1823, September 16—Queen Keōpūolani, the sacred wife of Kamehameha, becomes the first native Hawaiian to receive the Protestant rite of baptism. Missionary William Ellis administers the sacrament to Keōpūolani an hour before her death.

1823—A Hale Pa'i (Printing Office) is constructed in Honolulu near the Hale Pule (Mission House) to be the home of the Mission Press which will print millions of pages in the Hawaiian language. The first book, published in 1823, is *Na Himeni Hawaii (Hymns of Hawai'i).*

1823, November 27—Kamehameha II and Kamāmalu leave for England on the whaler *L'aigle.* Kuhina nui (premier) Ka'ahumanu is left in charge of the government.

1823, December 10—Moku'aikaua Church is dedicated in Kailua-Kona. Four thousand people assist in the construction of the new church built on the site of Hawai'i's first Christian church under the direction of Kuakini (John Adams), the brother of Ka'ahumanu.

1824, March 22—Ke'eamoku II, who had served as governor of both Maui and Kaua'i, dies in Honolulu.

1824, May 26—Kaumuali'i, who became ruler of Kaua'i in 1794, dies in Honolulu.

1824—Humehume, the son of Kaua'i's former ruler Kaumuali'i, challenges the rule of Kamehameha II with a surprise attack on Kaua'i's Waimea fort. His forces are defeated in a brutal confrontation known as 'Aipua'a ("Pig eater") that results in virtually all of Kaua'i's chiefs being replaced with O'ahu and Maui chiefs loyal to Kamehameha II.

1824— Kamāmalu (July 8) and Kamehameha II (July 14) die of measles in London, England.

1824—Chiefess Kapi'olani, a Protestant convert, leads a march from Kona to Kīlauea Volcano where she defies the volcano goddess Pele by proclaiming the power of Jehovah. When Kapi'olani is not engulfed by lava, at least 90 Hawaiians, including the high priest of the volcano, join the Hilo mission and convert to the Protestant religion. The English poet laureate Lord

In 1824, the devoutly Christian chiefess Kapi'olani and fifty attendants journeyed from Kona to Hilo. On the way, they climbed Kīlauea to see the famous lake of lava. According to Hilo missionary Joseph Goodrich, who later met Kapi'olani at the crater rim, some local Hawaiians "tried to dissuade Kapi'olani from going up to the volcano. They told her that Pele would kill her and eat her up if she went there. She replied that she would go, and if Pele killed and ate her up, they might continue to worship Pele, but if not, i.e. if she returned unhurt, then they must turn to the worship of the true God." Kapi'olani, undaunted, climbed to the edge of the crater. She led the party in a hymn. The party then descended and proceeded to Hilo.

Goodrich's first-hand account is matter-of-fact. Other missionaries embroidered the story, and later storytellers dramatized it even further, adding new characters and incidents. Still, even in its earliest and simplest form, the story is compelling. Kapi'olani was threatened with Pele's wrath and ignored the threats, confident that her new god was stronger than Pele. [*Kapi'olani Defying Pele* by Herb Kawainui Kāne]

Kamehameha III, Kauikeaouli, and his wife, Kalama Hakaleleponi Kapakuhaili, had two children, both of whom died as babies. The royal couple adopted three hanai children, including his nephew, Alexander Liholiho, who eventually ascended the throne as Kamehameha IV. During his long reign, the sandalwood trade declined, whaling grew and then declined, the sugar industry began, and the missionaries built churches and schools. [Hawai'i State Archives]

Alfred Tennyson later writes a poem entitled "Kapiolani" in commemoration of the event.

1825—First experimental sugar fields are set up in Mānoa Valley on O'ahu.

1825, May 3—The bodies of Kamehameha II and Kamāmalu arrive from London aboard the Navy frigate *Blonde* commanded by Lord George Anson Byron, who later writes *Voyage of H.M.S. "Blonde" to the Sandwich Islands, 1824-25.*

1825, June 6—Liholiho's brother, Kauikeaouli, becomes Kamehameha III, reigning for the next 30 years.

1825, December 4—Ka'ahumanu, wife of Kamehameha I and Queen Regent for Kamehameha II and III, is baptized along with her cousin Kalanimoku and his son Leleiohoku, her sister Pi'ia, Deborah Kapule, and Gideon La'anui.

1825—About 6,000 Hawaiians live in the village of Honolulu along with 300 foreigners. More than 150 trading and whaling ships arrive annually with thousands of sailors.

1825, October—Whalers angry at missionary-influenced restrictions attack the Lahaina home of Reverend William Richards.

1826—Captain James Hunnewell settles in Honolulu as agent for a Boston company trading sandalwood with China. By 1843 this firm will be C. Brewer & Co., the oldest firm in Hawai'i.

Humehume and Kaua'i's Last Rebellion

Prince George Kaumuali'i, also known as Humehume, was born about 1797 to Kaua'i's King Kaumuali'i and a commoner wife. As a child, he was sent to the United States for an education, but the money given to his guardian for his education was either squandered or lost. Humehume was enlisted in the U.S. Marine Corps during the War of 1812 and injured in a naval battle. In 1815 he enlisted in the Navy and sailed on the U.S.S. *Enterprise* to the Mediterranean. He then worked in the Boston Navy Yard and later studied at the Foreign Mission School in Cornwall, Connecticut.

On May 3, 1820, Humehume returned to Kaua'i to reunite with his father after many years apart. In 1824, after Kaumuali'i passed away on O'ahu, Humehume challenged the rule of King Kamehameha II with a surprise attack on the fort at Waimea, Kaua'i. The fort was successfully defended, and Humehume's troops retreated to nearby Wahiawā and Hanapēpē.

Kamehameha II was away in England at the time of the attack, leaving kuhina nui (premier) Ka'ahumanu in charge of the Hawaiian monarchy. In response to Humehume's rebellion, the well-armed troops of Ka'ahumanu's principal counselor Kalanimoku marched on Hanapēpē and the Wahiawā plains. Maui's Governor Hoapili commanded the warriors including 350 Maui soldiers and 1,000 soldiers from O'ahu.

Kalanimoku's warriors easily defeated Humehume's meager and ill-prepared forces which were armed only with spears and a few muskets. An estimated 50 to 130 of Humehume's group were killed, including women and children. Many of the dead were left on the battlefield to be eaten by pigs, and thus the event came to be known as 'Aipua'a ("Pig eater").

Humehume fled on horseback into the mountains with his wife and child, but was later captured. Ka'ahumanu replaced virtually all of Kaua'i's chiefs with O'ahu and Maui chiefs loyal to her and to King Kamehameha II. Humehume remained imprisoned on O'ahu until his death of influenza on May 3, 1826.

1826, January 16—The armed schooner *Dolphin,* the first American warship to visit Hawai'i, arrives in Honolulu to visit the Islands. On February 26, the *Dolphin's* crew along with other sailors, angry about a missionary-inspired ban on women visiting ships, break first into the home of Kalanimoku, the kālaimoku (counselor) of kuhina nui (premier) Ka'ahumanu, and then into the home of Reverend Hiram Bingham, known for his strict upholding of religious doctrine. He is protected from the unruly mob by Hawaiians.

1826, May 3—George Humehume Kaumali'i, who had left Hawai'i at a young age to return with the first 1820 group of American missionaries, dies.

1826, May 26—Kahakuha'akoi Wahinepio, wife of Kamehameha I and former governor of Maui, dies.

1826, June 17—Kalanipauahi, mother to Princess Ruth Ke'elikōlani, dies during an epidemic in Honolulu.

1826, October 21—The sloop of war U.S.S. *Peacock*, under the command of Captain Thomas Catesby Jones, arrives in Honolulu Harbor.

1826, December 21—Hawai'i's first general tax law is passed to provide revenue for shipbuilding and development.

1827, February 8—Kalanimoku, prime minister under Kamehameha I, II, and III, dies in Kailua-Kona.

1827, July 7—The first Catholic missionaries in Hawai'i arrive on the French ship, *La Comète.*

Boki and Liliha

Boki was governor of O'ahu under King Kamehameha II. His original name was Kamā'ule'ule ("The one who faints") but he was nicknamed Boki after King Kamehameha I's favorite dog, Poki ("Boss"). The handsome couple accompanied Kamehameha II and Queen Kamāmalu on their ill-fated visit to London in 1824, where this portrait was painted by John Hayter. After returning to the island, Boki became increasingly friendly with the foreign merchant community, which often put him at odds with Rev. Hiram Bingham and Queen Ka'ahumanu.

As governor of O'ahu, Boki initially supported them, giving land at Kawaiaha'o for their homes and a church, and at Punahou to establish a school for their children.

He came into conflict with kuhina nui (premier) Ka'ahumanu in the late 1820s when he converted to Catholicism which angered Ka'ahumanu who wanted all the chiefs to accept Protestantism and sought to forcibly deport Catholic priests. In May of 1827, Ka'ahumanu charged Boki with intemperance, fornication, adultery and misconduct, and fined him and his wife, Liliha. Heavily in debt, Boki decided in 1829 to sail to the South Pacific (New Hebrides) in search of sandalwood on the *Kamehameha* and the *Becket* which left Hawai'i on December 2 carrying 400 followers.

Near the Fiji island group the two ships became separated. The *Kamehameha* perished in a fire apparently started by a smoker who accidentally ignited gunpowder in the ship's hold and most of the crew of 250 died, including Boki. The crew of the *Becket* was decimated by disease and other mishaps, and finally returned to Honolulu on August 3, 1830 with just 20 survivors.

Liliha continued to oppose the religious and social controls of the Protestant mission. In 1831, she helped foment a brief, failed rebellion against the government of Queen Ka'ahumanu. [Hawai'i State Archives]

1827, July 14 (Bastille Day)—Reverend Alexis Bachelot leads Hawai'i's first Catholic Mass. On November 30, 1827, the child of Spaniard Francisco de Paula Marín, an advisor to Kamehameha, becomes the first foreign baby to be baptized in the Islands.

The Mission Houses

On September 15, 1821 a Hale Pule (Christian Meeting House) built to hold 3,000 people was dedicated in Honolulu at the future site of Kawaiha'o Church. Hawaiians framed and thatched the original structure, which had imported windows, doors, a pulpit, and a bell.

Also built nearby in the same year was the Hale Lā'au (Frame House), a two-story prefabricated structure brought by the missionaries which served as a residence for various missionaries, including Hiram Bingham, Gerrit Judd, and Elisha Loomis.

The other structure, still standing from the original headquarters, is Hale Kamalani, also known as the Chamberlain House. Constructed in 1831, it was built of coral blocks, and was home to the Mission's business agent, Levi Chamberlain (1792-1849) as well as used as a storeroom. Chamberlain had arrived in Hawai'i in 1823 and later helped found Punahou School (originally called Kapunahou).

On January 7, 1822, missionary Elisha Loomis used a second hand iron and mahogany Ramage press brought on the *Thaddeus* to complete the first printing in the North Pacific region at the grass-thatched Meeting House. Ke'eaumoku II (Governor Cox) pulled the lever to begin the printing process to create the first spelling book in Hawai'i.

In 1823, a new Hale Pa'i (Printing Office) was constructed of coral blocks that became home to the Mission Press, which eventually printed millions of pages in Hawaiian. Language teachers and translators utilized the lead-type press helped by Hawaiian assistants including John Papa 'Ī'ī. In 1823 the first book published in the Islands, *Na Himeni Hawaii* (Hymns of Hawai'i), came off the press. In the following years, Hale Pa'i produced books, broadsides, hīmeni (hymns), newspapers, rules, primers, and the first translation of the Bible into the Hawaiian language. It is considered the birthplace of the written Hawaiian language.

Today the complex of the original missionary buildings is known as the Mission Houses Museum. The Wood Frame House, the oldest wood frame house in Hawai'i, has been restored to reflect its original architecture and decor.

1827, December 7—Hawaiian chiefs agree on laws (kānāwai) banning murder, theft, rum selling, prostitution, and gambling.

1827, December 8—The British Consul General Charlton and a Honolulu merchants' group use their influence to change the laws of December 7. Laws prohibiting murder, theft, and adultery will go into effect in three months but laws prohibiting prostitution, gambling, and selling rum will be adopted later.

1827, December 14—A meeting with all chiefs marks the beginning of formal legislation in the Kingdom of Hawai'i. The resulting laws are to not kill, commit adultery, or steal.

1828, March 30—The *Parthian,* under the command of Richard D. Blinn, arrives with the Third Company of American missionaries.

1828—Hawai'i's first stone church, named Waine'e ("Moving water"), is constructed in Lahaina, Maui.

1829, December 2—The *Kamehameha* and the *Becket* leave Hawai'i for the South Pacific carrying Boki, who had been the governor of O'ahu under Kamehameha II, and more than 400 of his followers to look for sandalwood in the South Pacific. Fire and disease decimate the crews, and only 20 return.

1829—Missionaries select a 12-letter alphabet and outline a structure for the written Hawaiian language, adopting five vowels (a, e, i, o, and u) and seven consonants (h, k, l, m, n, p, and w) to capture the sounds of Hawaiian using English letters.

1829—Kuhina nui (premier) Ka'ahumanu orders that practicing Catholics be punished and sent to Kaho'olawe, which becomes a penal colony. In 1831, Ka'ahumanu expels Catholic priests from the Hawaiian Islands.

MOMENT IN HISTORY

PLANTING THE TRUE VINE OF GOD, THE ARRIVAL OF THE FIRST AMERICAN PROTESTANT MISSIONARIES MARCH 31, 1820

In 1819, the first group of missionaries set sail from Boston after attending church services. The voyage to the Hawaiian Islands on the brig *Thaddeus* took nearly six month. Sent by the American Board of Commissioners for Foreign Missions, the band of "brothers and sisters" included several ministers, teachers, a printer, a farmer—all with their wives, some just newly married. They had been instructed to set high standards, and to cover the land in schools, churches and homes under the banner of Christian civilization. Although three Hawaiian accompanied them as tutors in the native language, the missionaries knew little abut the people they intended to convert.

On a March afternoon in 1820, the ship approached the island of Hawai'i with its lofty summits of Mauna Loa and Mauna Kea. A boat sent to shore to prepare inhabitants for the arrival of the first missionaries returned with astonishing news. "Kamehameha is dead—his son Liholiho is king—the tabus are abolished—the images are destroyed—the heiau of idolatrous worship are burned, and the party that attempted to restore them by force of arms has recently been vanquished!" Reverand Hiram Bingham, unofficial leader of the Christian band, proclaimed that the hand of God had prepared the way for the mission.

The following morning the *Thaddeus* was surrounded by hundreds of natives in canoes, coming to greet the newcomers. Many Hawaiians had never before seen white women and were fascinated by their bonnets and high-necked dresses. The unashamed nakedness of the natives caused the Christian newcomers to shield their eyes or burst into tears.

"Can these bc human beings? asked Reverend Bingham. "Can such beings be civilized? Can they be Christianized?" Yes, he concluded, through the knowledge of faith. Thus began one of the most important, controversial, and at times painful transformations to affect the Native Hawaiian people.

Asa and Lucy Thurston, who arrived with the Binghams in the pioneer missionary company, devoted their entire lives to Moku'aikaua Church in the village of Kailua-Kona on Hawai'i Island. They were photographed in Honolulu on their 40th wedding anniversary in 1859. [Bishop Museum]

WITNESS TO HISTORY

A HAWAIIAN VIEW OF THE MISSIONARY LEGACY

During these years [the early 1820s reign of Kamehameha III], when a teacher became the leader for the kingdom of God in Hawai'i no one questioned the division between the old and the new religion. There was only one principle of division in the kingdom of God, all that did not belong to it was sin. God did not say this or that was wrong; it was the kingdom of God which was the dividing line. The kingdom of Hawai'i became a kingdom that worshipped God. The chiefs upheld the hands of Ka'ahumanu, and the nation turned to the truth. No one during those years could be seen worshipping in the old way; no one was to be seen inspired by a spirit, possessed by spirits, practicing sorcery; there was not much 'awa drinking; no fire places for burning in the kuni sorcery were to be seen, nor any of those ancient practices which had passed away at the time of free eating in Liholiho's day. It was a time when all Hawai'i turned to do homage to the kingdom of God. The plover flew in peace, the rat squeaked without fear in his hole, the shark showed his teeth unmolested in the wave, there had never been such peace before.

Some of the missionaries thought it wrong to protect this government of God; the kingdom of God is not a kingdom ruled by a king (they said). Perhaps this was not the king's thought in joining the kingdom which he ruled as chief with the kingdom of God. He did not mean to give up his rule as chief, but to make God the protector of the kingdom and of his rule over it. That was his real thought. God was to be the judge to set his kingdom to rights, and that was why he commanded the whole nation to learn to read and to turn to the word of God. Strange indeed were the hard thoughts of the missionary!...So they girded up their loins, sharpened their knives, and chose which part of the fish they would take one of the side piece, another the belly, one the eyes, another white meat, and another red meat. So they chose as they pleased. When the last man of them had come they were treated like chiefs; lands were parceled out to them; they were given the same honors as Ka-umu-ali'i. Yet they found fault. Now you want to close the door of heaven to the Hawaiians. You want the honors of the throne for yourselves—because you sit at ease as ministers upon your large land.

Samuel M. Kamakau, 1869
S.M. Kamakau, *Ruling Chiefs of Hawai'i*

In remote Waipi'o Valley, the traditional Hawaiian life was able to sustain itself throughout the nineteenth century. This etching is from a drawing by Reverend William Ellis, who in 1823 was the first foreigner to visit the royal village of Waipi'o. It shows a land still rich in cultivation. [Bishop Museum]

1830—The sandalwood era ends due to there being no more trees to harvest.

1830—Commercial ranching begins on Hawai'i Island when cowboys from Mexican California arrive to instruct Hawaiians on managing cattle. This is the beginning of the paniolo or Hawaiian cowboy, a word derived from the Spanish "españoles." Between 1835 and 1840, about 5,000 beef hides are exported annually.

1830, December 11—Lot Kamehameha (Kamehameha V) and son of Kekuanaoa and Kina'u, is born.

1831—The first archipelago census gives a population of 130,313.

1831—Liliha, the former wife of Boki (Kamā'ule'ule), instigates an unsuccessful revolt against Kamehameha III.

1831, June 7—The *New England*, under the command of Avery F. Parker, arrives carrying the fourth company of American missionaries.

1831, September—American Protestant missionaries start Lahainaluna Seminary on Maui to provide advanced education for young Hawaiian men to become preachers. More than 1,100 missionary schools are operating throughout the Islands with a total enrollment of more than 50,000 students, mostly adults.

1831, December 29—Naihe-Haiha, "Orator of the Nation" and chief counselor to Kamehameha, dies in Kona.

1832—The *Denmark Hill* becomes the first whaling ship to sail under the Hawaiian flag.

Lahainaluna High School was founded in 1831, to train Hawaiian men to be school teachers or assistant pastors of rural congregations. Rev. Lorrin Andrews was its only teacher until 1834. Under his direction the first pupils constructed and furnished the school's buildings. David Malo and Samuel M. Kamakau, best of the native historians, were early students. Many graduates rose to positions in the nation's government. Lahainaluna engraving. [Hawai'i State Archives]

1832—The Hawaiian translation of the *New Testament* is published, and missionary Hiram Bingham presents a copy to kuhina nui (premier) and former queen, Ka'ahumanu shortly before her death.

1832, May 17—The whaling vessel, *Averick*, under the command of Captain Swain, arrives carrying the fifth company of American missionaries.

1832, June 5—Ka'ahumanu, former queen as wife of Kamehameha, passes away at her Mānoa Valley home Puka'ōma'o, "Green opening" (the home had green shutters). She had served as kuhina nui (premier or regent) after the death of Kamehameha I, co-ruling from 1819 to 1832 with Kamehameha II and Kamehameha III during their reigns.

1833—Under the command of Captain Rice, the *Mentor* arrives carrying the sixth company of American Missionaries.

1834—Kamehameha III establishes the first police force, the predecessor of the Honolulu Police Department.

1834, February 9—Alexander Liholiho, Kamehameha IV, is born.

1834, February 14—Lahainaluna Seminary begins publication of a four-page Hawaiian language weekly, *Ka Lama Hawaii* (The Hawaiian Luminary), the first periodical printed in the North Pacific region.

1834, March 5—The Oahu Amateur Theater, Hawai'i's first community theater, has its first performance.

1834, December 5—*The Hellespont*, under the command of Captain Henry, arrives carrying the seventh company of American missionaries.

As the sandalwood trade waned, whaling became the economic mainstay of merchants in Hawai'i. Each season the crews of the American whaling fleets descended like locusts on the ports of Honolulu and Lahaina, seeking provisions and the sailors' traditional pleasures of the bottle and the flesh. It took boldness and strength to be a whaleman, and many lost their lives when the giant sea mammals smashed the tiny boats of their persecutors. [Hawai'i State Archives]

During Prince Kauikeaouli's young manhood, personal troubles worthy of a Greek tragedy embittered his life, for he and his sister, Princess Nahi'ena'ena, were very much in love. Shocking as this may seem to modern Western sensibilities, such unions were acceptable among the nobles of ancient Hawai'i, just as they were among the Egyptian pharaohs. Close relatives often married to keep the chiefly bloodlines pure and to ensure that children would have powerful mana or spiritual power. This word describes a Polynesian concept in which certain persons possess supernatural power and authority derived from their ancestors. Mana is accumulated by uniting persons or families with powerful mana, and offspring of these pure bloodlines were considered even closer to the divine than their parents. The greater the charge of mana, the greater his sacred power, the greater his right to rule. Tortured by love for her brother and guilt from newfound Christian beliefs that had made inroads into traditional Hawaiian ways, Princess Nahi'ena'ena drifted into despondency and died at the age of twenty-one. Long after Prince Kauikeaouli became King Kamehameha III, he regularly visited her grave in Lahaina. [Hawai'i State Archives]

1834, December 31—Kapi'olani, future wife of Kalākaua, is born.

1835, January 31—William Lunalilo, who will reign for thirteen months (1873-1874), is born.

1835—Kōloa Sugar Plantation becomes Hawai'i's first successful commercial sugar plantation.

1835—The first documented case of leprosy (Hansen's Disease) in Hawai'i is a woman named Kamuali on Kaua'i. The disease was likely present at least a decade earlier based on missionary descriptions of people with symptoms. In 1848 the diesease is confirmed in Honolulu.

1836, January 2—Emma Na'ea, later Queen Emma, wife of Kamehameha IV, is born.

1836, November 16—Kalākaua is born on O'ahu.

1836, November 16—Great Britain and Hawai'i negotiate a treaty signed by Kamehameha III.

1836, December 30—Nāhi'ena'ena, daughter of Kamehameha I and Keōpūolani, passes away.

1836—Reverend Lorrin Andrews, head of the Lahainaluna Seminary, publishes the first significant Hawaiian-English dictionary of 5,700 words, *Vocabulary of Words in the Hawaiian Language.*

1836, July 30—The four-page weekly *Sandwich Island Gazette and Journal of Commerce*, Hawai'i's first English-language paper, is published.

1837, April 9—The barque, *Mary Frazier*, under the command of Charles Sumner, arrives carrying

After the Kailua-Kona Church was destroyed in a terrible fire in December 1835, eager volunteers encouraged by Island of Hawai'i Governor Kuakini built Moku'aikaua Church in its place. The cornerstone was laid January 1, 1836, and almost one year later on January 31, the new church was completed. It was built to last with lava rock walls and a koa roof supported by 'ōhi'a beams. Benches were introduced for the first time, replacing floor mats. When they restricted space for the more-than-4,000-person congregation, a lānai was constructed around the sides of the building to provide additional seating. [Mutual Publishing]

Hulihe'e Palace, a two-story stone mansion in the Western-style, was built by Governor Kuakini in 1837-1838, on the seafront at Kailua-Kona. The building with a steeple is Mokuaikaua Church, also built in the 1830s by Kuakini. Hulihe'e Palace was the Kona residence of royal governors; the palace housed royalty of Hawai'i whenever they visited the Kona coast. Princess Ruth disliked the palace, and while governor of the Big Island, she lived either in her Hilo cottage or in a grass house on the Hulihe'e grounds. [Hawai'i State Archives]

the eighth company of American missionaries.

1837, Dec. 18—Kamehameha III issues an ordinance rejecting the Catholic religion, leading to a controversy with France.

1837, February 14—Kamehameha II marries Kalama in a ceremony performed by Reverend Hiram Bingham.

1837—Reverend John Diell organizes the O'ahu Bethel Church which holds 500 people and is Hawai'i's first church for foreigners. Diell and his wife Caroline distribute Bibles, religious tracts and spelling books to help sailors read.

1837—The O'ahu 'ō'ō bird (Moho apicalis) becomes extinct. Since ancient times, Hawaiians had valued the bird's plumage for use in their elaborate featherwork, including 'ahu 'ula (royal capes and cloaks) and mahiole (feather-crested helmets).

1837, Nov. 7—A tsunami generated near Chile hits Kahului, Maui, killing fifteen people and sweeping inland people, livestock, canoes, and the village's 26 grass houses. In Hilo, 100 houses are destroyed.

1838, September 2—Lydia Kamaka'eha, the future Queen Lili'uokalani and the last reigning monarch of Hawai'i, is born.

1838—Kuakini (John Adams), governor of Hawai'i Island, builds Hulihe'e Palace in Kailua, Kona. It is later home to Princess Ruth Ke'elikōlani, and then Kalākaua. In 1928, the palace is restored as a museum.

High Chief Kuakini, aka "John Adams," was the brother of Queen Ka'ahumanu. He served as the powerful governor of Hawai'i, building Hulihe'e Palace. He also served as governor of O'ahu during an 1831 uprising, and moved swiftly to close down grogshops, quell dissent, and enforce the Sabbath laws. "John Adams" Kuakini by Pellion, 1819. This sketch of Kuakini in Hawaiian costume appears to be a reworking of an engraving by Ellis. Kuakini is wearing an unconvincingly drawn Hawaiian feather cloak. [Hawai'i State Archives]

1838—An evangelical crusade led by Titus Coan converts more than 20,000 Hawaiians to the Protestant religion during a two year period known as "The Great Revival."

1839, April 4—Elizabeth Kahoʻanoku Kinaʻu, Kuhina Nui, dies.

1839, April 10—Kaikioʻewa, companion of Kamehameha I and governor of Kauaʻi, dies.

1839—Lahainaluna history teacher Reverend Sheldon Dibble *publishes A History and General Views of the Sandwich Islands Mission,* and then in 1843, *History of the Sandwich Islands,* based on research by students David Malo and Samuel Mānaiakalani Kamakau.

1839—Missionaries Amos Starr Cooke and his wife Juliette, a prominent music teacher, take charge of the Chiefs' Children's School (renamed Royal School in 1846). All five future rulers of the Hawaiian Kingdom attend the school, from Kamehameha IV to Liliʻuokalani as well as Princess Pauahi and the future Queen Emma.

1839, May 10—The first complete translation of the Bible into the Hawaiian language is completed in three volumes of over 2,331 pages.

1839, June 7—Kamehameha III issues a Declaration of Rights known as the Hawaiian Magna Carta. The document is a predecessor to Hawaiʻi's first formal constitution (1840) serving as its preamble. On June 17, the King issues an Edict of Toleration regarding religious differences, reversing his earlier stance banning the practice and teaching of Catholicism.

1839, June 8—The cornerstone of Kawaiahaʻo Church (originally known as Stone Church) is laid in Honolulu. More than 1,000 people construct the building, dedicated on July 21, 1842.

1839, July 9—The French Navy frigate *L'Artèmise* arrives under the command of Captain Laplace, commissioned by the French government to demand rights for French citizens in Hawaiʻi "with all the force that is yours to use," and to seek "complete reparation for the wrongs which have been committed."

Despite Kamehameha III's earlier Edict of Toleration, Laplace threatens war and makes a series of demands that include freedom of worship for Catholics, a site for a Catholic Church, and $20,000 in reparations (which is paid by local merchants). On July 17, Kamehameha III and Laplace sign the Convention of 1839 granting numerous protections to French citizens in Hawaiʻi.

Amos Starr Cooke (1810–1871) with daughter Mary Annis. [Hawai'i State Archives]

Opened in 1839 as The Chiefs' Childrens' School, Royal School educated Hawaiian monarchs until 1850. Missionary couple Amos and Juliette Cooke ran the boarding school, which taught subjects deemed necessary for future leaders. [Bishop Museum]

In 1843, the second Hawaiian licensed to preach by the missionaries was David Malo, a graduate of Lahainaluna School, and the author of a brilliant collection of oral histories *Hawaiian Antiquities*. Although a friend and outspoken defender of the missionaries, Malo was not ordained until 1852. Perhaps this reluctance to accept Native Hawaiians as full-fledged ministers contributed to his growing anti-foreign sentiments, which culminated in his desire to be buried high above Lahaina, far from the rising tide of foreigners. Malo was drawn in 1840 by A.T. Agate of the U.S. Exploring Expedition. [Hawai'i State Archives]

This is the first photograph of Kawaiaha'o Church, taken in 1857 by Hugo Stangenwald. It shows the arched entranceway and the wooden steeple, later removed. [Stangenwald/Bishop Museum]

Kawaiaha'o Church

O'ahu's largest church, Kawaiaha'o, was built in Honolulu on the site of a previous church known as the Christian Meeting House, or Hale Pule at the corner of South King and Punchbowl. Construction began in 1837 using plans drawn by Hiram Bingham.

Approximately 14,000 coral blocks, many weighing more than one ton, were cut using blunt axes from the ocean reef beneath 10 to 20 feet of water. Logs for the church were brought from north O'ahu to Kāne'ohe Bay by canoe, and then hauled over the mountain.

The cornerstone of the Church was laid on June 8, 1839. It was built in the New England style with Gothic influences. After more than four years of construction involving more than 1,000 people, the church was dedicated on July 21, 1842. Reverend Richard Armstrong presided over the dedication (Bingham had already left Hawai'i due to poor health).

In 1850 a clock tower (still in use today) was donated by James Hunnewell and installed in honor of King Kamehameha III.

The church served as the site of Kamehameha IV's coronation in 1854 and his marriage to Emma in 1856. It still reserves pews for descendants of Hawaiian royalty located at the rear of the church and marked with kāhili, the traditional royal standards. Portraits of Hawaiian royalty and important figures line the upper balcony walls. The church's spectacular pipe organ dominates the rear upper balcony.

Located just inside the main entrance gate is the Tomb of King Lunalilo, one of the first cement-block structures in the Islands. Many of Hawai'i's early missionaries are buried in a cemetery behind the church.

After the death of their stalwart supporter, Queen Ka'ahumanu, the missionaries looked to her successor to promote the cause of Christianity. As kuhina nui, Elisabeta Kīna'u continued to support the kingdom's mosaic laws. These had been established less than two decades before, and strict enforcement of the Sabbath often meant that on a Sunday, Honolulu was more sedate and devotional than any New England town of the same period. In this 1837 engraving by the French artist Louis-Jules Masselot, Queen Kīna'u and her retinue of mu'umu'u-clad ladies return from services at Kawaiaha'o Church. When she died just two years later in 1839, the Christian mission lost what Reverend Bingham described as "the kind, modest, firm, and sagacious patroness of the cause of reform at the Islands." [Hawai'i State Archives]

The frequent clashes between missionaries and merchants over the direction of the Hawaiian nation is captured in this 1837 drawing by Louis Masselot, "Assembly of Chiefs in Conference," at Halekauwila Palace in Honolulu. The one-room thatched government house, located near Honolulu Fort, was used for executive and judicial meetings during the reign of Kamehameha III. In the foreground, Captain DuPetit-Thouars of the French frigate *LaVenus* sits with other foreign dignitaries, demanding the rights of French priests to practice Catholicism in Hawai'i. King Kamehameha III sits in the armchair at the center background, listening intently to Kuhina Nui Kina'u on his left. Directly behind them is Rev. Hiram Bingham, accused by the French of prejudicing the Hawaiian rulers. Farther back are chiefs and chiefesses, some resting on mats. When the meeting concluded, two priests were given permission to remain in the Islands, and France and Hawai'i later pledged "perpetual peace and friendship." [Bishop Museum]

1840–1849

1840, May—Catholic missionaries Louis Maigret, Bishop Rouchouze, along with two other priests arrive in the Islands.

1840, June 6—The *Polynesian* weekly newspaper is published in Honolulu in English with some Hawaiian. The paper ceases printing on Dec. 11, 1841 and then begins again on May 18, 1844 under new editorship. Two months later it becomes the *Official Journal of the Hawaiian Government* and O'ahu's leading paper until 1861.

1840, September 23—Aboard the U.S.S. *Vincennes* that arrives in Hawai'i are the U.S. Exploring Expedition and its commanding officer Commodore Charles Wilkes.

1840, October 8—Kamehameha III and kuhina nui (premier) Kekāuluohi (Miriam 'Auhea) change Hawai'i to a constitutional monarchy via Hawai'i's first constitution, drafted in Hawaiian in 1839 and proclaimed (enacted) in 1840. The new government is based on American and British political models and provides for a Supreme Court (including the king), an Executive, a Legislative body of fifteen hereditary nobles, and seven representatives elected by the people and guarantees freedom of religious worship.

1840—Kamehameha III establishes a public school system.

1840, November 4—Hawai'i's first lighthouse is built at Keawa-iki in Lahaina, Maui.

1841—Samuel Kamakau establishes the Royal Hawaiian Historical Society.

1841, May 21—The *Gloucester*, under the command of Captain Easterbrook, arrives carrying the ninth company of American missionaries.

1842—Kawaiahao Congregational Church is built in Honolulu.

1842, January 13—Joseph Kaho'oluhi Nawahi, who will become a well-known artist, legislator, and principal advisor to Lili'uokalani, is born.

1842, May 15—Dr. Gerrit P. Judd, formerly a missionary, is appointed to the Treasury Board of the Hawaiian Kingdom. He is eventually appointed Secretary of Foreign Affairs.

1842, July 11—Punahou School is founded on O'ahu as a place of learning for the children of missionaries who had previously been sent back to New England for education. Reverend Daniel Dole and his wife are the school's first teachers.

1842—The United States recognizes the Kingdom of Hawai'i. In the summer of 1844, this recognition is reaffirmed.

1843, February 10—Lord George Paulet of Britain arrives on the frigate *Carysfort* and demands a military formal "provisional cession" of the Hawaiian Islands to Britain. Kamehameha III acquiesces to avoid bloodshed and allows the British flag to be raised.

1843, May 10—Kamehameha's Deputy Minister, Dr. Gerrit Parmele Judd (1803-1873), brings the King's public papers to the Royal Mausoleum at Mauna 'Ala for safekeeping where he uses the coffin of the late Ka'ahumanu as a desk to write appeals to London and Washington for help to resist Paulet's illegal actions.

1843, July 31—The provisional cession of the Hawaiian Islands to Britain is rescinded by Admiral Richard Thomas (1777-1851) who had been sent by Queen Victoria to restore control of the Hawaiian Islands to Kamehameha III. The British flag, which had flown over the Islands for five months, is lowered and replaced by the Hawaiian flag. Thomas declares Hawai'i an independent sovereign nation, and July 31 became Restoration Day.

1843, July 31—Kamehameha III recites what will become Hawai'i's national motto as part of his Restoration Day speech: "Ua mau ke ea o ka 'āina i ka pono." (The life of the land is perpetuated in righteousness.)

1843, November 28—Great Britain and France issue a joint declaration, signed in London, formally recognizing the independence of the Kingdom of Hawai'i (known then as the Sandwich Islands).

1845—The capitol is moved from Lahaina, Maui to Honolulu's Hale Ali'i, originally built by the high chief Mataio Kekūanaō'a for his daughter, Princess Victoria Kamāmalu. Kekūanaō'a gives Hale Ali'i to Kamehameha III and it serves for 33 years as the royal residence for the next four monarchs. Today it is the site of 'Iolani Palace.

1845—Theophilus Metcalf, Hawai'i's first commercial photographer, takes Daguerreotype photographs, considered the first ones in the Islands.

1845—Lahainaluna Seminary Press publishes the first English-Hawaiian

Honolulu Fort was established in 1816 in response to an abortive effort to raise the Russian flag over Honolulu harbor. It was of a simple rectangular design with twenty-feet thick walls constructed of coral blocks. The fort underwent significant renovations in 1831. Its numerous guns by 1853 had become outmoded. It fell briefly to British occupation in 1843 and to the French in 1849. Its troops were often needed to quell disturbances e.g. the "Sailor's Riot." With the construction of the Bethel police station and O'ahu Prison, its usefulness ended and was demolished in 1857. Governor Kekuanao'a's Office was located in the two-story building to the right. [*Interior of Honolulu Fort,* Paul Emmert 1853. [Bishop Museum]

Kekūanao'a, prominent chief and governor of O'ahu, was also father to Kamāmalu's brothers Alexander Liholiho (Kamehameha IV) and Lot Kapuaiwa (Kamehameha V). After returning from England Kekuanaoa married Pauahi, a granddaughter of Kamehameha I, who bore him Ruth Ke'elikōlani. When Pauahi died he married Elisabeta Kīna'u, Kamehameha's daughter, who bore him three sons, Moses, Lot, and Alexander, and a daughter, Victoria Kamāmalu. [Hawai'i State Archives]

Dictionary, *He Hoakakaolelo no na Hualelo Beritania (A Dictionary of English Words)*, edited by Artemas Bishop and J. S. Emerson.

1846, March—Kamehameha III passes the First Organic Act, establishing an executive branch of government as well as a Privy Council. The Second Organic Act is enacted on April 27, 1846, establishing a new system of land ownership. The Third Organic Act is enacted on January 10, 1848, reforming Hawai'i's judicial system.

1846, March 22—The French naval frigate *Virginie* arrives under the command of Rear Admiral Hamelin, who repays the $20,000 that Captain Laplace demanded and received in 1839.

1846, May 22—Under the command of Sir George W. Gordon, the British sidewheel steamer *Cormorant* becomes the first vessel to arrive by power rather than sail. Three years later the *Massachusetts* becomes the first steam-powered propeller vessel to arrive in the Islands.

1846—Whaling ship arrivals at Hawaiian ports peak with at least 596 whaling ships including 429 at Lahaina and 167 at Honolulu. During the 1840s and 1850s, thousands of Hawaiians work aboard the whalers.

1847, September 11—The 275-seat Thespian opens at King and Maunakea Streets, becoming Honolulu's first theater. The opening performances include The Adopted Child and Fortune's Frolic. The Thespian closes after just one

Lahaina and Lahainaluna, about 1848. [Bishop Museum]

season but is followed by the Royal Hawaiian Theatre in 1848.

1847, November—Hawai'i's first volunteer fire company is organized.

1847—A copper cent bearing the likeness of Kamehameha III is minted, becoming the first official coin of the Hawaiian Kingdom.

1847— Washington Place is built on Beretania Street by sea captain and merchant John Dominis, the father of Lili'uokalani's husband, John Owen Dominis. The senior Dominis disappears at sea circa 1850. When John Owen Dominis passes away in 1891 the queen inherits Washington Place where she lives until her death in 1917. In 1921, the Territory of Hawai'i purchases the stately Washington Place to use as a governor's mansion. It is now a museum with historical exhibits primarily dedicated to telling the story of Lili'uokalani and displaying her effects.

1848—Epidemics of influenza, whooping cough, and measles sweep through the Islands. Measles is brought to Hilo by an American warship, and in less than two years kills 10,000 people, an estimated ten to twenty-five percent of all Hawaiians.

1848, January 27—Kamehameha III begins the Great Māhele, which divides Hawai'i's land between the king and 245 chiefs, replacing Hawai'i's traditional land use practices with a new system of private property ownership. The Māhele ("Division") is completed on March 7, and the following day the king divides the remaining land between the king and the government. It ends with about 24 percent of Hawai'i's land owned by the king (Crown lands); 37 percent owned by the government; and 38 percent by ali'i (chiefs).

1848, February 14—As the deadline for filing claims with the Land Commission nears, an extension is allowed for the ali'i, but not for the maka'ainana (commoners).

1848, April—Two French ships arrive off Honolulu under the command of Rear Admiral Legoarant de Tromelin, who demands equality of worship and an end to duties on French imports claiming these acts violate an earlier treaty. Tromelin engages in reprisals that include taking over government buildings and ransacking Fort Kekuanohu in Honolulu. He departs ten days later.

1848, February 26—The barque *Samoset*, under the command of Captain Hollis, arrives with the twelfth and final company of American Missionaries.

1849—The royal brothers Alexander Liholiho and Lot Kamehameha set sail to tour the United States and Europe accompanied by Kamehameha III's Deputy Minister, Dr. Gerrit Parmele Judd. Racial prejudice experienced by the young royal brothers in the U.S. is formative in the decidedly pro-British reign of Kamehameha IV.

1849—German captain Heinrich (Henry) Hackfeld and his brother-in-law J. C. Pflueger start

Father Louis Maigret was a leader in the founding of the Catholic Church in Hawai'i and was its first bishop, serving for more than thirty years. [Hawai'i State Archives]

MOMENT IN HISTORY

THE MĀHELE TRANSFORMS THE LAND JANUARY 27, 1848

The merchants and traders who came to Hawai'i complained that the ancient land tenure system of ahupua'a thwarted their efforts to do business. Private property was nonexistent—the king retained legal possession of all land no matter who lived or worked on it. As more foreigners settled in the islands, their desire to own land led to frequent disputes. In 1843, a British subject claimed that his property had been illegally taken by King Kamehameha III. This inspired Lord Paulet to bring his man-of-war into Honolulu Harbor and seize the islands in the name of Queen Victoria. Although Hawaiian sovereignty was restored a few months later by Rear Admiral Thomas, government advisors pressed Kamehameha III to establish a Western form of land ownership.

One such advocate was the former physician missionary Dr. Gerrit P. Judd. As Minister of the Interior in the 1840s, he investigated ways to establish fee simple ownership. Finally, the privy council approved the Māhele, or land division, to allow for private property. In January 1848, two-hundred-fifty konohiki under the old system met to divide ownership of their parcels with the king. The division between chiefs and Kamehameha III was follwed by arrangements for giving land to Native Hawaiians who lived and worked on their kuleana, or small farms. This great revolution in land ownership was to have lasting ramifications on everyone's relationship to the 'āina.

a merchandising firm that later becomes American Factors Ltd. (Amfac), one of Hawai'i's "Big Five" companies.

1849-1851—The California gold rush creates a demand for potatoes, oranges, coffee, molasses, and other agricultural products from Hawai'i.

In 1849, Dr. Judd was appointed by Kamehameha III as special Commissioner and Plenipotentiary Extraordinary, empowered to travel to the United States and Europe and negotiate fair, equitable treaties. Accompanying him on this lengthy tour were Prince Alexander Liholiho (left) and Prince Lot Kamehameha (right), who enjoyed an outstanding opportunity to see the world beyond Hawai'i before each assumed the throne as Kamehameha IV and Kamehameha V. Dr. Judd grew to enjoy the accouterments of rank, including small gold crowns embroidered on his coat, but others viewed his use of power as despotic. In the face of growing criticism, he was forced to retire in 1853. [Hawai'i State Archives]

1850—The native Hawaiian population is 82,000 people.

1850—A group of Honolulu businessmen start the Royal Hawaiian Agricultural Society, whose goal is "to foster interest in the Agricultural and the Mechanical Arts" by educating farmers and land holders on the opportunities of cultivating their arable land. The Society eventually gains court influence leading to more liberal immigration policies.

1850, January 22—The Privy Council approves Thomas Square as the first park in the Islands. It is named for British Admiral Richard Thomas, who restored Hawaiian sovereignty after a five-month British occupation.

Rear Admiral Thomas led in the restoration of the monarchy after the rule of Paulet and remained in the Islands for six months. He was greatly liked and the site of the restoration, Thomas Square, bears his name. [Hawai'i State Archives]

1850, September 14—The first shipment of ice arrives in Hawaiʻi from Boston via San Francisco.

1850—The Kuleana Act is passed to define the land rights of makaʻāinana (commoners) on lands they have cultivated (kuleana). The Act authorizes a Land Commission to grant land titles. About 11,000 makaʻāinana are granted 28,600 acres, less than 1 percent of the available land, though much of it is prime agricultural acreage.

The Legislature also passes a law that allows non-Hawaiians (resident aliens) to own land. By 1890, more than 75 percent of lands originally granted to chiefs is owned by non-Hawaiians.

1850—Hawaiʻi's legislature passes the Masters and Servants Act, establishing a contract labor system to accommodate the importation of laborers to work on sugar plantations. It allows persons over twenty years of age to sign a contract binding them to an employer for up to five years.

1850—A Honolulu post office opens under postmaster Henry M. Whitney.

1850, December 12—Ten Mormons arrive from the California gold camps to become the first Mormon missionaries in the Islands. In 1855, one of them, George Q. Cannon, publishes a Hawaiian translation of the *Book of Mormon*, titled *Ka Buke a Moramona.*

1850, December 27—Kamehameha III signs an ordinance establishing the Honolulu Fire Department, Hawaiʻi's first fire department.

1851, February 1—Kamehameha III signs an agreement that places the Islands under the protection of the United States should French imperialism continue.

1851, October—The first printed postage stamps are issued. Henry M. Whitney, Honolulu's first postmaster, designs two, five and thirteen-cent stamps.

1851—The *Thetis* arrives from China with 195 men and 20 boys, the first contract laborers to come to the Islands to work on sugar plantations.

1852—The Honolulu Courthouse is built of coral blocks on Queen Street near the old Honolulu Fort. A second story is added one year later making it one of Hawai'i's largest buildings. The Supreme Court and the Legislature of Hawaiʻi both use the building, also the site of banquets, musical performances, church services and official ceremonies.

1852—About 50 foreign businessmen in Honolulu organize the Hawaiian Guard to keep the peace in Honolulu and stop riots. This group is considered the origin of today's Hawaiʻi National Guard.

1852—The arrival of whaling ships (519) and merchant ships (235) is at its peak.

1852—Kamehameha III adopts a new Hawaiian constitution, providing for a legislature of two houses, nobles appointed by the king, representatives elected by the people, and a supreme court. The constitution is designed by and favors American interests largely as the result of the king's American and European advisers, particularly Dr. Gerrit P. Judd.

1852, November 8—The death of imprisoned whaler Henry Burns causes thousands of sailors to riot and set fire to the Honolulu Police Station.

1853—David Malo, considered the first Hawaiians scholar, dies.

1853—Hawai'i's population is 73,134, including 2,119 foreigners.

1853—English language schools are established for Native Hawaiians. English language instruction for native peoples had been a pet cause of newspaper editor James Jarves for nearly a decade. Jarves' attempts to lobby for the schools are stymied by leading members of the missionary communities in the Islands. Eventually Jarves' opinion and the desires of the native population win out and schools begin to appear throughout the Islands.

1853—The first of several devastating smallpox epidemics infects about 10,000 people, taking the lives of approximately half that number. (Later epidemics take place in 1861, 1873, and 1881.) The outbreak has political ramifications as well. Dr. Gerrit Judd, a trusted adviser to the court of the Kingdom of Hawai'i, falls victim to rumor mongering by political rivals who seek greater access to the king. Judd is accused of withholding funds and material that would have helped stem the breadth of the smallpox cases. Judd is soon deposed from his role, allowing the Committee to begin steering the Kingdom towards overthrow and annexation.

1853—A sidewheel steamer, the 114-ton, 106-foot *S.B. Wheeler*, arrives from the United States. The ship is renamed the *Akamai*, and is used by the Hawaiian Steam Navigation Company for interisland trade becoming Hawai'i's first regular interisland steamer.

1853—The first steam-operated sugar mill opens in Līhu'e, Kaua'i.

1854, December 15—The death of Kamehameha III ends his 30-year reign. Prince Alexander Liholiho, the 21-year-old grandson of Kamehameha I, comes to the throne as Kamehameha IV.

1855, June 13—Abner Pākī, father of Bernice Pauhi Bishop, dies.

1855, August 11—Hilo is threatened by lava from an eruption of Mauna Loa.

1856, June 19—Kamehameha IV marries Emma Na'ea Rooke at O'ahu's Kawaiaha'o Church.

1856—*The Pacific Commercial Advertiser*, the forerunner of the *Honolulu Advertiser,* starts publishing initially as a weekly newspaper then as a daily in 1882.

1857, June 12—For the first time, a marine telegraph signals the downtown post office when a ship is sighted.

1857, July 2—Laura Kanaholo Konia, granddaughter of Kamehameha I and mother of Bernice Pauahi, dies.

1857—Lot Kamehameha, Minister of the Interior, forms the volunteer group, the Honolulu Rifles, to protect life and property against "lawless mobs." The Honolulu Rifles are later instrumental in supporting the Committee of Public Safety during the 1893 overthrow of the Hawaiian Monarchy.

1858, May 20—Birth of Prince Albert Edward Kauikeaouli, son of Kamehameha IV and Queen Emma.

Charles Reed Bishop and Bernice P. Bishop, circa 1850. [Bishop Museum]

1858, August 17—Charles Reed Bishop and W. A. Aldrich start Aldrich & Bishop, Hawai'i's first permanent, locally-owned bank. It is renamed Bank of Bishop & Co. Ltd., and is known today as the First Hawaiian Bank.

1858, November—Henry MacFarlane introduces gas lighting in his billiard saloon at the Commercial Hotel. On October 26, 1859, the Honolulu Gas Company begins providing gas lighting.

1859—The Episcopal Church is established with its first bishop arriving in 1862.

1859, May 20—The first formal outrigger regatta is held in honor of the first birthday of Crown Prince Albert.

Above, upper: View of Honolulu from the steeple of Fort Street Church looking up Nu'uanu Valley. Hugo Stagenwald, c. 1853. [Hawaiian Mission Children's Society Library]

Lower: Robert Crichton Wyllie, Hawai'i's Foreign Minister from 1845–1865 introduced the elegances and incongruities of European court etiquette. [Hawai'i State Archives]

Right, upper: A Kamehameha family portrait, c. 1852. To secure succession, Kamehameha III (center) and Queen Kalama (seated left), having lost their own two sons, adopted Kamehameha's nephew Alexander Liholiho (upper left) as son and named him heir to the throne. He became Kamehameha IV in 1854. His older brother Prince Lot (upper right) succeeded him in 1863, as Kamehameha V. Both Liholiho and Lot are sons of Kamehameha III's half-sister Kīna'u and Mataio Kekūanao'a. Their only daughter, Princess Victoria Kamāmalu (seated right), was named heir apparent by Lot, but she died ahead of him. [Bishop Museum]

Above center, left: Kamāmalu and her father Kekuanoa circa 1850s. [Bishop Museum] **right:** William Charles Lunalilo with his father, Charles Kanaina circa 1850. [Bishop Museum]

Lower: This 1856 view of King Street looking toward Waikīkī was taken from the corner of Fort Street in downtown Honolulu. The area just beyond was largely residential, occupied by such prominent citizens as Princess Bernice Pauahi and Charles Reed Bishop, whose two-story house with its spacious lanai, or veranda, is visible on the left. In later years the Bishop home was converted into the Arlington Hotel, the site of "Camp Boston," the 1893 headquarters for U.S. military troops during the overthrow of the monarchy. Kawaiaha'o Church, with its original wooden steeple, is in the distance. [H. Stagenwald/Bishop Museum]

WITNESS TO HISTORY

MISSIONARIES ARE THE WORST GOSSIPS
1858

Thus it is always with Honolulu society. It is full of jealousies and scandals. No one can live in it without subjecting his character to the severest test. The Missionaries are the worst gossips and the most inveterate scandal-mongers. Their wives and daughters are far beyond anything St. Paul ever condemned in the way of tittle-tattle and mischief making.

David Lawrence Gregg, U.S. Commissioner to the Hawaiian Kingdom, 1858
The Diaries of David Lawrence Gregg: An American Diplomat in Hawaii, 1853–1858

The Second Foreign Church, built in 1856 at Fort and Beretania Streets, mostly served Honolulu's foreign community. Also known as the "Fort Street Church," it was later combined with the old Seamen's Bethel Church and reorganized as Central Union Church. This old historic structure was replaced with a handsome new stone edifice in 1892 at the corner of Beretania and Richards Streets, directly across from Washington Place. [Gonsalves/Hawai'i State Archives]

The establishment of public hospitals in the Hawaiian Islands was first initiated by the kingdom's legislature in 1856 with the appropriation of $5,000 for a hospital in Honolulu. The construction of the hospital was delayed until 1859, when, through the efforts of Queen Emma, the Queen's Hospital was incorporated. Additional funds for the completion of the hospital facilities were collected by King Kamehameha IV, who obtained pledges of $14,000 from the citizens of Honolulu. The original two-story, 100-foot long by 47-foot wide stone building was finally completed in March 1860 at a cost of $13,500. Photographed soon after its opening from the slopes of Punchbowl, Queen's Hospital could initially accommodate only 100 patients. In the ensuing years, Queen Emma worked actively to raise additional private funds for the maintenance and ongoing expansion of the island's first hospital for Hawaiians. [Queen's Medical Center Creative Services]

1860, July 18—The steamer *Kilauea* begins making the first regular interisland run.

1860—Queen's Hospital is constructed at the corner of Punchbowl and Beretania Streets. It is named after Emma, the adopted daughter of her maternal aunt, Grace Kamaʻikuʻi Young Rooke and her husband, the English physician Dr. Thomas Charles Byde Rooke. Emma and Kamehameha IV originally established the Queen's Hospital in the late 1850s to help the Hawaiian people who were being devastated by foreign diseases.

1860— Emma and Kamehameha IV visit Kauaʻi with their son, Crown Prince Albert. The royal family stays at the large Hanalei Valley sugar plantation, estate of Robert Crichton Wyllie, the Foreign Minister of the Hawaiian Kingdom. To honor the young prince, Wyllie changes the name of his estate to Princeville Plantation. Tragically, Prince Albert dies in 1862 at the age of four.

1860—Rice seed is brought from South Carolina, beginning a new industry. By 1870, rice exports reach one million pounds per year, a decade later two million pounds per year, and in 1899 more than 33 million pounds.

Queen Emma and King Kamehameha IV had one child, Albert, Prince of Hawaiʻi. Beloved throughout the Islands, the little prince, in 1862, died at the age of four. He was the last child born to a Hawaiian monarch. [Hawaiʻi State Archives]

1861, March 8—A local amateur group performs Honolulu's first opera at the Royal Hawaiian Theatre.

1861, July 4—Walter Murray Gibson, who will play a leading role in politics under Kalākaua, arrives in the Islands.

1861, September 26—*The Ka Hoku O Ka Pakipika (Star of the Pacific),* debuts as the first Hawaiian-language newspaper published by native Hawaiians.

1861—Kamehameha IV signs a treaty of neutrality with the United States as a precaution in case the American Civil War extends into the Pacific.

1862—Lydia Kamakaʻeha Pākī, the future Queen Liliʻuokalani, marries John Owen Dominis.

1862, December—Kamehameha IV proclaims Christmas Day a general holiday.

Above, left: Lydia Kamaka'eha Pākī, 1860. [Hawai'i State Archives]

Right: John Owen Dominis, governor of O'ahu and Consort of Queen Lili'uokalani, died in August of 1891. The couple had been childhood friends since the days when he watched Princess Lydia on the grounds of the Royal School. They were married in 1862 and resided for many years at Washington Place, the Dominis family home. Her husband's death during the first year of her reign was a great personal loss for the queen. [Hawai'i State Archives]

1863, Nov. 30—Kamehameha IV dies, and is succeeded by his brother, Prince Lot Kapuāiwa Kamehameha, who becomes Kamehameha V. With the approval of kuhina nui (premier) Victoria Ka'ahumanu Kamāmalu and the Privy Council, Prince Lot proclaims himself king without opposition, but angers American interests and businessmen when he refuses to take an oath to uphold the Constitution of 1852.

On August 20, 1864, he proclaims a new constitution that gives greater power to the king but less control to the Privy Council and Legislative Assembly, and limiting their voting powers.

Lot has been called "the last great chief" of the olden type. He favored a stronger monarchy that amost verged on depotism although he was personally concerned for the welfare of his subjects. [Hawai'i State Archives]

1864—The government creates the Board of Immigration to aid in filling the need for immigrant labor. During the 1860s, a modest 1,439 arrive.

1864—Eliza McHutcheson Sinclair purchases the island of Ni'ihau for $10,000.

1864—Father Damien is ordained a Roman Catholic priest at Honolulu's Cathedral of Our Lady of Peace. In 1866, Hawai'i's first victims of Hansen's disease (leprosy) arrive at Kalawao on Moloka'i's Kalaupapa Peninsula beginning the practice of segregating patients at the remote site. Over the following decades nearly 9,000 Hansen's disease patients, many Hawaiians, are quarantined at Kalaupapa.

1865—The Royal Mausoleum is built in Nu'uanu, O'ahu at Mauna 'Ala ("Fragrant mountain"). The Mausoleum, planned by Kamehameha IV and Emma for their deceased son Prince Albert, is designed by Theodore Heuck, Honolulu's first resident architect. Other deceased royalty are later transferred from the Royal Mausoleum at 'Iolani Palace. It now holds the remains of Kamehameha II through Kamehameha V as well as Kalākaua, Lili'uokalani, and important nobles of Hawai'i's past.

1865, January 3—Kamehameha V and the Hawaiian Legislature pass the "Act to Prevent the Spread of

Father Damien before he came to Hawai'i intending to work among those suffering from Hansen's disease. [Hawai'i State Archives]

MARK TWAIN

... A Prose Poem on Hawaii ...

NO ALIEN LAND in all the world has any deep, strong charm for me but that one; no other land could so longingly and beseechingly haunt me sleeping and waking, through half a lifetime, as that one has done. Other things leave me, but it abides; other things change but it remains the same. For me its balmy airs are always blowing, its summer seas flashing in the sun; the pulsing of its surf beat is in my ear; I can see its garlanded craigs, its leaping cascades, its plumy palms drowsing by the shore; its remote summits floating like islands above the cloudrack; I can feel the spirit of its woodland solitude; I can hear the plash of its brooks; in my nostrils still lives the breath of flowers that perished twenty years ago.—MARK TWAIN. 7

The famous testimonial to Hawai'i by Mark Twain. [Baker-Van Dyke Collection]

Leprosy" authorizing land to be set aside for the isolation of Hansen's disease patients, at the time numbering more than 1,700. On January 6, 1866, the first patients are shipped to Moloka'i.

1866—A record export crop of 22,000 pounds of cotton is produced.

1866—Heads of cattle in the Islands number 60,000, many undomesticated. Bullock hunters from overseas are hired to help reduce their numbers.

1866, March 18—Samuel Langhorne Clemens, a.k.a. Mark Twain, a Missouri-born, California newspaper correspondent and former riverboat pilot arrives to write a series of travel letters about the whaling and sugar industries.

1866, May 29—Princess Victoria Kamāmalu, granddaughter of Kamehameha I, dies at age 27.

1866, July—Grace Kama'iku'i Rooke, adoptive mother of Emma Na'ea, dies at age 57.

1866, September 4—*The Hawaiian Herald* becomes Hawai'i's first daily newspaper.

1867—St. Andrew's Cathedral opens in Honolulu at Beretania and Queen Emma Streets (Queen Emma Square). Kamehameha IV and Emma build St. Andrew's after visiting Queen Victoria in 1861 and seeing the Church of England. It is built in the Gothic style with imported, prefabricated sandstone block. The choir section is completed in 1886.

1867—Steamship mail service is inaugurated between the Hawaiian Islands and San Francisco.

Honolulu from the lower part of town, looking towards Punchbowl, circa 1869. [Bishop Museum]

1868, April 2—An earthquake registering a magnitude of about 8.0 on the Richter scale destroys nearly every European-style home in the Ka'ū district and causes a mud flow that buries a village and kills 40 people. The earthquake also generates a localized tsunami that kills 48 people when waves surge up to 60 feet high and sweep away the village of 'Āpua in Puna.

1868, April 2—Mauna Loa erupts.

1868, November 24—Kekuanoao'a, father of Princess Ruth Ke'elikōlani, Kamehameha IV, Kamehameha V, and Princess Victoria Kamāmalu, dies.

1868—The *Scioto* arrives carrying the first Japanese to work on the sugar plantations. The initial migrants, 142 men and six women, are mostly tradesmen and craftsmen without contracts or government permission. They are called *gannenmono* ("first year men"), referring to the first year of Japan's Meiji era.

1868—The Spring Pioneer Omnibus Line begins operating horse-drawn carts in Honolulu beginning Hawai'i's first public transit service.

1869—More than 623,000 pounds of pulu are harvested and exported for sale as stuffing for mattresses and pillows. Pulu is the reddish-brown or golden-yellow silky hair that grows at the base of the pepe'e (young fronds) and at the bud stems of native hāpu'u (tree ferns).

1869—The first lighthouse at Honolulu Harbor begins operation.

WITNESS TO HISTORY

A TOWN OF SHADE TREES AND CATS, MARK TWAIN
1866

The further I traveled through the town the better I liked it. Every step revealed a new contrast—disclosed something I was unaccustomed to. In place of the grand mud colored brown fronts of San Francisco, I saw dwellings built of straw, adobes, and cream-colored pebble-and-shell-conglomerated coral, cut into oblong blocks and laid in cement; also a great number of neat-white-cottages, with green window-shutters; in place of front yards like billiard-tables with iron fences around them, I saw these homes surrounded by ample yards, thickly clad with green grass, and shaded by tall trees, through whose dense foliage the sun could scarcely penetrate; in place of the customary geranium, calla lily, etc., languishing in dust and general debility, I saw luxurious banks and thickets of flowers, fresh as a meadow after a rain, and glowing with the richest dyes; in place of the dingy horrors of San Francisco's pleasure grove, the "Willows," I saw huge-bodied, wide-spreading forest trees, with strange names and stranger appearance—trees that cast a shadow like a thundercloud, and were able to stand alone without being tied to green poled; in place of gold fish, wiggling around in glass globes, assuming countless shades and degrees of distortion through the magnifying and diminishing qualities of their transparent prison houses, I saw cats—Tomcats, Mary Ann cats, long-tailed cats, bob-tailed cats, blind cats, one-eyed cats, walleyed cats, cross-eyed cats, gray cats, black cats white cats, yellow cats, striped cats, spotted cats, tame cats, wild cats, singed cats, individual cats, groups of cats, platoons of cats, companies of cats, regiments of cats, armies of cats, multitudes of cats, millions of cats, and all of them sleek, fat, lazy and sound asleep.

I looked on a multitude of people, some white, in white coats, vests, pantaloons, even white cloth shoes made snowy with chalk duly laid on every morning; but the majority of the people were almost as dark-as negroes—women with comely features, fine black eyes, rounded forms, inclining to the voluptuous, clad in a single bright red or white arment that fell free and unconfined from shoulder to heel, long black hair falling loose, gypsy hats, encircled with wreaths of natural flowers of a brilliant carmine tint; plenty of dark men in various costumes, and some with nothing on but a battered stove-pipe hat tilted on the nose, and a very scant breech-clout—certain smoke-dried children were clothed in nothing but sunshine—a very neat fitting and picturesque apparel indeed.

Mark Twain, 1866
Samuel Clemens, *Mark Twain in Hawai'i*

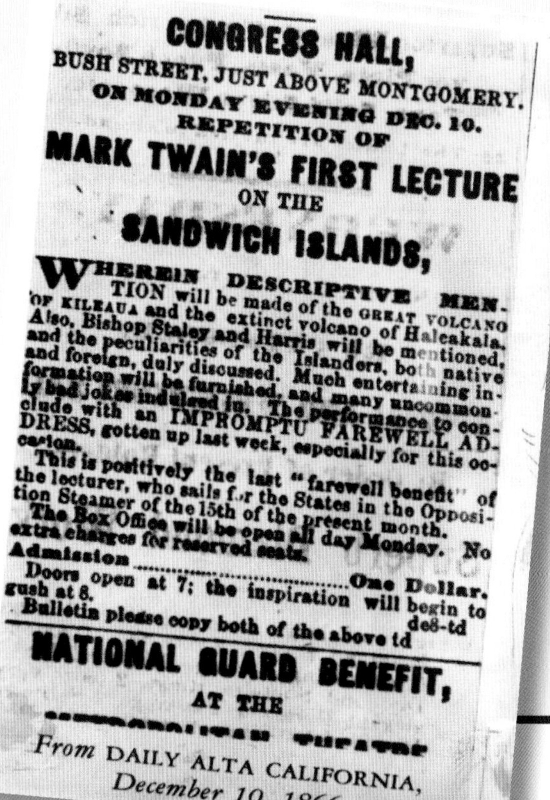

CONGRESS HALL,
BUSH STREET, JUST ABOVE MONTGOMERY.
ON MONDAY EVENING DEC. 10.
REPETITION OF
MARK TWAIN'S FIRST LECTURE
ON THE
SANDWICH ISLANDS,

WHEREIN DESCRIPTIVE MENTION will be made of the GREAT VOLCANO OF KILEAUA and the extinct volcano of Halcakala. Also, Bishop Staley and Harris will be mentioned, and the peculiarities of the Islanders, both native and foreign, duly discussed. Much entertaining information will be furnished, and many uncommonly bad jokes indulged in. The performance to conclude with an IMPROMPTU FAREWELL ADDRESS, gotten up last week, especially for this occasion.

This is positively the last "farewell benefit" of the lecturer, who sails for the States in the Opposition Steamer of the 15th of the present month.

The Box Office will be open all day Monday. No extra charges for reserved seats.

Admission .... One Dollar.

Doors open at 7; the inspiration will begin to gush at 8.

Bulletin please copy both of the above td de8-td

NATIONAL GUARD BENEFIT,
AT THE

From DAILY ALTA CALIFORNIA, *December 10, 1866*

The missionaries could not have succeeded in promoting Christianity, literacy and education without strong supporters among all ranks of the native population. John Papa Ī'ī was a close friend, assisting Reverend Bingham in translating the *Bible* into Hawaiian, and serving as an advisor and a judge for the kingdom. He is shown here as an older man in an 1867 photo. [Hawai'i State Archives]

Queen Emma (1836-1885) was born and raised in Honolulu, but her roots lay in Kawaihae on the Big Island, the home of her grandfather, John Young. During the Māhele, the land division of the 1840s, when lands were distributed to the king, chiefs, and commoners, Emma's uncle Keoni Ana, John Young's son, was given half of the Kawaihae ahupua'a; the other half was crown land. Emma later inherited Keoni Ana's Kawaihae landholdings, making her the largest landowner in the ahupua'a. [Baker-Van Dyke Collection]

1870, May 2—John Papa ʻĪʻī, a chiefly Hawaiian scholar and intellectual, passes away at age 69.

1870, May—Ice cream is sold commercially at the Criterion Coffee Saloon.

1870, September 20—Kalama, wife of Kamehameha III, dies at age 53.

1870—Queen Emma and an entourage of 100 retainers and servants visit her Kaua'i estate and journey up to Kaua'i's highland forests of the Alaka'i Swamp and Kōke'e. The royal party eventually reaches the end of the trail where the overlook called Kilohana ("Lookout Point") provides spectacular views of Kaua'i's north shore. In honor of her mountain journey, Emma renames her Lāwa'i estate Mauna Kilohana.

1870—Samuel Thomas Alexander and Henry Perrine Baldwin establish the firm of Alexander & Baldwin, later one of Hawai'i's "Big Five" companies.

1870—Queen Emma starts St. Andrew's Priory School for Girls for Hawaiian girls with nursing is promoted as a major career goal.

1870s—Waikīkī is dominated by rice fields planted primarily by Chinese immigrants.

1871, March 26—Prince Jonah Kūhiō Kalaniana'ole Pi'ikoi, future Hawai'i delegate to Congress, is born.

1871, June 11—Kamehameha V proclaims a holiday in memory of his grandfather, Kamehameha I.

1871, July 22—Rollerskating comes to Hawai'i when the Honolulu Skating Rink opens on Hotel Street.

1871—An early Arctic freeze north of the Bering Strait destroys the North Pacific whaling fleet,

The beloved Royal Hawaiian Band was formed in 1872. In the summer of 1879, they posed on the steps of the bandstand in Emma Square for their earliest known photograph. Wishing not to be too conspicuous, bandmaster Heinrich Wilhelm (Henry) Berger stands in the top row, second from the left. He helped to organize the Royal Hawaiian Band in 1872 and assumed full leadership in 1877. For over thirty-five years, he led the musicians in numerous performances until his retirement on June 30, 1915. [Hawai'i State Archives]

including seven Hawai'i-owned ships.

1871—The medieval-looking 'Iolani Barracks, designed by German immigrant Theodore Heuck, is constructed with firing loops built into the walls and archery parapets located atop the building. It was originally known as Halekoa and used by the Kingdom's army, known as the Household Troops, comprised of 60 soldiers. The inner courtyard area of 'Iolani Barracks was used for roll call.

1871—The Kamehameha V Post Office Building is constructed on Merchant and Bethel Streets and serves as the main Honolulu Post Office until 1922. Designed by J. G. Osborne in the Renaissance Revival style, the structure is the US's oldest reinforced concrete building.

1872—The first true hotel in Honolulu, the "Hawaiian Hotel," is built by the government. It is described as the finest in hotels this side of Chicago.

1872—Hawai'i's population is 56,897 people.

1872, June 11—The Royal Hawaiian Band gives its first concert under the lead of Heinrich "Henry" Berger, who had been brought from Germany. A royal proclamation by Kamehameha V declares June 11 Commemoration Day in honor of Kamehameha I. The annual holiday later becomes known as King Kamehameha Day.

1872, October 19—An electric telegraph begins operation in downtown Honolulu.

1872, December 11—Kamehameha V dies.

1873, January 8—William Charles Lunalilo ascends to the throne as King Lunalilo after being elected king by a vote of the Legislature when Kamehameha V dies without naming a successor. Lunalilo immediately begins to amend the Constitution of 1864, including ending the property qualification for voting. He dies just one year after being elected king, the shortest reign of any Hawaiian monarch.

1873, January 25—Scottish author Isabella Bird Bishop (1832-1904) begins her travels around the Hawaiian Islands, later publishing *The Hawaiian Archipelago: Six Months Among the Palm Groves, Coral Reefs, and Volcanoes of the Sandwich Islands.*

1873, September 7—The Household Troops, the army of the Hawaiian Kingdom, rebel against their officers. After six days, Lunalilo

On the day he be came king, Kalākaua named his younger brother, William Pitt Leleiōhoku II, as heir, hoping to assure the future of his dynasty. [Hawai'i State Archives]

convinces the troops to lay down their arms and then disbands the army.

1873—The Belgian Father Damien (Joseph Damien DeVeuster) volunteers to minister to the needy at the Kalaupapa Hansen's disease (leprosy) colony, where he serves until he succumbs to the disease in 1889.

1874, February 12—After the death of Lunalilo on February 3, 1874, David La'amea Kalākaua is elected king by a Legislative vote of 39 to 6, causing supporters of Emma to ransack the courthouse and beat legislators leaving many injured and one dead. American and British warships provide armed marines to restore order and Kalākaua takes an oath of allegiance to the 1864 Constitution of Kamehameha V.

1874—Honolulu's Ali'iōlani Hale is built and becomes the new seat of Hawai'i's government due to the extensive damage of the Honolulu Courthouse caused by supporters of Emma in protest of the election of Kalākaua. Ali'iōlani Hale will also house the National Museum when it opens on November 8, 1875.

The visitor to the Territory of Hawai'i in the first decades of the twentieth century had several choices of hostelry which blended genteel elegance with Polynesian hospitality. The grand Hawaiian Hotel in downtown Honolulu had been the landmark since it opened its doors on February 29, 1871 with a lavish grand ball and banquet. Built by the Kingdom of Hawai'i at a cost of $150,000, the hotel earned its reputation as the "Royal" Hawaiian Hotel with its large, breezy lānai, observatory cupola, highly polished rare Hawaiian woods, plush couches and glistening crystals. The hotel occupied an entire city block of four acres bounded by Hotel, Richards, Beretania, and Alakea Streets. When competition from the newly constructed Alexander Young Hotel and the Moana Hotel cut into is business in the early 1900s, the Hawaiian Hotel added the semi-circular lānai, shown in this early photograph, and additional cottages to accommodate nearly 200 guests. By 1917, however, the hotel's business slackened and the building was remodeled as the Army-Navy YMCA. On December 20, 1926, a wrecking ball put an end to the history of the Hawaiian Hotel as a new Armed Forces YMCA building was constructed on the site. [National Archives]

1874, February 14—Kalākaua names his younger brother Prince William Pitt Leleiōhoku his successor. Two new princesses are designated—Princess Kamakaʻeha Dominis (the future Queen Liliʻuokalani) and Princess Likelike. After Prince William Pitt Leleiōhoku passes away in 1877 at the age of only 22, Kalākaua declares Princess Liliʻuokalani Kamakaʻeha Dominis the heir apparent.

1874, November 17—Kalākaua and a royal party leave for San Francisco on the steamer *Benicia* for a goodwill tour of the United States and to promote the Reciprocity Treaty, which had been repeatedly delayed. Kalākaua is the first king to visit the U.S., including Washington D.C. He arrives back in the Hawaiian Islands on the U.S.S. *Pensacola* on February 15, 1875.

1875, October 16—Princess Victoria Kaʻiulani, daughter of A.S. Cleghorn and Princess Miriam Likelike, is born.

1876—Hawaiʻi's population is 53,900 people.

1876—The song *Hawaiʻi Ponoʻī* (Hawaiʻi's Own), with lyrics written by Kalākaua in 1874, and music by Captain Heinrich "Henry" Berger, becomes Hawaiʻi's national anthem. In 1967 the song is designated as the anthem of the State of Hawaiʻi.

1876, August 15—The Reciprocity Treaty is ratified, allowing Hawaiʻi to export to the U.S. sugar and other products without custom duties.

1876—Princess Pauahi travels to England with her husband, Charles Reed Bishop. The couple is presented at Queen Victoria's Court and is later received by Pope Pius IX in Rome.

In 1872, two future kings posed with the California poet, novelist, journalist, and essayist Charles W. Stoddard during one of his frequent trips to the Islands. Prince William Lunalilo (second from the left, in the front row), soon to be the first elected king in Hawaiian history, sits on the right of Stoddard, as Prince David Kalākaua (far right in the front row) sits on his left. Others are Major Moehonua (front row, far left), and (left to right, standing) Dave McKinley, J.J. Kekoulahao, and Fred K. Beckley. The Hawaiian princes often impressed visiting literati with their lively and informed conversations on literature, music, and the arts. [Hawaiʻi State Archives]

1877—Kalākaua dedicates Kapiʻolani Park, named in honor of his wife, Kapiʻolani. The park is used for band concerts, polo games, horse races, and in later years, car races. Today it is home to the Kapiʻolani Bandstand, the Waikīkī Shell, and the Honolulu Zoo.

1877, April 19—Prince Leleiohoku dies and Princess Liliʻuokalani is proclaimed heir.

1877—Charles H. Dickey installs Hawaiʻi's first commercial telegraph system between his stores in Haʻikū and Makawao on Maui. Under his direction the first telephone line is installed in 1878 between Wailuku, Maui and Kahului by the East Maui Telegraph Company.

1877, May 9—A large earthquake occurs near Peru, resulting in a tsunami that arrives in Hilo before dawn, destroying 37 houses and killing 45 people.

1878, January 12—A charter is granted to C.H. Dickey and C.H. Wallace for the Hawaiian Telegraph Co.

1878—Hawaiʻi's first telephone line is installed between Wailuku, Maui and Kahului by the East Maui Telegraph Company under the direction of Charles H. Dickey.

1878—Portuguese workers arrive aboard the *Priscilla* from Madeira Island, beginning an influx of Portuguese plantation laborers that

WITNESS TO HISTORY

THE HAWAIIAN WAHINE

The women are free from our tasteless perversity as to colour and ornament, and have an instinct of the becoming. At first the holoku, which is only a full, yoke nightgown, is not attractive, but I admire it heartily now, and the sagacity of those who devised it. It conceals awkwardness, and befits grace of movement; it is fit for the climate, is equally adapted for walking and riding, and has that general appropriateness which is desirable in costume. The women have a most peculiar walk, with a swinging motion from the hip at each step, in which the shoulder sympathizes. I never saw anything at all like it...A majestic wahine with small, bare feet, a grand, swinging, deliberate gait, hibiscus blossoms in her flowing hair, and a lei of yellow flowers falling over her holoku, marching through these streets, has a tragic grandeur of appearance, which makes the diminutive, fair-skinned haole, tottering along hesitantly in high-heeled shoes, look grotesque by comparison.

Isabella Bird, 1873
Six Months in the Sandwich Islands

During the mid-nineteenth century, Honolulu's famed pāʻū riders were Hawaiian women in long skirts, or pāʻū. On Saturday afternoons they often enjoyed "furious riding" on King Street, and onward out of town on the distant shores of Waikīkī. [Baker-Van Dyke Collection]

will total 20,000 by 1913. Virtually all Catholics, they strengthen the presence of the Catholic church in the Islands.

1878—The Bank of Bishop & Company Building (Bishop Bank Building) is constructed at 63 Merchant Street in Honolulu. The architect is Thomas J. Baker, and the building is constructed of brick, featuring a corner entry and a fortress-like parapet. Today the Bishop Bank Building is the only remaining Northern Italian Renaissance Revival style building still standing in Honolulu. It is now called the Harriet Bouslog Building.

1878, October—Marshmallows brought from San Francisco as Sunday treats are introduced to Hawaiʻi by Emma Louise Dillingham.

1879—Portuguese contract laborers arriving on the *Ravenscrag* bring a stringed instrument called the *cavaquinho* (in mainland Portugal) or *braguinha* (on Madeira). A local variant of the instrument known as the ʻukulele, quickly becomes popular.

1879, July 1—The first artesian well in the Hawaiian Islands is bored by James Campbell (1826-1900) near his ranch in Honouliuli, Oʻahu. Soon other wells are bored, providing water for the cultivation of sugarcane on thousands of acres of ʻEwa, Oʻahu.

Campbell was born in Ireland, ran away at age 13, and was later stranded on a South Sea island after

King Kalākaua's reputation for enjoying soirées, dances, drinking, horse racing, lavish parties, and gambling—although often exaggerated by his enemies—was not without basis. Kalākaua entertained friends and visitors of the Royal Boat House at Honolulu Harbor far from the watchful eyes of the missionary community. [Hawai'i State Archives]

a wreck of his whaling vessel. He eventually became an extremely successful businessman, owning much of Lahaina. He engaged in many business ventures, and supported the first electric-light and telephone companies in the Hawaiian Islands.

1879—Prince Henry of Prussia visits Kalākaua.

1879—The Hawai'i State Library opens on King Street. A new building is constructed in 1911 and additions are built in 1930. Particularly notable is the library's entrance, consisting of 20-foot-high Tuscan columns and 18-foot arches.

1879, July 20—The Kahului & Wailuku Railroad begins operating on Maui, becoming Hawai'i's first common rail carrier. It allows central Maui's sugar and pineapple crops to be brought to Kahului which will replace Lahaina as Maui's primary port.

1879, December 31—The cornerstone is laid for 'Iolani Palace in midtown Honolulu. Completed in 1882, it serves first as a royal palace, and later as the capitol building of the Republic of Hawai'i, the Territory of Hawai'i, and then the State of Hawai'i.

Above, upper: Wailuku Plantation with 'Īao Valley in the background, 1875. [Baker-Van Dyke Collection]

Lower: In 1876 the Kapiolani Park Association was organized to lease lands and establish the area as a suburban development. On June 11, 1877 Kalākaua dedicated the park for his consort Queen Kapi'olani. Originally used for horse racing, after 1898 the U.S. Army occupied much of the park. [Bishop Museum]

Ali'iōlani Hale

Ali'iōlani Hale's construction was completed in 1874. The two-story building on South King Street was initially planned as a palace for Kamehameha V.

After the Honolulu Courthouse was extensively damaged in a riot by supporters of Emma when she lost the monarchial election to King Kalākaua, Ali'iōlani Hale became the new seat of the Hawaiian government housing the Supreme Court, Legislature, and House of Nobles. Built with concrete blocks, it was the first major Western-style building constructed by the Hawaiian monarchy. It was designed by architects Thomas Rowe and Robert Stirling in the Renaissance Revival style including a distinctive four-story clock tower.

On November 8, 1875, the National Museum opened in Ali'iōlani Hale with Charles Reed Bishop as its first supervisor. Its collection included many royal artifacts which were later transferred to the Bernice Pauahi Bishop Museum. In January of 1893 after the overthrow of the monarchy, Ali'iōlani Hale was the site of the announcement by Sanford Ballard Dole that a Provisional Government had been formed. The Provisional Government of Hawai'i renamed Ali'iōlani Hale the "Court House," but it became known as the "Judiciary Building" for which purpose it has been used ever since. The House of Representatives and the House of Nobles met at Ali'iōlani Hale until 1896 when they moved to 'Iolani Palace, which was renamed "The Executive Building."

By 1911, Ali'iōlani Hale was in disrepair due to termite damage and as part of its remodeling it had to be set on fire so only the exterior walls remained. Architects Ripley and Reynolds designed a new floor plan that included a rotunda and double staircase. Today, it houses the Kamehameha V–Judiciary History Center of Hawai'i (founded in 1989), that provides educational judicial exhibits.

The Kamehameha I statue stands in front of Ali'iōlani Hale.

'Iolani Palace

The cornerstone for 'Iolani Palace was laid on December 31, 1879. 'Iolani means "Hawk of heaven," or "Royal hawk," referring to the flight of the 'io (Hawaiian hawk), considered a sign of royalty. A project of King Kalākaua, the Palace was completed in 1882 in the "American Florentine" architectural style. Measuring 140 long and 100 feet wide it cost $360,000. It served as the royal palace for Kalākaua from 1882 to 1891 and then for Lili'uokalani until her 1893 overthrow.

Kalākaua, who once met Thomas Edison, was very interested in new technology and installed electric lights at 'Iolani Palace on July 21, 1886 at least four years before the United States' White House. The palace was ahead of its time in other ways including flushing toilets and bidets, hot and cold running water, and copper-lined tubs. It utilized beautifully crafted native and Polynesian-introduced woods along with other fine hardwoods.

The main floor of the Palace was used for formal functions while the royal family resided on the second floor. The basement housed the Palace kitchen and its storeroom. It could accommodate more than 40 servants, and had a room for the kāhili, the royal feather standards.

'Iolani Palace also served for seven months as the prison chamber of Lili'uokalani after her overthrow. It was then used as the capitol building of the Republic of Hawai'i (1893-1900), of the Territory of Hawai'i (1900-1959), and of the State of Hawai'i (1960-1969). In great disrepair, the Palace underwent extensive renovations in 1969, and was opened as a museum in 1978.

Ali'iōlani Hale (House of the Heavenly Chief) was originally designed as a palace for Kamehameha V, but the plans were altered to created an administration building across from the palace. Built of concrete blocks, at that time a fairly new material, it housed the kingdom's House of Nobles, House of Representatives, the Supreme Court and Judiciary Department, the Law Library, and the National Museum of the Hawaiian Kingdom. To the left is Kapuāiwa, the Board of Health building, completed in 1884. On the far right is a portion of the opera house, completed in 1881 at the corner of Mililani and King streets. [Hawai'i State Archives]

'Iolani Palace was the crowning achievement of King Kalākaua's "new departure in Hawaiian politics." The cornerstone of the structure was laid on Queen Kapi'olani's birthday in 1879. Since the king was a member of the Masonic Order, its secret rituals were incorporated into the elaborate ceremony. Three years later, the completed palace was inaugurated with a formal banquet for the Masonic fraternity. The official coronation of King Kalākaua took place on February 12, 1883 from the Coronation Pavilion erected in front of the palace.

In this view from the tower of Ali'iōlani Hale, the wooden bungalow called Kīna'u Hale is visible just to the left of 'Iolani Palace. The king and queen actually spent more time in Kīna'u Hale than the palace, preferring the informality of the smaller and more comfortable bungalow. [Chase/Bishop Museum]

1880, August 14—A besotted Kalākaua appoints to his cabinet Celso Casesar Moreno as Minister of Foreign Affairs. An Italian-American confidence artist recently arrived in the Islands, Moreno curries favor from the king by making vague assurances about his political connections as well as promising to increase trade with China thereby overflowing Hawai'i's coffers. Moreno's tenure at court is short lived however, as Kalākaua dismisses him from his post four days later.

1880—Lava flows from Mauna Loa Volcano reach the edge of Hilo. After Kamehameha I's granddaughter, Princess Ruth Ke'elikōlani, travels to the area and offers chants and gifts to supplicate the wrath of the volcano goddess Pele, the lava flow stops just on the edge of town.

1880—St. Louis College, a Catholic high school for boys, is established, later supplemented by Chaminade College, now called Chaminade University.

1880—Kuan Yin Temple opens in Honolulu on land now part of Foster Botanical Gardens. The Buddhist temple is devoted to the Chinese goddess of mercy, Kuan Yin (also spelled Guanyin), meaning "one who sees and hears the cry from the human world."

1880—Kalākaua revives the hula by encouraging its performance at public events.

1881—Kalākaua leaves on an around-the-world journey calling on eleven heads of state including leaders of the United States, Japan and Great Britain. He is the first ruler of any country to circumnavigate the world.

1881—The Music Hall Theater is founded on King Street, across from 'Iolani Palace, next to Ali'iōlani Hale. After closing due to a smallpox epidemic, the theater reopens as the Royal Opera House in 1883.

In 1877, Princess Ruth Ke'elikōlani was photographed with ali'i Samuel Parker of the Parker Ranch and John Cummins of Waimānalo Plantation. The half-sister of Kamehameha IV and Kamehameha V, she received all the Kamehameha lands after the deaths of her brothers. Her heir was Princess Bernice Pauahi Bishop, the last of the direct descendants of the great conqueror. [Hawai'i State Archives]

Seated left to right: Miss Laura Cleghorn, Lili'uokalani (Mrs. John O. Dominis), Princess Likelike (Mrs. Archibald S. Cleghorn), Mrs. Elizabeth Achuck (Keawepoole) Sumner. Standing: Mr. Thomas Cleghorn, Gov. John O. Dominis, Hon. Archibald S. Cleghorn, circa. 1880. [Dickson/Bishop Museum]

1881—William Herbert Purvis introduces Australian macadamia nuts.

1881, August 21—Hawai'i's first electric lights are demonstrated at Mill Number One at Maui's Spreckelsville Plantation.

1881, December 30—The Hawaiian Bell Telephone Company is incorporated.

1882, May 1—The weekly *Pacific Commercial Advertiser* becomes a daily.

1882—Captain William Matson purchases his first schooner, the *Emma Claudina*, for travel between

Claus Spreckels, refiner, planter, and "king" of Hawaiian sugar, gained undue influence in Kalākaua's government by allowing the King to become heavily indebted to him. The Spreckels mansion on Punahou Street. Sumptuous and baronial, it was built at a cost of $100,000. During the height of Spreckels' power, this Victorian palace was the scene of lavish dinner parties and dances. [Hawai'i State Archives]

Spreckels cornered the 1877 Hawaiian sugar crop and rose to a position of power in the affairs of the Hawaiian Kingdom. As an advisor to King Kalākaua, he helped promote many dubious financial and political schemes. He purchased his power by bank rolling the free-spending king's pet projects at high rates of interest. In the end, Kalākaua found himself almost totally indebted to Spreckels. The shrewd Spreckels lost favor with the king through his displays of dictatorial behavior. Finally, he was bought off and left the Islands. A ruthless and unscrupulous businessman, he nevertheless contributed greatly to the expansion of the Hawaiian sugar industry. [Hawai'i State Archives]

the Hawaiian Islands and the United States beginning Hawai'i's tourism industry.

1883—Princess Ruth Ke'elikōlani, the granddaughter of Kamehameha I, passes away. Her will bequeaths to Princess Bernice Pauahi Bishop 353,000 acres of Kamehameha lands—nearly nine percent of all land in the Islands.

1883, February 12—King Kalākaua has an official coronation on the grounds of the newly completed 'Iolani Palace in midtown Honolulu. The coronation marks the beginning of King Kalākaua's support of traditional Hawaiian practices, including the revival of hula. A statue of Kamehameha I is unveiled.

1883, September 30—Seventy-two mongooses from Jamaica arrive in Hilo. The predatory animals are brought by Mr. J. Tucker, sponsored by the Hilo Planter's Association, to control the rats plaguing sugar plantations. Unfortunately the mongooses are nocturnal and end up preying on native birds, decimating numerous species.

1883, November 8—Mother Marianne arrives in Hawai'i with six Sisters of St. Francis to care for those with leprosy.

1884—Hawai'i's population exceeds 80,000 people, but the native population continues to decline.

1884—Princess Pauahi dies, leaving 434,000 acres of land in perpetual trust for the establishment of schools bearing the Kamehameha name. Kamehameha School for Boys opens in Honolulu on October 4, 1887, and Kamehameha School for Girls opens in Honolulu on December 19, 1894.

1885, February 8—The *City of Tokio* arrives in Honolulu with the first official (government sponsored) Japanese contract workers, 676 men and 158 women, the result of a treaty signed by Kalākaua with Japan's Emperor Meiji permitting the large-scale immigration of Japanese plantation laborers.

1885, April 25—The Dowager Queen Emma dies at age 49.

1886, November— Kalākaua's 50th birthday jubilee is held at 'Iolani Palace.

1886—The passage of the Hawaiian Kingdom Chinese Exclusion Act halts the importation of Chinese laborers.

1886—A three-day fire engulfs eight blocks of Honolulu's Chinatown

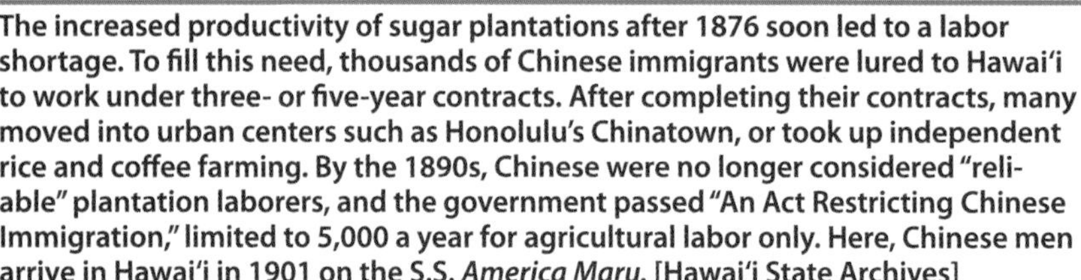

The increased productivity of sugar plantations after 1876 soon led to a labor shortage. To fill this need, thousands of Chinese immigrants were lured to Hawai'i to work under three- or five-year contracts. After completing their contracts, many moved into urban centers such as Honolulu's Chinatown, or took up independent rice and coffee farming. By the 1890s, Chinese were no longer considered "reliable" plantation laborers, and the government passed "An Act Restricting Chinese Immigration," limited to 5,000 a year for agricultural labor only. Here, Chinese men arrive in Hawai'i in 1901 on the S.S. *America Maru.* [Hawai'i State Archives]

Above, left: In 1881, King Kalākaua became the first head of state in history to circumnavigate the globe. His journey through Asia, the Middle East, Europe and North America included a visit with the Emperor of Japan at the Imperial Palace in Tokyo. In a private meeting, the king proposed an alliance to establish an Oceanic Empire in the Pacific. It was supposed to form a bulwark against United States encroachment into Hawai'i. The Meiji Emperor declined this intriguing suggestion, which would have radically transformed history in the Pacific. King Kalākaua was photographed sitting next to Prince Yoshiaki (left) and Yoshi Amatami, Minister of Finance. Standing in the second row are, from left to right: Charles H. Judd, Ryosuki Sugai, First Secretary of Finance; and William N. Armstrong, who wrote *Around the World with a King,* a narrative of the journey. [Bishop Museum]

Right: David La'amea Kamanakapu'u Mahinulani Naloiaehuokalani Lumialani Kalākaua—"Cry Out O Isles with Joy" (This hymn was sung at his coronation). [Hawai'i State Archives]

Honolulu's Chinatown was first destroyed by flames on April 18, 1886, when a fire broke out at a restaurant on the corner of Smith and Hotel Streets. Three days later, the raging fire had burned the homes of 7,000 Chinese and 350 Hawaiians, leaving eight blocks of the district a smoldering heap of charred remains. In the background, at the corner of Smith and Beretania Streets, the twin spires of Kaumakapili Church stand unharmed by the blaze. Although strict fire codes were enacted by the legislature after the conflagration, the rebuilding of Chinatown was so fast that little attention was paid to the regulations. Fourteen years later, Chinatown would burn to the ground again, this time consuming Kaumakapili Church. [The Hawaiian Historical Society]

district burning the homes of 7,000 Chinese and 350 Hawaiians, causing $1.5 million in damage.

1887—Kamehameha Schools is founded.

1887—A political organization of American merchants called the Hawaiian League instigates the Bayonet Constitution, which Kalākaua is forced to sign. It severely curtails his power and ends 23 years of rule under the previous constitution of Kamehameha V.

1887—Kalākaua leases Pearl Harbor to the United States for eight years as part of the Reciprocity Treaty allowing Hawaiian products to be sold in the United States without customs or duties.

1887— Kapiʻolani attends the jubilee of Great Britain's Queen Victoria in England, and later visits President Grover Cleveland.

1888, Jan. 14—The Hawaiian League attempts to have heir apparent Princess Liliʻuokalani Kamakaʻeha Dominis take the throne from Kalākaua, but she refuses.

1888—Benjamin F. Dillingham forms the Oʻahu Railway & Land Company, where the first train runs on September 4, 1889. In 1961, Oʻahu Railway & Land Company merges with Hawaiian Dredging and Construction Company to become the Dillingham Corporation.

1888—Honolulu's gasoline lamp street lights are replaced with electric lights and Princess Kaʻiulani starts the generators to light downtown Honolulu. In 1889 a government electric plant produces power for the incandescent lighting of homes and buildings.

1888, December 28—A mule-drawn tram becomes the first streetcar in Honolulu. The mule-car service is offered by Hawaiian Tramways, Ltd., which is taken over in 1900 by the Honolulu Rapid Transit & Land Co. (HRT).

1888—Mother Marianne Cope moves to Kalaupapa to minister to Hansen's disease patients serving there for 30 years until she passes away in 1918 at age 80.

1889, April 15—Father Damien dies of leprosy.

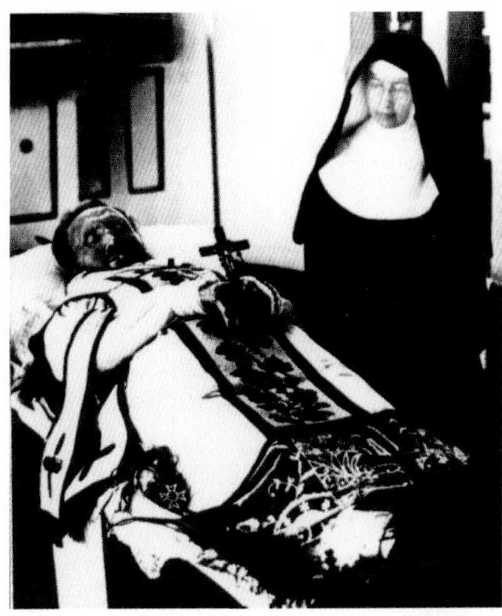

Mother Marianne in April 1889 at the bier of Father Damien. She was already in charge of the Bishop Home for Leprous Women and Girls. [*Pilgrimage and Exile*]

1889—To honor the memory of his wife Charles Reed Bishop founds the Bernice Pauahi Bishop Museum. He constructs Polynesian Hall and Hawaiian Hall on the same site as Kamehameha Schools.

1889—Renowned Scottish author Robert Louis Stevenson and his family arrive in Waikīkī on the chartered yacht *Casco* and stay for five months. Stevenson visits the Hawaiian Islands again in 1893. Already famous for such works as *Treasure Island* and *Dr. Jekyll and Mr. Hyde*, Stevenson began

The first Kaumakapili Church opened on a Sunday in 1888 on Beretania Street in downtown Honolulu. When King Kalākaua laid the cornerstone some years earlier in 1881, he explained why a Hawaiian Protestant Church should have two steeples, not the customary one. "A man has two eyes so he can see better, and two ears so he can hear better. My church must have two steeples so that I can find God better!" The main structure is made of brick, mortar, wood, and stained glass. Its spires were made of wood. Up the broad double stairways ascended the Native Hawaiian Protestant worshippers, who also used the church for political meetings during the troubling days ahead. [Hawai'i State Archives]

This memorable photograph was taken at a lū'au held at the Henry Poor residence in Waikīkī in February 1889. At center is King David Kalākaua. On his right are Princess Lili'uokalani (later Queen) and writer Robert Louis Stevenson. Seated at the king's left is Mrs. Thomas Stevenson, mother of the famed writer. The lū'au was an important feature of Hawaiian culture; it symbolized welcome and hospitality for the visitor. With everyone seated on the floor or the ground, it was certainly an easy way to put all at ease in getting to know each other. Despite the presence of kings, princesses, and renowned luminaries, a lū'au is, by its very nature, a relaxed setting where enjoyment of food and good conversation takes precedence over formality. [Baker–Van Dyke Collection]

writing some of his finest stories during his time in Hawai'i including *The Isle of Voices* and *The Bottle Imp*.

1889, July 30—Robert W. Wilcox leads 150 armed insurgents in a revolt against Kalākaua's signing of the 1887 "Bayonet Constitution." Wilcox takes over Ali'iōlani Hale (the judiciary building) and the grounds of 'Iolani Palace. Shots are exchanged between Wilcox's group and government forces, who place sharpshooters in the tower of Kawaiaha'o Church and surrounding buildings. Government forces throw dynamite onto the grounds of 'Iolani Palace to scatter the rebels. Wilcox surrenders and is tried for treason, but is later acquitted claiming the king sanctioned his actions.

1889—A railroad line built by the O'ahu Railway and Land Company begins operating between O'ahu cane fields and Honolulu docks with the rail line eventually extending to Pearl City, Wai'anae, Waialua, and Kahuku. In 1927, the O'ahu Railway & Land Train Terminal opens at 325 North King Street near the Honolulu Harbor pier.

1889, November 2—Hawai'i's first successful manned hot-air balloon flight takes place at Kapi'olani Park when Joseph Lawrence Van Tassel ascends to an altitude of one mile and then parachutes back to Earth. Van Tassel attempts the same thing from Punchbowl Crater on November 18, but drowns in Ke'ehi Lagoon when winds blow him off course. He is Hawai'i's first air fatality.

1889—The first interisland undersea cable connects Moloka'i and Maui. In November of 1900, the first interisland radio message is sent from Honolulu to Moloka'i, via a kite flying on Maui.

1880s (late)—Duck ponds replace many areas of Waikīkī that were formerly taro patches and fishponds in land that now includes the Ala Moana Shopping Center.

MOMENT IN HISTORY

THE *IKKAISEN,* OR FIRST COMPANY OF JAPANESE IMMIGRANTS FEBRUARY 8, 1885

After two weeks at sea the City of Tokio finally arrived at Honolulu Harbor in February 1885. Over nine-hundred government contract laborers disembarked to work on the sugar plantations. A smaller group of gannen mono, or "first-year men," had been recruited in 1868, but the experiment ended as a dismal failure. Poor working conditions and harsh treatment by sugar planters resulted in further immigration to Hawaiʻi being banned. King Kalākaua successfully restored harmonious diplomatic relations with Japan.

Newspaper reports described the new immigrants as having "robust, healthy appearances. They all wore a cheerful, contented look…and soon settled down into their shore quarters and made themselves at home."

After several days in quarantine, they were greeted by Kalākaua. A festival was held with demonstrations of kendo, or Japanese fencing, and sumo wrestling. Each new immigrant was given a dollar by Kalākaua; tubs of sake were opened. One reporter wrote, "Such people on a plantation would help make things lively, and there certainly was a fine display of muscle, pluck and good nature."

Over the next two decades, tens of thousands of men and women from Japan ventured across the Pacific. Others emigrated from China, Okinawa, Korea, and Philippines, and from as far away as Europe. All contributed to the wealth of the sugar industry and helped transform Hawaiʻi into a rich, multicultural mosaic.

In 1893, a group of Japanese contract laborers walked across the "China Bridge," carrying their personal belongings to the Quarantine Island where all immigrants were required to spend 18 days. The Immigration Station was located about a mile offshore on a sandy outcropping (later enlarged into today's Sand Island) in Honolulu Harbor, accessible to the newcomers by this footbridge. After being examined for communicable diseases, and cleared, immigrants were sent to various sugar plantations throughout the Islands to complete a three- to five-year contract for field labor. [Hawaiʻi State Archives]

The Wainaku homes of Japanese plantation workers were built of local materials, but resembled Japanese farmhouses rather than Hawaiian hale. The banners at the center of the photograph may have marked a community bath. A wooden flume and pipes brought water from the hill. Circa 1890. [Bishop Museum]

WITNESS TO HISTORY

THE CORONATION OF A KING, FEBRUARY 12, 1883

"On the day of the Coronation," wrote Isobel Strong Field, step-daughter of Robert Louis Stevenson, "natives passed our house in eager groups, dressed in their best...We saw silken holokus of every color, the long trains thrown over the arm; all hats were garlanded with flowers and every neck was encircled with a bright golden lei...It was a glorious day, sunny and vivid, with the cool breath of the sea that makes the climate of the islands so perfect."

A huge throng gathered on the grounds of recently completed 'Iolani Palace. The grand edifice, a showcase for the royal Hawaiian family, had been built under the direction of King Kalākaua. Four thousand guests sat in chairs around the special Coronation Pavilion festooned with banners, flags and flowers. Four thousand more onlookers stood farther back. Two thrones awaited the royal couple. Across the street the newly unveiled statue of King Kamehameha gleamed golden in the morning sun. The ceremony commenced with the Royal Hawaiian Band performing *Hawai'i Pono'ī*, the new national anthem.

His Majesty first placed a magnificent, jewel-bedecked crown on the head of his consort, Kapi'olani. Then pronouncing himself King Kalākaua of the Hawaiian Islands, he placed his own crown upon his head. Following the ceremony, ancient hula dances were performed in honor of the occasion throughout the day and into the night. The spectacular festivities had a sense of royal grandeur inspired by a Hawaiian visionary who sought to restore the pride and spirit of his race.

Above: King Kalākaua's Coronation, February 12, 1883. [Bisop Museum]

Right: In 1887, the heir apparent Princess Lili'uokalani and Queen Kapi'olani attended Queen Victoria's Jubliee in London. [Hawai'i State Archives]

Statue of King Kamehameha I

In 1883, an eight-and-a-half-foot bronze statue of Kamehameha I was installed in Kapa'au, in the Kohala region where the monarch had been born and raised. A new railroad running along the North Kohala coast had just been finished, so the railroad was ceremonially opened and the statue unveiled at the same time. The honors were performed at a grand spectacle.

The statue representing Kamehameha at forty-five years of age had been commissioned by the kingdom's legislature five years earlier, to beautify Honolulu—not Kohala. The sculptor chosen for the project, American Thomas Gould, lived in Italy. Upon completion, the nine-ton statue based on an early engraving, was shipped on the *G.F. Haendel,* which sank off the Falkland Islands. The Legislature ordered a replica made, but meanwhile divers had salvaged the original statue, which had suffered only minor damage. A ship captain purchased the statue, brought it to the Islands, and resold it to Kalākaua for a handsome profit. The replacement arrived while the original was being repaired.

Hawai'i Island's governess, Princess Kekaulike, suggested that the repaired original go to Kohala and the pristine replica remain in Honolulu. The original arrived on May 1, 1883, in Kohala. Kalākaua followed five days later, aboard a Russian warship that fired a crashing royal gun salute when it sailed into Māhukona. The King's entourage—Russian officers, more than one hundred guardsmen, government officials, royalty, and the Royal Hawaiian Band—filled all six coaches of Kohala's new train. Several days of festivities culminated in the statue's unveiling on May 8, 1883 in Kapa'au in front of the North Kohala Civic Center near Kamehameha's birthplace. King Kalākaua opted to return to Māhukona by horseback. However, the teak passenger wagons from London in which he had traveled would go into history as "the Kalākaua cars." (When the railroad closed in 1955, the cars were shipped to California to be restored. Only one car remained, on Maui.) **[Hawai'i State Archives]**

Above: This omnibus for Punahou School went from downtown to the Mānoa campus. A similar omnibus took people to Waikīkī. In 1886, the kingdom's legislature granted to Hawaiian Tramways Company, Ltd. the right to construct and operate a street rail system in Honolulu. By 1888, the first tracks were laid and service commenced on January 1, 1889. Mule- or horse-drawn trams carried passengers down King Street between Pālama and Pa'awa at eight miles per hour. Crowds that formed to ride were large. In a few years, twelve miles of track were laid through city streets that were rapidly becoming congested. [Bob Ebert]

Left: Princess Kalaniana'ole standing in front of Kamehameha Statue on Kamehameha Day. [Bishop Museum]

The Bayonet Constitution

In 1887, a political organization of American businessmen called the Hawaiian League, that included Sanford Ballard Dole, instigated the Bayonet Constitution drafted by Kalākaua's own Minister of Interior, Lorrin A. Thurston. The League considered Kalākaua to be corrupt and when his government sold its opium monopoly to a Chinese interest, the Americans sought to restrict his power.

At a mass meeting, the League demanded that Kalākaua's Cabinet be dismissed and that Kalākaua sign a new constitution. A radical faction of the League wanted to march to 'Iolani Palace with guns and annex Hawai'i to the United States, but Dole and the majority only wished to limit Kalākaua's monarchical powers. Kalākaua later signed a new constitution given the nickname "The Bayonet Constitution" implying the document was signed at gunpoint. Accounts vary on the actual threats made to the king to sign.

The new document severely curtailed Kalākaua's power and ended 23 years of rule under the previous constitution of Kamehameha V. According to the Bayonet Constitution a vote of the Legislature was necessary to replace Cabinet members. Nobles were to be elected by those who owned large amounts of land which significantly reduced the power of Asians and native Hawaiians. The constitution also allowed the Legislature to override the king's veto and extended voting rights to all Europeans and Americans willing to take an oath to support the new constitution.

The new constitution was meant to support commercial interests consisting of the Chamber of Commerce, sugar planters and merchants whose aim was to abrogate the monarchy, declare Hawai'i a Republic, and annex Hawai'i to the United States. Politically known as the "down-town party," they sought to drastically reduce Kalākaua's sovereign power and end the corruption allegedly taking place among his Cabinet particularly by his premier and minister of foreign affairs, Walter Murray Gibson.

WITNESS TO HISTORY

PROGRESS IN THE PACIFIC 1886

Fifty years ago the tide flowed where now are some of our busiest streets; a small coasting schooner anchored where now may be seen steam vessels carrying the Hawaiian flag across the ocean...Kalo patches and grass huts, unshaded by any tree, except where the cocoanut fringed the shore, have been replaced by substantial buildings and busy streets, and the whole shaded by such a wealth of lovely foliage...busy haunts of a commerce...brought with rapid strides to its present high condition by the wise and patriotic effort of the King whose jubilee we now celebrate.

Walter Murray Gibson, Prime Minister of the Hawaiian Kingdom,
delivering a speech on "Progress of Hawaii since 1836," on November 18, 1886,
at Kaumakapili Church in honor of the jubilee birthday of King Kalākaua
The Diaries of Walter Murray Gibson, 1886, 1887

Princess Pauahi and Charles Reed Bishop

Princess Bernice Pauahi Bishop (1831-1884) was the great granddaughter of Kamehameha I, and his last direct descendant. Supposedly she had been engaged to the young Lot Kamehameha before he became Kamehameha V but instead chose to marry Charles Reed Bishop. They wed on June 4, 1850 and lived in their Honolulu home known as Haleakalā built by her father in 1847 near King and Bishop streets.

Just an hour before Kamehameha V passed away on December 11, 1872, he offered to name her as his successor, but she declined.

When Princess Ruth Ke'elikōlani died in 1883, her will bequeathed to Princess Pauahi her elaborate Emma Street mansion, Keōua Hale, as well as approximately 353,000 acres of Kamehameha lands, nearly nine percent of all land in the Islands. In 1885, Princess Pauahi inherited Haleakalā from her parents, Abner Pākī and Konia. Princess Pauahi also inherited approximately 25,000 acres of land from her parents and her aunt, 'Akāhi.

In 1876, she traveled to England with her husband, and the couple was presented at Queen Victoria's Court. They were later received by Pope Pius IX.

When Princess Pauahi died in 1884, her will left 434,000 acres of land in perpetual trust to assist in the establishment of two schools in the Kamehameha name. Under the terms of the endowment, the Kamehameha School for Boys opened in Honolulu on October 4, 1887, and the Kamehameha School for Girls on December 19, 1894. The Bishop Estate still operates Kamehameha Schools including its 600-acre Kapālama campus in Honolulu as well as smaller ones on Maui and Hawai'i Island. The Estate's vast land holdings and investments are worth more than $9 billion.

Charles Reed Bishop (1822-1915) was born in Glen Falls, New York on January 25, 1822. Orphaned as a child and raised by his grandparents he worked on his grandparents' farm and at various jobs. At age 24, he sailed around Cape Horn bound for Oregon, but remained in the Islands when the ship stopped to take on provisions.

Bishop first posted books for the government and then in 1849 became Honolulu's Collector General of Customs. He later opened a mercantile business with W.A. Aldrich, forming the firm of Aldrich and Bishop in 1858. They initially worked out of an office on the Honolulu waterfront, and the company later became the Bank of Bishop & Co. Ltd. Much of the bank's initial business involved loans to the whaling and sugar industries.

Bishop served on the Board of Education under Kamehameha V, Lunalilo, and Kalākaua, and then joined the Privy Council of Queen Lili'uokalani. He was known for his philanthropy, served on numerous charitable boards, and contributed generously to needy causes. After Bernice Pauahi Bishop passed away in 1884, he played a major role in carrying out her wishes including the establishment of Kamehameha Schools.

To honor his wife, he founded in 1889 the Bernice Pauahi Bishop Museum, constructing Polynesian Hall and Hawaiian Hall on the same site as Kamehameha School. When the school was relocated in the 1960s, Bishop Hall became part of the Bishop Museum, which was established to complete the Kamehameha Schools education. The Bishop Museum's collection materials initially came from three prominent women who passed away in the mid-1880s: Princess Ruth Ke'elikōlani, the granddaughter of Kamehameha I; Bernice Pauahi Bishop, the great-granddaughter of Kamehameha I; and Emma, the wife of Kamehameha IV.

When Bishop passed away in 1915, his ashes were interred next to his wife in the Kamehameha Tomb at the Mauna 'Ala Royal Mausoleum. Honolulu's Bishop Street, Hawai'i's business and finance center, is named after him. In 1969, the Bank of Bishop & Co. Ltd. was renamed First Hawaiian Bank, and is the oldest financial institution in the state.

When the U.S.S. *Charleston* returned the remains of King Kalākaua, his loyal friend John Adams Cummins (center, with a long white beard) was one of the waiting mourners. The king's casket was taken from the ship and placed in a hearse, which then moved quietly through the crowds on a last journey to 'Iolani Palace. [Bishop Museum]

On February 15, 1891, the funeral procession of King Kalākaua moved solemnly down King Street as his native subjects carried large kāhili, or feather standards, on all four sides of his koa wood casket, partially draped in a magnificent yellow feather cape. The King's Guard, several military companies, Hawaiian legislators, and the fraternal societies of the kingdom marched in measured cadence as Queen Kapi'olani rode in a closed and shrouded carriage behind her husband's casket. [The Hawaiian Historical Society]

1890—Due to foreign-introduced diseases less than 40,000 native Hawaiians remain from an estimated population of more than 300,000 before contact with Westerners in 1778.

1890—Kapi'olani Maternity Hospital (Home) opens at Beretania and Makiki Streets later moving to Punahou Street in 1929. The hospital is originally sponsored by a society called Ho'oulu a Ho'ōla Lāhui ("Propagate and Perpetuate Nation"), whose first president was Kapi'olani.

1890—Passage of the McKinley Tariff by the United States eliminates the advantages of Hawai'i's sugar producers over foreign producers.

1890, November 25—Kalākaua departs for San Francisco on the U.S.S. *Charleston.*

1891—The Hawaiian Electric Company begins providing service.

1891, January 20—Kalākaua dies in San Francisco.

1891, January 29—Princess Lili'uokalani becomes queen. Under pressure from her cabinet Lili'uokalani takes the oath of office and unwillingly pledges allegiance to the Bayonet Constitution. During the next two years Lili'uokalani works to promulgate a new constitution that restores autonomy of her kingdom by setting aside provisions of the Bayonet Constitution that had limited the power of the monarch. Opposing her is the Hawaiian League with its stated goals of deposing the queen, overthrowing the monarchy and annexing Hawai'i to the United States.

1891—Princess Ka'iulani is proclaimed heir apparent.

1892, January 11—At the first official meeting of the Hawai'i Historical Society, Charles R. Bishop is selected as the first president.

1893—The Sans Souci Hotel opens in Waikīkī along the shoreline of Kapi'olani Park, and hosts Robert Louis Stevenson for a five week visit.

1893, January 14— Lili'uokalani informs her Cabinet that she

Queen Kapi'olani knelt in prayer at the casket of King Kalākaua, which lay in state for over two weeks in the Throne Room of 'Iolani Palace. [The Hawaiian Historical Society]

When it was learned that Queen Lili'uokalani was intending to abrogate the Constitution of 1887, a 13-member Committee of Public Safety was formed on January 14, 1893. It issued her a warning that any attempt to interfere with the current constitution would be met with resistance. Later the thirteen men were commemorated in this display, which featured (center) Henry E. Cooper (Chairman), (clockwise from top) Henry Waterhouse, Lorrin A. Thurston, Ed Suhr, F. W. McChesney, John Emmeluth, William R. Castle, William O. Smith, John A. McCandless, Crister Bolte, William C. Wilder, Andrew Brown and Theodore F. Lansing. Only five of them were actually citizens of Hawai'i, the others retaining citizenship of the United States, Scotland or Germany. Chairman Cooper, who was a recent arrival to the Islands, never became a citizen of the Kingdom of Hawai'i. [Bishop Museum]

plans to proclaim a new constitution at the request of a majority of the Hawaiian people. After the prorogation (closing) of the Legislature at Ali'iōlani Hale, she instructs her Cabinet Ministers to go to 'Iolani Palace to sign the new constitution. When her cabinet refuses to sign the new constitution, she defers any action. In a speech from the lānai of 'Iolani Palace she tells the many, who had gathered in anticipation of a new constitution being announced, to go home peacefully as she is unable to declare a new constitution. In response, the Hawaiian League's Committee of Safety declares the Queen's actions treasonous and makes plans for a Provisional Government with the goal of annexing the Hawaiian Islands to the United States.

1893, January 15—In consultation with U.S. Minister to Hawai'i John L. Stevens, the Committee of Public Safety is assured that troops from the U.S.S. *Boston* will land if any danger is posed to American lives or property.

1893, January 16—In an official proclamation Lili'uokalani declares that changes to the constitution will only be made with the consent of the Legislature.

1893, January 16—Two mass meetings are held, one by supporters of annexation, the other by the Queen's supporters.

1893, January 16—Under orders from U.S. Minister Stevens, troops from the U.S.S. *Boston* come ashore at 5 p.m. and march down King Street past Ali'iōlani Hale to Arion Hall across from 'Iolani Palace. They are quartered at the Arlington Hotel in downtown Honolulu, the former home of Princess Bernice Pauahi Bishop. The hotel becomes known as "Camp Boston" when martial law is declared by the provisional government. The 162 soldiers are supposed to only protect American property and lives during anticipated political upheavals. Lili'uokalani protests that a majority of the troops are quartered directly across from Ali'iōlani Hale, the government building almost across from 'Iolani Palace, an area where no Americans resided or owned property. The troops are in an excellent position to defend the leaders of the revolution who are about to declare a provisional government.

1893, January 17—A Provisional Government is proclaimed by members of the Committee of Public Safety which includes Sanford Dole, who will become the Provisional

On the evening of January 16, 1893, troops of the U.S.S. *Boston* landed. They were quartered at the Arlington Hotel in downtown Honolulu, the former home of Princess Bernice Pauahi Bishop. The hotel became known as "Camp Boston" when martial law was declared by the provisional government. The 162 soldiers were supposedly only to protect American property and lives during anticipated political upheavals. Queen Lili'uokalani protested that a majority of the troops were quartered directly across from Ali'iōlani Hale, the government building almost across from 'Iolani Palace, an area where no Americans resided or owned property. The troops were in an excellent position, however, to defend the leaders of the revolution who were about to declare a provisional government. [Hawai'i State Archives]

Queen Lili'uokalani poses solemnly for the camera on the grounds of Washington Place in 1893, following the overthrow of the monarchy. [Baker–Van Dyke Collection]

Government's first president. U.S. Minister Stevens quickly recognizes the Provisional Government as Hawai'i's lawful government. That evening about 100 armed men gather around Ali'iōlani Hale in support of the annexationists posting guards around Ali'iōlani Hale, the new headquarters of the Provisional Government. They hold drills on King Street in front of 'Iolani Palace. Martial Law is declared, and troops from the U.S.S. *Boston* remain nearby.

1893, January 17— Lili'uokalani unsuccessfully requests assistance from U.S. Minister Stevens in opposing the newly formed "Provisional Government." The Honolulu Rifles, an armed volunteer group, assembles in Aliiolani Hale in opposition to the loyalist guard across the street at Iolani Palace.

1893, January 17— Lili'uokalani is dethroned and a provisional government is established.

1893, February 1—U.S. Minister Stevens raises the United States flag over Hawai'i and troops from the U.S.S. *Boston* take over as official guards of Ali'iōlani Hale, the center of the Provisional Government.

1893, March 4—Democrat Grover Cleveland succeeds Benjamin Harrison as U.S. President,

Officers of the Provisional Government of Hawai'i after the overthrow of the monarchy and shortly before the establishment of the short-lived Republic which was followed by U.S. annexation. Shown here are (left to right), James A. King, Sanford B. Dole (president of the Republic and first territorial governor), William O. Smith, and Peter C. Jones. [Baker–Van Dyke Collection]

replacing his Republican pro-annexation administration.

1893, March 29—By order of the U.S. President, James H. Blount arrives from Washington to investigate the events leading to the overthrow of the monarchy. He gives orders for the American flag to be taken down and the Hawaiian flag raised. U.S. naval forces are sent back to their ships.

1893, June—The President of the Provisional Government, Sanford Ballard Dole, orders that the government's executive departments be moved to ʻIolani Palace, with its garrison occupying adjacent ʻIolani Barracks. The Provisional Government also passes a resolution renaming ʻIolani Palace the "Executive Building," and Aliʻiōlani Hale the "Court House" (it was often called the "Judiciary Building").

1893, October 18—The Blount Report blames the overthrow of the monarchy on U.S. Minister Stevens and suggests restoring the Hawaiian government. President Cleveland denounces the overthrow as lawless and achieved under "false pretexts."

1893, November 4—President Cleveland gives orders to restore the power of Liliʻuokalani. He also sends word that he regretted the "unauthorized intervention" that took away the queen's sovereignty.

1893, November 4—The Provisional Government refuses to restore Liliʻuokalani to the throne saying that only armed conflict will force them to give up power. President Cleveland, while not supporting annexation, is reluctant to use force against Americans.

Refusing President Grover Cleveland's demand that the Hawaiʻi Provisional Government return authority to Queen Liliʻuokalani, the American businessmen who had overthrown the monarchy formally established the Republic of Hawaiʻi on July 4, 1894. Their plan was to wait for the election of a president sympathetic to their goal, which occurred in August 1898 when President McKinley declared that Hawaiʻi would become part of the United States. [Hawaiian Historical Society]

1894, May—The Provisional Government calls a Constitutional Convention to draft the constitution of the "Republic of Hawaiʻi." In the courtroom of the Supreme Court at Aliʻiōlani Hale the new constitution is written by nineteen delegates appointed by the Provisional Government along with 18 elected delegates.

Commercial Advertiser.

ANNEXATION!

"HERE TO STAY!"

And the star-spangled banner
In triumph shall wave,
O'er the Isles of Hawaii
And the homes of the brave.

CERVERA'S FLEET IS ANNIHILATED

Attempted to Run the Blockade at Santiago. He Is a Prisoner—Heavy Losses.

1894, July 4—When efforts to annex Hawaiʻi to the United States were thwarted by President Grover Cleveland and anti-imperialist members of the Democratic Party, the Provisional Government declares itself the Republic of Hawaiʻi. Sanford B. Dole is elected president.

1894—Lāʻie, Oʻahu resident Joseph Kekuku develops the steel guitar and a unique playing style that allows better harmonics, glissandos, and slurs not previously possible. The steel guitar, or kīkā kila (kīkā means guitar; kila means steel), is considered one of just two major instruments invented in the United States (the other is the banjo).

1895, January 6—As its leaders prepare to celebrate the second anniversary of the Hawaiian Kingdom's downfall, Robert Wilcox, Samuel Nowlein, and a coalition of Hawaiians and royalist

On July 4, 1894, when efforts to annex Hawai'i to the United States were thwarted by President Grover Cleveland and anti-imperialist members of the Democratic Party, the provisional government declared itself the Republic of Hawai'i. Sanford B. Dole was elected president. Six months later, in January of 1895, as its leaders prepared to celebrate the second anniversary of the Hawaiian kingdom's downfall, Robert Wilcox, Samuel Nowlein, and a coalition of Hawaiians and royalist sympathizers attempted to overthrow the republic. Wilcox had intended to land guns at Sans Souci beach on the evening of January 6, 1895. Informers tipped off the sheriff and his deputies. Gunfire broke out on the beach at Waikīkī as the revolutionists broke rank and scattered toward Diamond Head and up into Pālolo and Mānoa valleys. Honolulu was placed under martial law. Wilcox is pictured here in his flamboyant self-designed uniform. The photo was taken after an earlier arrest, in 1889, when he led an uprising against the signing of the "Bayonet" Constitution. [Hawai'i State Archives]

On January 16, 1895, Queen Lili'uokalani was arrested at her Washington Place home and taken to 'Iolani Palace, where she spent eight months under house arrest. [Hawai'i State Archives]

sympathizers attempt to overthrow the republic. Wilcox had intended to land guns at Sans Souci beach on the evening of January 6, 1895 but informers tipped off the sheriff. Gunfire breaks out on the beach at Waikīkī as the revolutionists broke rank and scattered toward Diamond Head and up into Pālolo and Mānoa valleys. Honolulu was placed under martial law.

1895, January 24— Lili'uokalani is forced to abdicate the throne.

1895, January 6—A small group of royalists, mostly native Hawaiians, attempt a counterrevolution to overthrow the Republic and restore the queen. The uprising allegedly takes place without any participation by Lili'uokalani who denies any involvement. Hundreds of men are arrested, including Robert W. Wilcox who is condemned to death but later pardoned.

1895, January 7—Martial Law is declared and a military commission is appointed to court martial Lili'uokalani and others.

1895, January 16— Lili'uokalani is imprisoned in 'Iolani Palace.

1895, January 24— Lili'uokalani signs a formal abdication calling for the recognition of the Republic of Hawai'i as the lawful government. She later claims that the abdication was invalid due to coercion and that she signed the document only to spare the lives of her supporters.

1895, February 5— Lili'uokalani is arraigned before the military commission for treason, a charge that will be later changed to misprision of treason (knowing of treason, i.e. the attempted counterrevolution, but not disclosing it).

1895, February 27— Lili'uokalani is found guilty of misprision of treason and sentenced to a $5,000 fine and five years hard labor. The sentence is not carried out though Lili'uokalani remains imprisoned in 'Iolani Palace for seven months until September 6, 1895. She is then confined to Washington Place until February 6, 1896, and then island-restricted until October 6, 1896.

1895, March 19—Martial Law in Hawai'i ends. In all, 37 people are found guilty of treason and open rebellion, 141 guilty of treason, and 12 guilty of misprision. Twenty-two people are exiled to the United States.

1897—President McKinley succeeds President Cleveland. Lili'uokalani visits Washington D.C. to petition McKinley to restore the rights of the

In 1897, four years after being deposed, Lili'uokalani took her cause before the American people in a journey to Washington, D.C. and New York. This photograph was taken just before her departure to the United States. [Hawai'i State Archives]

Hawaiian people, but her petition is not acted upon.

1897—The Provisional Government also sends a pro-annexation petition to Washington D.C., which is acted upon, unlike Liliʻuokalani's petition which opposes annexation and seeks the restoration of the Hawaiian monarchy.

1897, June 16—President McKinley sends an annexation treaty to the Senate. Liliʻuokalani submits a formal protest which is ineffective. The United States Senate later claims that President McKinley's act of sending the bill to the U.S. Senate amounted to a recognition of Hawaiʻi's Provisional Government. While acknowledging that the Hawaiian monarchy was overthrown, they claim that McKinley's recognition of the Provisional Government meant that the facts would not be reviewed further by the United States.

1897—Hawaiians organize Hui Pākākā Nalu in Waikīkī, charging tourists for ocean canoe rides. This is the forerunner of the Waikīkī Beachboys, a renowned group of water sports instructors, who from the 1920s to the 1950s work on the beaches fronting the Royal Hawaiian and Moana Hotels.

1897, February 5—The Hawaiian Opera House shows Hawaiʻi's first silent movies.

1897, July 14—Refusing President Grover Cleveland's demand that the Hawaiʻi Provisional Government return authority to Liliʻuokalani, the Republic of Hawaiʻi is formally established. The plan is to wait for the election of a president sympathetic to their goal. (In August 1898 President McKinley declares that Hawaiʻi is to become part of the U.S.)

1897, September 7—Two native Hawaiian groups, Hui Kalaiʻāina and Hui Aloha ʻĀina, hold a mass rally attended by thousands of native Hawaiians at Palace Square in front of ʻIolani Palace to launch an anti-annexation petition drive on all the Islands. In December of 1897, native Hawaiian representatives travel to Washington D.C. and present petitions against annexation to the U.S. Senate. Numerous pro-annexation senators are persuaded to change their minds leaving the Senate twelve votes short of passing an annexation treaty.

1898—Two Edison photographers record the first motion picture scenes filmed in the Islands.

1898, April 24—Spain declares war against the United States. U.S. troops are temporarily stationed at Camp McKinley in Kapiʻolani Park.

The United States wasted no time consolidating their power in the Islands. Four days after annexation, the 1st New York Volunteer Infantry and the U.S. Volunteer Engineers arrived in Honolulu. The New Yorkers, photographed at their official posting, Camp McKinley in Kapi'olani Park, spent several months in the Islands before returning to the mainland. When Camp McKinley was vacated the military paid over three thousand dollars to repair damage to the grounds. [U.S. Army Museum of Hawai'i]

The melancholy, imposing funeral of Hawai'i's beloved Princess Ka'iulani took place on the Sunday following her death, March 6, 1899. The streets surrounding Kawaiaha'o Church were crowded with spectators and mourners early in the day. The catafalque moved slowly from the church 'Ewa down King Street to Alakea then up to Emma and Vineyard and along Vineyard to Nu'uanu Avenue to Mauna'ala Mausoleum. An estimated 25,000 persons lined the march. [Hawai'i State Archives]

1898—Chang Apana becomes a member of the Honolulu Police Department. His skill and determination in solving cases and his Asian ancestry later inspire the creation of the character "Charlie Chan."

1898—Hawai'i's first golf course is built in Moanalua Valley on O'ahu.

1898—Recordings of "My Honolulu Lady" and "Honolulu Cake Walk" become the earliest known Hawaiian music recordings. (A 1901 Columbia Records catalog later lists the song "Pua i Kaoakalani" as well as "Aloha 'Oe," written by Lili'uokalani in 1878.)

1898—Princess Ka'iulani hosts a feast to persuade several U.S. Congressional legislators sent to Hawai'i to review the U.S.'s new Pacific Territory to reverse annexation.

1898, June 15—The Spanish-American War extends to the Philippines, making the Hawaiian Islands a strategically important coaling base for the United States fleet. This gives renewed impetus toward U.S. annexation of Hawai'i.

1898, July 6—Annexation by a Joint Resolution of the United States is passed.

1898, August 12—Power is officially transferred from the Republic of Hawai'i to the United States. United States Minister Harold M. Seawall accepts the transfer of sovereignty from President Dole of the Republic of Hawai'i.

1899, March 6—Princess Ka'iulani, the niece of Lili'uokalani and Kalākaua, passes away at the young

The heart of Honolulu's shopping district in the 1890s was Fort Street, photographed here near the corner of Hotel Street. In 1903, the mule- and horse-drawn trolleys of Hawaiian Tramways Ltd. were replaced with the electric cars of the Honolulu Rapid Transit & Land Co. [Hawai'i State Archives]

The first Lunalilo Home was constructed in Makiki at a site now occupied by Roosevelt High School. It opened its doors on March 30, 1883. Forty years later, in 1923, the old home was demolished and its elderly residents moved to the second Lunalilo Home in Maunalua Valley, now known as Hawai'i Kai. [Baker–Van Dyke Collection]

age of 23. Though her death is attributed to a fever, many believe she died of a broken heart as the last Hawaiian princess and heiress to a vanished throne.

1899, October 8—Hawai'i's first automobiles, two "Wood Electrics," arrive in Honolulu for Edward D. Tenney and H. P. Baldwin.

1899, December 12—An epidemic of bubonic plague breaks out in Honolulu.

1899—The Hilo wharf is constructed.

The Waikīkī Beachboys

In 1897, Hawaiian watermen organized Hui Pākākā Nalu in Waikīkī, charging tourists for ocean canoe rides. This was the forerunner of the Waikīkī Beachboys, a name given to water sports instructors offering their services in front of the Royal Hawaiian and Moana Hotels from the 1920s to the 1950s. The first Waikīkī Beach Patrol was organized in the 1930s.

Many of the Beachboys had colorful names such as Toots, Chick, Steamboat, and Turkey. One of the most famous was the legendary Duke Kahanamoku. Duke and other local surfers founded Hui Nalu (Club of the Waves) in 1911, and many of the club members eventually became Waikīkī Beachboys. Their clients included wealthy visitors who wanted to surf or ride an outrigger canoe in the waves and Hawaiian royalty as well as the general public. They included many gifted musicians. Rumors of the Beachboys' amorous adventures abounded.

After the Japanese attack on Pearl Harbor in 1941 martial law ended the carefree beachboy lifestyle. The golden era of the Waikīkī Beachboys was over.

MOMENT IN HISTORY

THE OVERTHROW OF A NATION
JANUARY 17, 1893

Days of political rallies throughout Honolulu had increased tensions in the city. The forces of revolution mounted under the direction of the Committee of Safety, thirteen businessmen led by lawyer W.O. Smith and journalist-businessman Lorrin A. Thurston. The group learned that Liliʻuokalani intended to promulgate a new constitution for the Hawaiian Kingdom—restoring the monarch's prerogatives and the people's voting rights which had been severely curtailed by the 1887 or "Bayonet" Constitution. The Committee of Safety informed the queen that if she proceeded, they would take necessary actions to stop her.

Threatened by an uprising of wealthy business leaders, the queen decided not to press for a new constitution. Hundreds of her subjects gathered outside ʻIolani Palace. Speaking from the balcony, she announced that despite petitions from the Hawaiian people, she would postpone action until some future time. The Committee of Safety seized this opportunity to negotiate with U.S. Minister John Stevens—an ardent promoter of American annexation of Hawaiʻi—and gained his support in creating an alternate form of government. Despite protests by the queen, over a hundred fifty officers and men from the U.S.S. *Boston* landed in Honolulu. They bivouacked across the street from the palace. On January 17, the Committee of Safety announced the establishment of the Provisional Government of Hawaiʻi. The proclamation was read in public with U.S. military troops standing guard.

Realizing that resistance to this illegal proclamation could result in bloodshed, Liliʻuokalani yielded "to the superior force of the United States of America." Her strongly worded letter of protest noted that she did so "until such time as the Government of the United States shall, upon the facts being presented to it, undo the action of its representatives and reinstate me in the authority which I claim as the constitutional sovereign of the Hawaiian Islands." A century later, her nation and native subjects still await restitution of their sovereignty.

The official ceremonies of the U.S. annexation of Hawaiʻi took place before noon on August 12, 1898, when the Hawaiian flag was lowered from ʻIolani Palace "like the fluttering of a wounded bird." The president of the Hawaiian Republic, Sanford Dole then took an oath of allegiance. During the transfer of authority, the National Guard of Hawaiʻi stood at attention in front of troops from the U.S.S. *Philadelphia* and *Mohican*. At noon a thirty-six-foot American flag was hoisted above the renamed Executive Building as "The Star-Spangled Banner" was played. A twenty-one gun salute from ship batteries on the shore and in the harbor followed. A century later, the legality of U.S. annexation would be challenged by Native Hawaiians. [Hawaiʻi State Archives]

WITNESS TO HISTORY

"THE LAST DROP OF BLOOD," QUEEN LILI'UOKALANI 1896

Oh, honest Americans, as Christians hear me for my down-trodden people! Their form of government is as dear to them as yours is precious to you. Quite as warmly as you love your country, so they love theirs. With all your goodly possessions, covering a territory so immense that there yet remain parts unexplored, possessing islands that, although near at hand, had to be neutral ground in time of war, do not cover the little vineyard of Naboth's, so far from your shores, lest the punishment of Ahab fall upon you, if not in your day, in that of your children, for "be not deceived, God is not mocked." The people to whom your fathers told of the living God, and taught to call "Father," and whom the sons now seek to despoil and destroy, are crying aloud to Him in their time of trouble; and He will keep His promise, and will listen to the voices of His Hawaiian children lamenting for their homes.

It is for them that I would give the last drop of my blood; it is for them that I would spend, nay, am spending, everything belonging to me. Will it be in vain? It is for the American people and their representatives in Congress to answer these questions. As they deal with me and my people, kindly, generously and justly, so may the Great Ruler of all nations deal with the grand and glorious nation of the United States of America.

Queen Lili'uokalani, 1896
Hawai'i's Story by Hawai'i's Queen

The police reluctantly take an oath of allegiance to the United States following the annexation ceremonies on August 12, 1898. [Hawai'i State Archives]

The Newlands Resolution Annexing Hawai'i to the United States

"Whereas, the Government of the Republic of Hawai'i having, in due form, signified its consent, in the manner provided by its constitution, to cede absolutely and without reserve to the United States of America all rights of sovereignty of whatsoever kind in and over the Hawaiian Islands and their dependencies, and also to cede and transfer to the United States the absolute fee and ownership of all public, Government, or Crown lands, public buildings or edifices, ports, harbors, military equipment, and all other public property of every kind and description belonging to the Government of the Hawaiian Islands."

"Resolved by the Senate and House of Representatives of the United States of America in Congress Assembled, that said cession is accepted, ratified, and confirmed, and that the said Hawaiian Islands and their dependencies be, and they are hereby, annexed as a part of the territory of the United States and are subject to the sovereign dominion thereof, and that all and singular the property and rights hereinbefore mentioned are vested in the United States of America."

"The existing treaties of the Hawaiian Islands with foreign nations shall forthwith cease and determine, being replaced by such treaties as may exist, or as may be hereafter concluded, between the United States and such foreign nations."

Approved July 7th, 1898
William McKinley

MOMENT IN HISTORY

THE ANNEXATION OF HAWAIʻI
AUGUST 12, 1898

Leaders of the Provisional Government had worked strenuously for the annexation of the Islands by U.S. President Benjamin Harrison. However, their best efforts were thwarted by the new administration of President Grover Cleveland. After investigating the actions of U.S. representatives in Hawaiʻi, Cleveland retracted the annexation treaty submitted to the Senate and asked for the restoration of Liliʻuokalani. The Provisional Government ignored this request. Instead its leaders established the Republic of Hawaiʻi and waited for an American administration more sympathetic to their goals. With the election of President McKinley, a new annexation treaty was submitted. Yet a petition from over 38,000 Native Hawaiians and loyalists of all races had also been sent to the U.S. Congress, protesting the annexation. This aroused anti-imperialist opposition in the Senate, which would need a two-thirds majority for passage. Supporters of annexation saw that approval was doomed, but they managed to have Congress pass a joint resolution. In August 1898, President McKinley declared that Hawaiʻi would become part of the United States.

To insure a peaceful transition, marines and sailors from the American warship Mohican stood guard at the ceremonies at ʻIolani Palace. Renamed the Executive Building, it was crowded with supporters of the new American regime. Liliʻuokalani had been invited to attend, but declined and remained in seclusion.

Sanford B. Dole, President of the Republic of Hawaiʻi, took an oath of allegiance to the American government. His cabinet members did the same. With this simple ceremony, the sovereignty of the Republic was transferred to the United States. "Scarcely an Hawaiian face was to be seen in the not too large assemblage," one supporter of the queen wrote. "This last gesture was a silent protest of the Hawaiian people. They could do no more."

Opposite page: Following annexation, a commission of U.S. congressmen was sent to the Hawaiian Islands to assess the new territory. Along with island representatives, such as newly appointed Governor Dole, the commission visited all the Islands. The commission repeatedly needed to state that annexation was not a temporary war measure due to the conflict between the U.S. and Spain, but represented permanent status for the Islands. The town meetings turned out to be poorly attended.

One person who faithfully accompanied the commission on their travels, much to the surprise of its members, was Queen Lili'uokalani who wanted to meet the commissioners informally and remove any prejudice against her from their minds. The commissioners had to be impressed with enthusiasm towards her by her former subjects.

Formal petitions against annexation were not just from Hawaiians but from all population groups. Accompanying the rising chorus of protest against annexation, the commissioners were treated with an outpouring of aloha by the Hawaiian community each time a petition was presented.

One big effort to persuade the U.S. commissioners to accept the anti-annexation protests was a feast hosted by Princess Ka'iulani at her 'Āinahau home in Waikīkī. Over the years, the photo's accompanying caption stated that Princess Ka'iulani was "hosting the commission to an elaborate feast," implying that Hawaiians had acquiesced to annexation. In reality, the feast was part of an effort by loyalists to reverse annexation. [Hawai'i State Archives]

Princess Ka'iulani
Heir to a Vanquished Throne

Princess Ka'iulani, the niece of Lili'uokalani and Kalākaua, was proclaimed heir apparent to the Hawaiian Kingdom when Lili'uokalani ascended to the throne in 1891. The young princess attended boarding school in England, and was a talented artist, musician, horseback rider and swimmer. She was also active in many charitable causes.

On March 6, 1899, at the age of 23, the last Hawaiian princess passed away at 'Āinahau, where her favored flowers grew and her peacocks roamed. The princess had become ill after going horseback riding in a rainstorm, and though her death was attributed to a fever, many believe that she died of a broken heart as the last Hawaiian princess and heiress to a vanished throne. On the night she died her peacocks were purported to have made extremely loud vocal displays of their grief.

Robert Louis Stevenson had visited Princess Ka'iulani in Waikīkī, and when she departed for England he wrote this celebrated poem:

Forth from her land to mine she goes,
The island maid, the island rose,
Light of heart and bright of face
The daughter of a double race.
Her islands here in Southern sun
Shall mourn their Kaiulani gone.
And I, in her dear banyan's shade,
Look vainly for my little maid.
But our Scots Islands far away
Shall glitter with unwanted day,
And cast for once their tempest by
To smile in Kaiulani's eye.

—Robert Louis Stevenson, 1889

Upper and center: Ka'iulani was beautiful both as a child and as a young woman. [Hawai'i State Archives]

Lower: As a mature woman Ka'iulani's beauty bewitched all who saw her. The daughter of Governor Archibald Cleghorn and Princess Miriam Likelike, the adored princess died on March 6, 1899, three years after this photo was taken. [Hawai'i State Archives]

Annexation—The Kū'ē Petitions

After the 1893 overthrow of the Hawaiian monarchy, a small but powerful group of Hawai'i's residents led the movement for annexation of the Hawaiian Islands to the United States. Many in Washington D.C. also supported annexation, including President McKinley, an avowed imperialist who was eager to increase the international prominence of the United States.

A large number of native Hawaiians opposed annexation just as they had opposed the overthrow of the Hawaiian monarchy. On September 7, 1897, two native Hawaiian groups held a mass rally at Palace Square in front of 'Iolani Palace to begin a petition drive against annexation. The two groups were Hui Kalai'āina, formed in 1887 by native Hawaiians opposed to Kalākaua's signing of the Bayonet Constitution, and Hui Aloha 'Āina, formed in support of Lili'uokalani after the 1893 overthrow. Thousands of native Hawaiians united in their opposition to annexation attended the rally and then set about getting signatures from residents throughout the Islands.

The Hui Aloha 'Āina petition against annexation titled "Palapala Hoopii Kū'ē Hoohui 'Āina a Ka Lahui" Petition of the Nation Protesting Annexation contained 21,269 signatures. The Hui Kalai'āina petition contained 17,000 signatures and called for the restoration of the Hawaiian monarchy. The two signed documents became known as the Kū'ē Petitions (kū'ē means "to oppose, or protest").

Agreeing that the main goal was preventing annexation, group leaders decided to present only the Hui Aloha 'Āina petition to the U.S. government in order to avoid showing a division of opinion. James Keauiluna Kaulia, the president of Aloha 'Āina, and David Kalauokalani, the president of Hui Kala'āina, after consulting with Lili'uokalani in December of 1897 traveled to Washington D.C. to present the petitions to Senators Hoar and Pettigrew. The 566 pages of signatures were sent to the Senate Foreign Relations Committee and then discussed on the Senate floor before the whole Senate.

On June 17, 1897 Lili'uokalani also presented an Official Protest to the Treaty of Annexation. Her protest stated (in part), "I declare such a treaty to be an act of wrong toward the native and part-native people of Hawai'i, an invasion of the rights of the ruling chiefs, in violation of international rights both toward my people and toward friendly nations with whom they have made treaties, the perpetuation of the fraud whereby the constitutional government was overthrown, and, finally, an act of gross injustice to me."

When the native Hawaiian representatives left Washington D.C. in February, 1898, they had succeeded in persuading numerous pro-annexation senators to change their minds, leaving the Senate twelve votes short of passing the treaty (a 2/3 majority was required for ratification) and successfully stalling the political process of annexation. Some Senators pushed for a vote among the residents of the Hawaiian Islands, but pro-annexation Senators opposed this as they knew a vote would doom their cause.

On June 15, 1898 when the Spanish-American War spread to the Pacific's Spanish Philippines the Hawaiian Islands became strategically important as a coaling base. On July 6, 1898, a simple majority passed a Joint Resolution of Congress approving annexation. Known as the Newlands Resolution, it was signed by President McKinley on July 7, 1898, and thus the Hawaiian Islands were annexed to the United States.

The official transfer of power from the Republic of Hawai'i to the United States took place on August 12, 1898. The Hawaiian flag at 'Iolani Palace was replaced with the U.S. flag. Sanford Ballard Dole became the first governor of the Territory of Hawai'i. Annexation also ceded about 1.8 million acres of Hawaiian Crown lands and government lands to the US.

Plantation towns were lonely isolated places in the midst of vast sugar cane fields far removed from other towns and cities. The homes of the workers were dominated by the mill structures. Shown here at the turn of the century is Maui's Wailuku Sugar Mill in central Maui. [Hawai'i State Archives]

20TH CENTURY

On the morning of January 20, 1900, fires were set to burn out plague-infested houses near Beretania and Nu'uanu Streets. High winds suddenly began to gust as the flames leaped to the Waikīkī spire of Kaumakapili Church. As the fire department worked frantically to control the flames, the other spire exploded into a fiery inferno as flames leaped over Beretania Street and raced uncontrolled towards the harbor. Panic-stricken residents fled down King Street as citizen guards used ax handles, baseball bats and pickets torn hastily from fences to keep the crowds from leaving the quarantined sections of town. This photograph taken looking 'Ewa down King Street from Bethel Street shows the residents of Chinatown fleeing the area with their belongings. When the fire had finally burned itself out, the devastation was staggering. Thirty acres of the city, looking mauka towards Beretania Street, were nothing but charred rubble. Kaumakapili Church was left a burned-out shell. Thousands of Chinese, Japanese and Hawaiian residents of the populated district were left homeless, most of their belongings destroyed in the conflagration. While many of the victims bitterly suspected that the fire had been started deliberately by the authorities to destroy the Asian section of town, the process of rebuilding Chinatown with more fire-resistant materials soon began. [Bishop Museum]

On June 5, 1900, the Territory of Hawai'i was inaugurated. 'Iolani Palace, renamed the Executive Building, was bedecked with the colorful bunting of "Old Glory." The former kingdom's flag was given a subordinate role as a territorial emblem for the doorway. Thousands of supporters of this new American presence gathered on the Palace grounds to witness Sanford Ballard Dole, former president of the provisional government and the Republic of Hawai'i, take his oath of office as governor of the territory. U.S. troops formed a perimeter around the pro-American crowd. For the majority of Hawaiians loyal to the monarchy, this "glorious day" was one of deep bitterness. At the end of the twentieth century, their descendants would critically examine the historic events leading to annexation, and actively seek restoration of their sovereign rights. [Hawai'i State Archives]

1900—Hawai'i's population is 154,001 people: about 25 percent Hawaiian or part-Hawaiian; 40 percent Japanese; 16 percent Chinese; 12 percent Portuguese; and 5 percent Caucasian.

1900, January 20—A fire is intentionally set in Honolulu's Chinatown to rid the area of disease-infected tenement homes harboring the bubonic plague. The fire accidentally gets out of control and burns more than 38 acres, displacing more than 4,000 residents.

1900—The National Guard of the Republic of Hawai'i officially becomes part of the United States military and its members take an oath of allegiance to the United States. The Guard's nine companies include a total of about 525 men.

1900—An electric trolley (tram line) begins operation in Honolulu, replacing horse-driven and mule-driven tram cars. Operated by Pacific Heights Electric Railway Company, Ltd., the electric streetcars are open-sided, carrying thirty passengers, and initially run between Pacific Heights and upper Nu'uanu Avenue.

1900, April 30—President McKinley signs the Organic Act establishing a Territorial government in Hawai'i.

1900—*The New China Daily Press* becomes Hawai'i's first Chinese newspaper.

"The First Lady of Waikīkī," the Moana Hotel, was the first successful overnight accommodation on these famed shores. The original hotel, a five-story wooden building fronting Kalākaua Avenue, opened in 1901. By 1918 the original hotel was expanded with the addition of two wings to accommodate the growing number of tourists seeking the "magic of Waikīkī." [Baker-Van Dyke Collection]

James Drummond Dole, on the right, plows his first pineapple field in 1901 near Wahiawā, beginning immense pineapple plantations that once covered much of O'ahu's central plateau. [Hawaiian Pineapple Company]

After the death of Lili'uokalani, the Hawaiian royal legacy was kept alive by Prince Jonah Kūhiō Kalaniana'ole. Born on Kaua'i in 1871, he had been named by the Queen as an heir to the throne before the overthrow of 1893. Two years later, he participated in the royalist uprising against the Republic of Hawai'i, an action for which he was charged with treason and sentenced to a year in prison. After the annexation, he entered politics and in 1902 was elected the Territory's delegate to congress. He was instrumental in the passage of the 1919 Hawaiian Homes Commission Act, which made Native Hawaiians eligible for lands at practically no cost. Often celebrated as "Prince Cupid" due to his good looks and friendly manner, Prince Kūhiō died on January 7, 1922 at the age of fifty. His final ceremony at the Royal Mausoleum in Nu'uanu was the last state funeral given to an ali'i. [Bishop Museum]

1900, June 14—The Hawaiian Islands are officially incorporated as a Territory of the United States.

1900, November—Robert W. Wilcox, a member of the Home Rule Party and a participant in two attempted revolutions, is elected as the Territory's first delegate to Congress as a non-voting member.

1901—Leahi Hospital opens in Honolulu to treat tuberculosis victims.

1901, March 2—Commercial radio service is established allowing communication between the Islands.

1901, March 11—The Moana Hotel, known as the "First Lady of Waikīkī" opens. It is the tallest building in the Islands.

1901, December 4—James Drummond Dole forms the Hawaiian Pineapple Company with the first pineapple harvest in 1903.

1902—Prince Jonah Kūhiō Kalaniana'ole Pi'ikoi (1871-1922), running as a Republican, is elected as Hawai'i's second delegate to the United States Congress.

1902—An electric trolley (tram line) is built to connect Waikīkī and downtown Honolulu. This replaces the horse-driven tram cars. The hotel and tram line construction begins the process of popularizing Waikīkī as a resort destination, and is also the impetus for building the Ala Wai Canal to drain the wetlands.

1904—Prince Kūhiō restores the Royal Order of Kamehameha. On June 11, 1904 the celebration of Kamehameha Day is re-established for the first time since the overthrow of the Hawaiian monarchy.

1902, December 28—The Hawaiian Islands are linked to the United States by a Commercial Pacific telegraph cable beneath the Pacific Ocean between Honolulu and San Francisco. The first message is sent from Waikīkī on January 1, 1903.

1903—President Theodore Roosevelt designates the Northwestern Hawaiian Islands as a seabird refuge. Midway Atoll is placed under the control of the United States Navy. In 1909, Roosevelt designates the Hawaiian Islands as a National Wildlife Refuge.

1904, March 19—The Waikīkī Aquarium is founded at the far end of Waikīkī along the shoreline of Kapiʻolani Park. It is initially operated by the Honolulu Rapid Transit and Land Company as an end of the streetcar line attraction. It is the oldest aquarium west of the Mississippi River, and the United States' third oldest public aquarium, exhibiting more than 2,500 organisms.

1905—Kahauiki Military Reservation is established in Honolulu, becoming Hawaiʻi's first permanent United States Army post. The post is renamed Shafter Military Reservation in 1907 in honor of Civil War Medal of Honor winner, Major General William R. Shafter (1835-1906).

1905—Duke Kahanamoku surfs Waikīkī beginning the rebirth of Hawaiian surfing, which had largely disappeared after New England missionaries discouraged the sport.

1905—After 18 months of construction, the Kohala Ditch is completed on Hawaiʻi Island, tapping the streams of the Kohala mountains to irrigate the region's sugar plantations. The engineering feat includes flumes and tunnels spanning 17 miles.

1906, August 23—The Territorial Archives Building (Old Archives Building) is constructed on the grounds of ʻIolani Palace, becoming the first U.S. building built for the sole purpose of preserving public archive materials. The building is designed by architect Oliver Green Traphagen in the Renaissance Revival style.

1906, December 20—The first fifteen Filipino farm workers, known as *sakada,* arrive on the *Doric* to work on the sugar plantations. It is the start of waves of immigration from the Philippines that reach 120,000 workers by 1931 as Filipinos replace Japanese as the majority of sugar field workers.

1907—Honolulu's Kapālama Basin is dredged to enlarge Honolulu Harbor with the landfill used to create Sand Island.

1907, May 21—Authors Jack London and his wife Charmian arrive on the ketch *Snark* for a four-month tour of the Islands. Both write about Hawaiʻi, including Jack's article "A Royal Sport: Surfing at Waikiki." The Londons return for another visit in 1915.

1907—The Outrigger Canoe Club is established in Waikīkī.

1907—Rice is the second largest crop in the Islands, with more than 41 million pounds produced on about 9,400 acres.

The growth of Maui's sugar industry led to the development of Wailuku which became the island's commercial center. A new courthouse opened in 1907, making Wailuku the island's governmental headquarters as well. [Bishop Museum]

1907—The College of Agriculture and Mechanic Arts (renamed The College of Hawai'i in 1911) is established in downtown Honolulu through a resolution introduced in the legislature by Senator William Joseph Coelho. The College opens on September 15, 1908, and in 1920 is renamed the University of Hawai'i.

1908—The Matson Navigation Company purchases the luxurious 51-passenger steamship *Lurline* to carry tourists to the Hawaiian Islands. The 146-passenger *Wilhelmina* joins the fleet in 1910. Captain Matson passes away in 1917 at the age of 67.

1908, November—Joseph James Fern, a stevedore boss working for the Inter-Island Steam Navigation Company, becomes the first mayor of the newly established City and County of Honolulu. Elected as a Democrat, he is re-elected in 1910, 1912, 1917, and 1919.

1909—Makapu'u Lighthouse is constructed at Makapu'u Point. The lighthouse on Moloka'i's Kalaupapa Peninsula installs a Fresnel lens that is the brightest in the Pacific, visible 21 miles out to sea.

1909—Schofield Barracks Military Reservation is established on 14,000 acres in Wahiawā, O'ahu, eventually becoming the biggest permanent United States Army post. The Barracks are named for President Andrew Johnson's Secretary of War, Lieutenant General John M. Schofield.

1909—The Yokohama Specie Bank Building is constructed at the corner of Merchant Street and Nu'uanu Avenue, becoming Hawai'i's first major Japanese bank. It has separate entrances for Chinese, Japanese, and Caucasian customers. The architect of the Renaissance-style building is Harry Livingston Kerr who designed more than 900 Honolulu buildings and considered the Yokohama Specie Bank the finest building in Honolulu. After the 1941 Pearl Harbor attack, the U.S. Alien Custodian Agency confiscates the building and uses its first floor as a storehouse for seized goods.

In 1903, the area at the juncture of McCully and Kalākaua was banana, rice, and taro patches. The mule-drawn cars of the Hawaiian Tramways Company were replaced by the electric trolleys of the Honolulu Rapid Transit Company, which gave both visitors and residents easier access to Waikīkī's popular bathing beaches. [Baker-Van Dyke Collection]

Established in 1909, the 14,400 acres of Schofield Barracks, located in the center of the island of O'ahu, constituted the largest U.S. military base. It was home to the Hawaiian Division of the U.S. Army, which during the 1930s had been reinforced to a strength of over twenty thousand soldiers. In addition to Schofield Barracks, the Hawaiian Division included airbases at Wahiawā's Wheeler Field and Luke Field on Ford Island at Pearl Harbor, and a coastal and harbor defense system at Fort DeRussy, Fort Ruger, and Fort Armstrong. U.S. troops were stationed at the entrance to Pearl Harbor at Fort Kamehameha, and the entire operations were headquartered at Fort Shafter. With the U.S. Army's Hawaiian Division under General Walter C. Short and the Pacific Fleet of the United States Navy at Pearl Harbor under Admiral Husband E. Kimmel, the military believed, in 1941, that America's might in the Pacific was invincible. [National Archives]

The Organic Act

On April 30, 1900, President McKinley signed the Organic Act establishing a Territorial government in Hawai'i and on June 14, 1900 the Hawaiian Islands were officially incorporated as a Territory of the United States. The Territory's first governor was Sanford Ballard Dole (1844-1926), one of the original revolutionaries of the 1893 overthrow of the monarchy. Dole served as president of the Provisional Government from 1893 to 1894, as President of the Republic of Hawai'i from 1895 to 1898, and as governor of the Territory of Hawai'i until 1903. In November of 1900, Robert W. Wilcox, a member of the Home Rule Party and previously a participant in two attempted revolutions, was elected as the Territory's first delegate to Congress (as a non-voting member).

As a Territory, Hawaiian residents became U.S. citizens, although not allowed to vote in presidential elections. Hawai'i was allowed to send a non-voting representative to Congress. While Hawaiian voters elected a Territorial House of Representatives and Senate, the U.S. Congress could veto any bill passed by the Hawai'i Legislature.

Above, upper: The H. Hackfield Co. building constructed in 1899. The company was founded in 1850. In 1978, this was the location of Irwin Park and Nimitz Highway (right) 1902. [Baker-Van Dyke Collection]

Lower: One of the favorite pastimes of visitors to Honolulu in the 1880s was taking a leisurely carriage to the summit of Pūowaina, or the "Hill of Sacrifice." From the slopes of this ancient volcanic crater known also as "Punchbowl," there were stunning views of the town, the 'Ewa plains and the districts of Makiki, Kamō'ili'ili, Waikīkī and Diamond Head. On the slopes of the crater was a battery of small cannon used to salute arriving and departing ships, to honor special events and to mourn the passing of kings. [Gonsalves/Hawai'i State Archives]

Above, upper: After annexation, the U.S. military moved swiftly to transform the Islands into a Western defense perimeter for the expanding U.S. presence in Asia. Parades, reviews, and marching cavalry were frequent in downtown Honolulu. [Hawai'i State Archives]

Lower: Sunday baseball at 'A'ala Park, circa 1908. The bandstand was built in 1906. Nu'uanu River's embankments were completed in 1900. [Hawai'i State Archives]

J.C. "Bud" Mars, after making the first airplane flight in Hawai'i at the polo field on the Damon Estate at Moanalua December 31, 1910. [Baker-Van Dyke Collection]

1910—Hawai'i's population is 191,874, including 26,041 Hawaiians and 12,056 part-Hawaiians.

1910, October—Malcolm and Elbert Tuttle build and fly a glider becoming "Honolulu's First Bird-Men."

1910, December 31—About seven weeks after the Wright brothers' famous first flight at Kitty Hawk, North Carolina, Hawai'i's first airplane flight takes place at O'ahu's Moanalua Polo Field when J. C. "Bud" Mars flies a Curtiss P18 biplane, the *Honolulu Skylark*, to an altitude of 500 feet. On a subsequent flight, Mars reaches 1,500 feet.

1911, June 10—Hawai'i's first airplane crash occurs when Clarence H. Walker hits a tree during landing.

1911, October—A case of yellow fever appears in Honolulu. The city mobilizes an army of military and civilian personnel to seek out and destroy mosquito breeding places.

1911—Duke Kahanamoku and his friends organize Hui Nalu (Club of the Waves), a swimming, paddling, and surfing club.

1911—Duke sets three world records in freestyle swimming at Honolulu Harbor.

Hawai'i's first international celebrity was Duke Kahanamoku, world-champion swimmer, surfer, Olympic gold medalist and beloved denizen of Waikīkī. His quiet dignity, radiating aloha and pride of heritage symbolized the Hawaiian virtues, which would sustain his people through a century of dispossession. Duke Kahanamoku's perfect form was photographed during a practice session in preparation for the 1912 Olympics. [Hawai'i State Archives]

1912, July 6—Duke Kahanamoku wins an Olympic gold medal and a silver medal in swimming in Stockholm, Sweden, setting a world record in the 100-meter freestyle event.

1913—*Shark God* and *Hawaiian Love* become the first Hollywood movies shot on location in the Islands.

1913—The *Honolulu Star-Bulletin* is formed when the *Evening Bulletin* merges with the *Hawaiian Star*.

1914—The Honolulu Zoo opens in Kapiʻolani Park.

1914, August—The first German merchant vessel—the steamer ship *Setos*—arrives in Honolulu Harbor.

1914—The *Matsonia* begins service between Honolulu and San Francisco

1915—The Honolulu Rapid Transit & Land Company begins offering bus service.

1915, March 25—The first submarine disaster in American naval history occurs when the Navy submarine *Skate (F-4)*, one of four based in the Islands, explodes and sinks 306 feet to the bottom of Honolulu Harbor, killing its 21-man crew.

1915, August 5—Talking pictures are shown for the first time at the Bijou in Honolulu.

1916—The 25-mile-long Waiāhole Ditch is completed, diverting up to 27 million gallons of water daily from Windward Oʻahu to the sugarcane and pineapple fields of Leeward and Central Oʻahu.

1917, April 16—The United States declares war on Germany entering

Above: This 1914 meeting of Sanford B. Dole, Lucius B. Pinkham (governor of the Territory of Hawai'i), and Lili'uokalani was arranged by Henry Berger (standing), leader of the Royal Hawaiian Band. Berger brought everyone together in the interests of patriotic solidarity and to elicit public support of American aid to the Allied cause in World War I. Dole was instrumental in the forceful overthrow, which brought an end to the Hawaiian monarchy and later subjected the queen to the humiliation of house arrest in an apartment in her own 'Iolani Palace. Each felt that he or she was perfectly justified in his or her actions. In the twenty years that had passed before this gathering was recorded, they resumed their original friendship. [Hawai'i State Archives]

Below: In 1911, Lili'uokalani agreed to attend the dedication of Pearl Harbor to support the U.S. military. She sat in the grandstand amidst American military and civilian authorities of the Territory of Hawai'i. Seated next to her in the top hat is Governor Lucius Pinkham. A bevy of children watch the proceedings from below the stands. [Baker-Van Dyke Collection]

The dining room of the Halekūlani Hotel 1930 [Baker-Van Dyke Collection]

World War I which began in 1914. At least 179 men and women of the Hawaiian Islands are killed as soldiers in World War I.

1917, November 11— Liliʻuokalani, the last monarch of the Hawaiian Kingdom, passes away from a stroke at the age of 79. A state funeral is held for her on November 18.

1917—The Halekūlani ("house befitting heaven" or "house befitting royalty") Hotel opens in Honolulu. Originally consisting of a beachfront house and five bungalows, it grows over the years and in 1981 is rebuilt as a modern, world-class hotel.

1917—The island of Lānaʻi is sold to the Baldwin family for use as a cattle ranch.

1917—The United States Government purchases Ford Island in the middle of Pearl Harbor for joint use by the Army and Navy.

1918—Honpa Hongwanji Mission is built in Honolulu to commemorate the Shin sect of Buddhism's 700th anniversary. Dr. Syngman Rhee, who was in exile in Hawai'i but later became South Korea's first president, founds the Korean Christian Church on Liliha Street in Honolulu. The Liliha Street church is completed in 1938, with its front replicating the Kwang Wha Mun gate in Seoul, Korea.

1918, March 15—Major Harold M. Clark of the Fort Kamehameha Aero Squadron completes Hawaiʻi's first interisland flight, from Honolulu to Molokaʻi and back.

Three years after Japan annexed Korea in 1910, Dr. Syngman Rhee came to Hawaiʻi to serve as an educational minister. Instrumental in the Don Ji Hoi, a nationalist political organization for the Korean Independence Movement, Rhee lived on Hawaiʻi Island where he initiated a charcoal enterprise in Mountain View to help finance Korea's cause. By 1919, about three thousand Koreans had raised $34,000, and Rhee left Hawaiʻi the following year. He eventually became the Republic of Korea's first president. [Hawaiʻi State Archives]

A Matson poster portrays the lures of the Islands. [Baker-Van Dyke Collection]

1918, June 1—Most members of the army stationed in Hawaiʻi are dispatched to France, and the Hawaiʻi National Guard is mobilized to protect the Islands.

1918, November 19—Corporal Mark Grace of the Sixth Aero Squadron becomes Hawaiʻi's first aviation fatality when his plane goes into a tailspin and crashes.

1919, June 11—A historical procession marks the 100th anniversary of the death of Kamehameha I.

1919—The building of the Ala Wai Canal begins. Completed during the next nine years to drain the marshlands of Waikīkī, the prominent waterway spans 25 blocks, separating Waikīkī from Honolulu and creating some of Hawaiʻi's most valuable real estate.

1919, August 21—Josephus Daniels, U.S. Secretary of the Navy, formally dedicates the Pearl Harbor dry-dock.

1919—A massive Lahaina fire destroys two blocks of commercial structures.

1919, November 27—Costing $500,000, the first Mormon temple built outside of the continental United States is dedicated in Lāʻie at the base of the Koʻolau Mountains.

The U.S. annexation of the Hawaiian Islands in 1898 had been justified by its supporters as a necessary strategy for the protection of American interests in the Pacific. By establishing a naval base at Pearl Harbor, the United States would have a powerful dominion over the future of the Pacific region. The construction of a dry dock at Pearl Harbor was essential to making Hawaiʻi the center of operations for the U.S. Pacific Fleet. On August 21, 1919, the dry dock was finally opened with an elaborate ceremony. [National Archives]

Floral parade, 'Iolani Palace grounds, 1913 [Baker-Van Dyke Collection]

Above, left: The Alexander Young Hotel building shortly after its construction in 1902 or 1903. Bishop Street had not yet been cut through. [Baker-Van Dyke Collection]

Above, right: Paper boys selling the *Pacific Commercial Advertiser* on Alakea Street near Hotel Street, 1916. [Baker-Van Dyke Collection]

Left: With the rapid growth of Honolulu, the harbor area was filled in to expand for much-needed commercial services such as those provided by the Honolulu Iron Works. Since the 1850s, the Honolulu Iron Works had provided the building materials essential for the successful construction of sugar mills, commercial structures, and residential housing. Eventually the residential districts near the harbor, including Iwilei and Kaka'ako, would also become industrial areas with acres of warehouses, fuel tanks and supply yards. [Bishop Museum]

Completed in 1927, the Waikīkī Natatorium War Memorial was built to remember the men and women who served during World War I. It was built in the Hawaiian Beaux-Arts architectural style. Now in disrepair, its future use is being debated. [Hawai'i State Archives]

1920—Hawai'i's population is 255,881 people, with 42.7 percent of the population of Japanese descent.

1920—Duke Kahanamoku wins two Olympic gold medals in Antwerp, Belgium, breaking his own 100-meter freestyle world record and helping to set a world record in the freestyle relay.

1920, February—The only train robbery in Hawai'i occurs.

1920—The United States military begins using the island of Kaho'olawe as a bombing range for ships and aircraft.

1921—Kīlauea National Park is established on Hawai'i Island.

1921, July 9—The Hawaiian Homestead Commission Act, initiated by Prince Jonah Kūhiō in 1919, is enacted by the U.S. Congress with the goal of providing farming and homesteading land (203,000 acres of public land) to persons with at least 50 percent native Hawaiian ancestry. In 1959, the Act is adopted into the State of Hawai'i Constitution. In 1996, the Hawai'i Supreme Court rules that homesteaders may rent their land only to native Hawaiians. As of 2011 there were 9,875 homestead leases, 85 percent of which were residential, 11 percent agricultural and 4 percent pastoral. More than 26,000 persons are on the waiting list.

1922, January 7—Prince Jonah Kūhiō Kalaniana'ole, the last prince of the monarchy and a Hawai'i delegate to the U.S. Congress, dies.

1922—A new Hawai'i Theatre is built at 1130 Bethel Street at a cost of $500,000. The Theatre stages live performances and also shows the new entertainment medium of movies. Designed by architects Emory & Webb in the Classical Revival/Art Deco style, it is then one of the most modern American theaters. Today, a renovated Hawai'i Theatre is a cultural and performing arts center.

1922—James Drummond Dole purchases 98 percent of the island of Lāna'i for $1,100,000, and soon produces almost one-third of the world's pineapple crop. He is known as the "Pineapple King" and the pineapple industry dominates Lāna'i for the next 65 years, producing as many as 250 million pineapples annually.

1923—The Territorial Legislature designates an emblem for each Hawaiian Island.

1924, September 9—Sixteen Kaua'i Filipino sugarcane plantation workers and four Hanapēpē police officers die when an eight-month strike is brutally suppressed. The event, which becomes known as the Hanapēpē Massacre, began when police attempted to rescue two workers held by the strikers to be forced to join the walkout.

1924—The Federal Immigration Act prohibits immigration from Japan as Japanese immigrants total about 200,000 since they began arriving in 1885.

1924—At the Paris Olympics, Duke Kahanamoku (at age 34) takes the silver medal in the 100-meter freestyle losing to Johnny Weissmuller who later becomes famous as the actor who plays Tarzan.

1925, June 14—Duke uses his surfboard to single-handedly save

Dole Pineapple Co., Honolulu, 1928.

eight lives from a capsized boat in Corona del Mar, California—one of many ocean rescues with which he is credited.

1925, August 31—Commander John Rodgers and his four-man crew fly a two-engine PN-9 Navy seaplane from near San Francisco toward the Hawaiian Islands attempting the first flight between Hawai'i and the mainland. The plane runs out of gas 300 miles from Maui, and the crew uses improvised sails and tow assistance to reach Kaua'i's Ahukini Harbor on September 10, 1925.

1926—Honolulu Stadium opens at the corner of King and Isenberg Streets. For the next 50 years is used for polo games, rodeos, high school football games, stock car racing, hula festivals, and spiritual crusades. Sports stars performing in the stadium include Jesse Owens, Babe Ruth, and Lou Gehrig, while musical performers include Irving Berlin and Elvis Presley. The structure eventually falls into disrepair and is dubbed the "Termite Palace" before being demolished in 1976 when Aloha Stadium opens.

1926, June 9—Sanford B. Dole, President of the Republic of Hawai'i and first governor of the Territory of Hawai'i, dies.

1926, September 25—Aloha Tower opens on the waterfront at Honolulu Harbor becoming Hawai'i's first skyscraper and the tallest building in the Islands topped with a 40-foot flagstaff and seven-ton clock.

1927—The War Memorial Natatorium is built at the eastern end of Waikīkī as a memorial to Hawaiian residents that died in World War I. It includes a 20-foot high Memorial Archway and a 100-meter-long, tide-fed, saltwater pool. Scheduled restoration work costing $6 million was cancelled by Honolulu mayor Mufi Hannemann on January 3, 2005, his first day in office. Current plans are to convert the site to a beach, keeping the arch intact.

1927, February 1—The Royal Hawaiian Hotel opens in Waikīkī with the Royal Hawaiian Band playing for 1,200 guests. The hotel, nicknamed the "Pink Palace of the Pacific," costs $4 million and features elegant chandeliers, high ceilings, pink stucco walls and pink turrets.

1927, March 21—John Rodgers Airport, Hawai'i's first official civilian airfield, is dedicated in Honolulu. It is later renamed Honolulu International Airport.

1927, June 28, 29—Albert Hegenberger and Lester Maitland, two lieutenants in the United

The Honolulu Advertiser
Hawaii's Territorial Newspaper

HONOLULU, TERRITORY OF HAWAII, WEDNESDAY MORNING, SEPTEMBER 10, 1924 — PRICE FIVE CENTS

17 DEAD, MANY INJURED AS POLICE, STRIKERS CLASH

dmiral Announces Plans He Is To Make For Fleet's Coming

CHANG MOVES BIG ARMY TO SHANHAIKWAN

Marshal Tuan Denounces Peking Government Urging People To Oust Tsao Kun

FIRE IN PEKING?

Shanghai Hit by strong Wind, Rain Storm: Report Says Lu Is Nearing City

Sonoma Gets S.O.S. From Steamer Piled on Reef

Kauai Scene Of Wholesale Slaying When Filipinos At Hanapepe Resent Arrests

MACHINE GUN SQUADS HERE GO TO KAUAI

National Guardsmen Will be sent to Trouble Zone Today

Four Police Among Those Killed; Sheriff Crowell Wounded; Dead Are Left on Roadside As Injured Rushed To Hospital; Arrest Hundreds

LIHUE, Kauai, Sept. 9 (10:00 p.m.).—The death list in today's rioting reached 17 tonight when five more Filipino participants died at the Makaweli hospital. Police succeeded in rounding up a big majority of the rioters and have placed all of them under arrest here. Two truck loads of the rioters were brought to the county jail from Hanapepe this afternoon while all leaders are being held pending an investigation.

Makaweli hospital tonight resembled scenes appropriate to a field hospital at a battle front with the wounded filling all beds while all doctors on the island have been called to assist in the first aid work. All types of transportation was pressed into service to rush the wounded here and only those seriously wounded were moved ...

PUBLIC BATHS MANAGEMENT IS UNDER FIRE

OAHU WATER PROVES BEST IN THE WORLD

FREITAS GETS THREE YEARS FOR ASSAULT

As immigrant communities in the Islands matured, they began to demand higher wages, better working conditions, and collective bargaining. The earliest strikes were essentially wildcat shutdowns initiated by disgruntled workers on individual plantations. However, in 1909, the Japanese labor force organized an island-wide strike on O'ahu that shocked plantation owners and cost the sugar industry a million dollars. The great strike of 1920 was another unsuccessful attempt by Japanese workers to improve wages, although some demands were met. In 1924, violence erupted on Kaua'i during a Filipino strike led by labor activist Pablo Manlapit. Yet in these early years ethnic jealousies between unions were difficult to overcome; the "divide and rule" strategy of plantation owners invariably succeeded in averting strikes. [Hawai'i State Archives]

States Army, complete the first non-stop flight to the Hawaiian Islands (Wheeler Field at Schofield Barracks, Oʻahu) from the U.S. mainland (Oakland, California) in a Fokker C-2-3 Wright 220 tri-motor plane *Bird of Paradise*. The flight takes 25 hours and 50 minutes.

1927—The Matson Navigation Company purchases the *Malolo*, a lavish passenger steamship and the fastest ship in the Pacific at the time, to bring visitors to Hawaiʻi from the West Coast. The success of the route leads to the construction of three new, larger ships between 1930 and 1932: the *Mariposa*, the *Monterey*, and the *Lurline*.

1928—Hilo Airport is dedicated.

1928, September 18—Nineteen-year-old Myles Yutaka Fukunaga abducts and kills the son of Caucasian businessman Frederick Jamieson, vice president of the Hawaiian Trust Company. Racial tensions rise as the Japanese community is targeted during a search for the boy whose body is found on the following day. Fukunaga is later caught using the ransom money, and National Guardsmen with bayonets are needed to control a crowd of 20,000 people gathered around the police station as he is brought in. Fukunaga, who stated that he sought revenge against Hawaiian Trust for demanding rent from his parents, is hanged on November 19, 1929.

1928, October 8—Interisland airmail service is established.

Early Waikīkī was a charming place of rolling surf, cool breezes, lush taro farms, and abundant fish ponds. Both Hawaiian royalty and the business elite retreated to its relaxing shores. When tourism began in the twentieth century, Waikīkī was the natural site for new hotels, such as the Moana, the Seaside, and the Royal Hawaiian. The 1920s construction of the Ala Wai Canal allowed Waikīkī's wetlands to be drained, paving the way for further development. Already, the bungalow-style houses that would characterize Waikīkī's neighborhoods had begun to proliferate on the mountain side of the street. These quaint cottages would eventually disappear amid the high-rise construction frenzy of the sixties and seventies. Circa 1927-1930. [Baker-Van Dyke Collection]

1929—Built in 1927, Honolulu Hale opened in 1929, to serve as Honolulu's City Hall with offices for the mayor and city council. Located on South King Street, the building was designed by architects Charles William Dickey and Hart Wood, and modeled after Florence, Italy's 13th century Bargello Palace featuring pillars and arches, decorative balconies, ceiling frescoes, and a tiled roof.

1929—The Dillingham Transportation Building is constructed at 735 Bishop Street. The architect is Lincoln Rogers, and the building is constructed in the Italian Renaissance/Mediterranean Revival style. A plaque on the building commemorates Benjamin Franklin Dillingham, founder of the Oʻahu Railway & Land Company.

1929, May 1—Lei Day becomes an official holiday of the Territory of Hawaiʻi. In 1934, the city of Honolulu begins sponsoring an annual Lei Day celebration.

1929, November 9—The first interisland airline begins regular sightseeing trips between the Hawaiian Islands. Two days later, Silver Star Navy pilot Stanley C. Kennedy starts Inter-Islands Airways Ltd. (later renamed Hawaiian Airlines), and begins Hawaiʻi's first scheduled air service using two Sikorsky S-38-C 7-passenger amphibians and a Bellanca monoplane. The planes initially make three weekly round trips between Honolulu and Hilo, with stops on Maui.

The fertile sugar fields of the districts of Hāmākua and 'Ōla'a rapidly expanded as capital, labor and technology poured into the windward coast of the island of Hawai'i. The commercial center of sugar industry growth was Hilo town, as new small ethnic businesses, automobiles, construction and congestion transformed the main thoroughfare, Kamehameha Avenue. 1926. [Baker-Van Dyke Collection]

Bishop Street became Hawai'i's financial center as most of the companies and financial institutions located along its wide, palm tree-lined sidewalks. The Dillingham Transportation Building is still located at Queen and Bishop Streets. The Dillingham companies controlled O'ahu's railroad transportation. [Hawai'i State Archives]

WITNESS TO HISTORY

DOWNTOWN HONOLULU, W. SOMERSET MAUGHAM 1921

Along the streets crowd an unimaginable assortment of people. The Americans, ignoring the climate, wear black bowlers. The kanakas, pale brown, with crisp hair, have nothing on but a shirt and a pair of trousers; but the half-breeds are very smart with flaring ties and patent-leather boots. The Japanese, with their obsequious smile, are neat and trim in white duck, while their women walk a step or two behind them, in native dress with a baby on their backs. The Japanese children in bright colored frocks, their little heads shaven, look like quaint dolls. Then there are the Chinese. The men, fat and prosperous, wear their American clothes oddly, but the women are enchanting with their tightly-dressed black hair, so neat that you feel it can never be disarranged, and they are very clean in their tunics and trousers, white, or powder blue, or black. Lastly there are the Filipinos, the men in huge straw hats, the women in bright yellow muslin with great puffed sleeves.

W. Somerset Maugham, 1921
Trembling of a Leaf

During a 1920 Outrigger Canoe Club regatta, spectators throng the finish line on the beach in front of the canoe club. In the background is the Moana Hotel. Years later the Outrigger Canoe Club would move to the Diamond Head end of Waikīkī Beach as its old grounds became the site of the Outrigger Hotel. Hawaiian water sports such as surfing and canoeing had greatly declined by the end of the nineteenth century due to a variety of factors, including the notion that idle sport in the surf had little benefit to the social or spiritual welfare of the surfer. Alexander Hume Ford, a South Carolinian journalist who had moved to Honolulu, was dismayed at the neglect of the ancient sport of riding waves. Through his efforts, the Hawaiian Outrigger Canoe Club was established in 1908 on the beach at Waikīkī near the site where the ʻĀpuakehau Stream emptied into the sea. The club revived the arts of surfing and canoeing, initiating canoe regattas, which became a staple feature of Waikīkī Beach activities. [Baker-Van Dyke Collection]

The Honolulu waterfront in 1929 was dominated by the four-year-old Aloha Tower, which rose ten stories over the esplanade for arriving and departing passenger ships. The cement and steel structure contained four bronze clocks, each costing $190,000, weighing seven tons and guaranteed to be accurate within thirty seconds per month. A symbol of hospitality, the tower also served as a shoreline beacon with its 5,550-candlepower light visible twenty miles at sea. In the waning days of 1941, few could imagine that this symbol of Hawai'i's aloha would soon be painted in drab camouflage color. [Hawai'i State Archives]

By the start of the twentieth century, Hawai'i's multiethnic mixture was applauded by social scientists as a "living laboratory of human relations." Extensive immigration from Asia, the Pacific Islands, Europe, and the Americas to support the sugar plantation economy, and the subsequently high interracial marriage rates, had created a fascinating cultural mosaic popularized as the "Melting Pot." Photographs of young Islanders, such as this 1920 portrait of numbered and ethnically identified women, were frequently published as evidence that the Hawaiian Islands were truly the "Crossroads of the Pacific." [Hawai'i State Archives]

"Hawaii's" ~~THE~~ MELTING POT"

~~KAWAIAHAO SEMINARY~~

HONOLULU, T. H.

1—Hawaiian.
2—Ehu Hawaiian.
3—Japanese.
4—Chinese.
5—Korean.
6—Russian.
7—Filipino.
8—Portuguese.
9—Polish Russian.
10—Hawaiian-German.
11—Hawaiian-Chinese.
12—Hawaiian-Russian.
13—Hawaiian-American.
14—Hawaiian-French.
15—Hawaiian-Portuguese.
16—Hawaiian-Filipino-Chinese.
17—Hawaiian-Indian-American.
18—Hawaiian-Japanese-Portuguese.
19—Hawaiian-Portuguese-American.
20—Hawaiian-Spanish-American.
21—Hawaiian-German-Irish.
22—Hawaiian-~~Chinese~~-German. Spanish
23—Hawaiian-Chinese-American.
24—Hawaiian-Portuguese-Irish.
25—Hawaiian-Japanese-Indian.
26—Hawaiian-Portuguese-Chinese-English.
27—Hawaiian-Chinese-German-Norwegian-Irish.
28—South Sea (Nauru)-Norwegian.
29—African-French-Irish.
30—Spanish-Porto Rican.
31—Guam-Mexican-French.
32—Samoan-Tahitian.

1930—Hawai'i's population reaches 368,336.

1930—Mary Foster passes away, bequeathing six acres at Nu'uanu Avenue and Vineyard Boulevard, Honolulu for a city park and botanical garden, now called Foster Botanical Garden. The Garden was initially planted by Prussian doctor William Hillebrand (1821-1886), a royal physician at Queen's Hospital. Mary Foster, who was part Hawaiian, was the daughter of Rebecca Prever and James Robinson, and the wife of Thomas Foster, an organizer of the Inter-Island Steam Navigation Company.

1930—The first radio broadcast to California from Hawai'i takes place when KGMB transmits a ten-minute Christmas program.

1931, September 12—Thalia Massie, the wife of a U.S. Navy lieutenant, is allegedly beaten and sexually assaulted after a party at Honolulu's Ala Wai Inn. Five accused local men are later set free due to lack of evidence and a deadlocked jury. Fueling racial tensions among Island residents as well as between the military and local residents, the event garners national attention. Massie's husband and friends kill one of the accused men and are indicted for second degree murder, but are convicted only of manslaughter and their sentences commuted. These events will contribute to racial antagonism in the Islands for years to come.

Thalia and Lt. Thomas Massie became the center of the sensational Massie murder trial, one of the Associated Press's top ten stories of 1932. The famed Chicago defense attorney Clarence Darrow argued his last and most ignominious case in Honolulu. [Hawai'i State Archives]

Buster Crabbe, swimming champion and star of "Tarzan" and "Flash Gordon" films, leaves for college with his brother, 1927. [Baker-Van Dyke Collection]

1931, September 13—The Ala Wai Golf Course opens. Initially the course consists of just nine holes, but another nine holes are added in 1937.

1932—Swimmer Clarence "Buster" Crabbe competes at the Los Angeles Olympics, winning a gold medal in the 400-meter freestyle. Crabbe was Hawai'i's only medalist in the 1928 Amsterdam Olympics, winning a bronze in the 1,500-meter freestyle.

1933—The last electric trolley runs in Honolulu as buses become the predominant mode of public transit.

1933—The amount of land in the Islands for sugar production peaks, totaling more than 250,000 acres. About 96 percent of the sugar crop is controlled by the "Big Five" companies: Theo H. Davies; American Factors (Amfac); C. Brewer & Co.; Alexander & Baldwin; and Castle & Cooke.

1934—The Jones-Costigan Act allows the U.S. Secretary of Agriculture to set quotas for agricultural production throughout the U.S. and its territories. Hawai'i sugar planters protest that the quotas violate their right to operate their businesses as they see fit and undermine

Duke Kahanamoku shares a pineapple with Amelia Earhart, Waikīkī, 1935. [Baker-Van Dyke Collection]

All the nostalgic appeal of the "Hawaii Calls" radio show is captured in this photo from the 1930s. Hilo Hattie is second from the left. [Hawai'i State Archives]

competitiveness and prices for their product. These protests are summarily dismissed by the U.S. Congress who quickly determine that "the Congress has plenary power to legislate for and against the territory if it sees fit to do so." Many in the Islands consider this an arrogant and paternalistic statement, causing further resentment among those living in the territory.

1934, February 3— Hawai'i's first recorded bank robbery occurs.

1934, July 26—Franklin Delano Roosevelt becomes the first U.S. president to visit the Hawaiian Islands arriving in Honolulu aboard the cruiser *Houston*.

1935—The first union newspaper, *Voice of Labor*, is published.

1935, January 11, 12—Amelia Earhart completes the first solo flight from Hawai'i (Wheeler Field, O'ahu) to the mainland of the United States (Oakland, California) in a single-engine Lockheed Vega monoplane.

1935, July 3—The *Hawaii Calls* radio series begins. Webley Edwards produces and directs the show from beachside at Waikīkī's Royal Hawaiian Hotel and later the Moana Hotel. *Hawaii Calls* features top Hawaiian music, including live performances by top Hawaiian artists. The show is broadcast on hundreds of radio stations all around the world and runs until 1975, making it the longest running radio program ever.

1935, July 29—Shirley Temple arrives in Honolulu aboard the *Lurline* and

SQUADS HERE GO TO KAUAI

PUBLIC BATHS MANAGEMENT IS UNDER FIRE

DESTITUTE BY KAUAI MASSACRE BURY DEAD: EYE WITNESS TELLS OF BATTLE

Single Funeral Held For 15 Filipinos: Buried In Trench: Guard Against Reoccurrence

Officer Who Took Part In Rioting Gives Vivid Tale Of Horror Clash

For A United Labor Front

The Voice of Labor

HAWAII'S ONLY WORKING-CLASS NEWSPAPER

Don't Forget To Register!

HONOLULU, T. H., THURSDAY, AUGUST 4, 1938 — PRICE FIVE CENTS

"THEY EVEN SHOT MEN IN THE BACK"

Nationwide Protests Deluge Poindexter and Washington

Editorial

"Ripped Their Bodies With Bayonets; Shot Men Picking Up Their Wounded Comrades"

The headline of the August 4, 1938, *Voice of Labor* protests the police brutality of the August 1 clash between police and strikers in Hilo remembered as the Hilo Massacre. Seventy police officers attacked two hundred unarmed demonstrators, fifty of whom were injured, some severely. [Hawai'i State Archives]

MOMENT IN HISTORY

THE INFAMOUS MASSIE CASE
SEPTEMBER 13, 1931

In the early hours of September 13, 1931, two separate incidents were logged by the Honolulu Police Department. A local couple reported being in a near-accident and altercation with a group of local men. One hour later, Thalia Massie, wife of U.S. Navy officer Lt. Thomas Massie, reported being abducted off of a Waikīkī street by a group of local men, beaten, and raped. Police linked both incidents and arrested the owner of the automobile involved in the accident, as well as his four companions. Considering the race of the victim, her husband's connection to the military, and the sensationalism of the alleged crime, the five defendants were automatically considered guilty by the non-local community. When a mixed-race jury failed to reach a verdict, a mistrial was declared and racial tensions in the city reached a fever pitch.

In January 1932, Joseph Kahahawai awaited retrial on the rape charges. Unexpectedly, he was kidnapped by Lt. Massie, his mother-in-law Grace Fortesque, and two others, taken to a bungalow in Mānoa, tortured for a confession, and then murdered. Massie and the others were arrested later trying to dispose of the body in their "Blowhole" on O'ahu's southern coast. The subsequent trial of the Massie group was a courtroom drama that attracted national attention, with famed lawyer Clarence Darrow representing the defendants. All four were found guilty of manslaughter and sentenced to ten years in prison. Under pressure from Washington, D.C. and the U.S. military, Governor Judd of Hawai'i commuted the sentences to one hour, served with police escort in his offices at 'Iolani Palace. Native Hawaiians and other nonwhite Islanders saw the Massie case as representing a dual system of justice based on an institutional racism which mocked the older, prevailing spirit of aloha. The facade of ethnic harmony had been stripped away.

Famed Chicago defense attorney, Clarence Darrow, at the courthouse with his co-defendants Lt. Massie and Grace Fortesque, the mother of Thalia Massie, argued his last and most ignominious case in Honolulu. [*Honolulu Star-Bulletin*]

The Honolulu Advertiser EXTRA

Hawaii's Territorial Newspaper

HONOLULU, TERRITORY OF HAWAII, U.S.A., WEDNESDAY MORNING, APRIL 17, 1935. PRICE FIVE CENTS

CLIPPER LANDS AT 8:00

Thousands See Flight's Start At Golden Gate

Heavily-Laden Ship In Graceful Takeoff from Bay Waters; Routine Job to Crew

An Early Morning Caller

Reaches Honolulu At 7:04; Cruises Over Island Until Crowds Arrive At Air Base

Giant Plane Sets New Record for Westbound Hop; Could Easily Have Made Better Time But Delayed Landing for Spectators

Advertiser Signs Wood

Correspondent On North Haven to Write for You

Here's Log Of Clipper Since Hop From Coast

Receptions Ready Today

Naval And Civilian Officials To Greet Men

performs "On the Good Ship Lollipop."

1936, February 19—Hawai'i's first traffic signal is installed at the intersection of Nu'uanu Avenue and Beretania Street.

1936, October 21, 22—Pan American World Airways flies a Martin M-130 flying boat, the *Hawaii Clipper*, from San Francisco to Honolulu.

1938, August 1—The Hilo Longshoremen's Association goes on strike against the Inter-Island Steamship Navigation Company. Police attack the striking workers at Hilo wharf with bayonets, guns, tear gas and hoses, injuring 51 people. The event comes to be known as "Bloody Monday," and leads to strikes and violence spanning a two-year period and shutting down the docks of the Inter-Island Steamship Company.

Above, left: The 72nd Bombardment Squadron flying near Pearl Harbor on February 26, 1932. On December 7, 1941, the base at Pearl Harbor was on a minimum state of alert. The total number of combat aircraft in the Islands on December 6, however, was just 221, with only 119 in commission, the others were being overhauled to send to the Philippines. [U.S. Army Museum of Hawai'i]

Above, right: When Japanese dignitaries visited Wheeler Air Force Field in the 1930s, the clouds of war were already gathering in Manchuria. [Baker-Van Dyke Collection]

Left, upper: Lei sellers vended their colorful creations on Honolulu's downtown street. Business was especially brisk on Boat Day as residents rushed to buy greeting leis for newly arrived visitors. Circa 1900s. [Hawai'i State Archives]

Left, lower: "Steamer Day" in Honolulu was an exciting weekly opportunity to welcome home old friends, greet arriving visitors, or simply check out the new tourists. As the passenger ships rounded Diamond Head, the word spread through town and lei-sellers, well-wishers, and the curious crowded the wharf at Pier 10 ready to enjoy the carnival atmosphere that included hula dancers and music by the Royal Hawaiian Band. [Baker-Van Dyke Collection]

Above, upper: Union Street in downtown Honolulu district. In a few months it would be braced for an invasion with all windows taped to prevent shattering from explosions. [Baker-Van Dyke Collection]

Left: While many Honolulu buildings were constructed to reflect American tastes, the architects C. W. Dickey and Hart Wood developed a distinctive "Hawaiian architecture" suitable to Honolulu's Polynesian and Asian character and tropical climate. Envisioning a unique urban setting which reflected Island themes, they designed such masterpieces as the Alexander & Baldwin Building built in 1930 on Bishop Street. Its high-pitched roof, Mediterranean stucco façade, Asian motifs and palm-tree landscaping were features of "Hawaiian architecture." [Hawai'i State Archives]

Right: The Young Men's Christian Association at the corner of Hotel and Alakea Street (1939) was later known (1978) as the Merchandise Mart Building.

Above, upper: Duke Kahanamoku (far right) and his brothers (left to right: Bill, Sam, Louis, David, and Sergeant) pose with their surfboards in front of the old Moana Bathhouse in 1931. A strong traditionalist, Duke also favored the 16-foot, solid koa wood surfboards of ancient design. [Bishop Museum]

Lower: Pineapple workers on the assembly line at Dole Cannery. [Tongg Publishing]

The cattle swim at Kailua Bay. Since the main market for beef was in Honolulu, Big Island cattle had to be herded to boat landings, and then swam out to waiting vessels. Strong paniolo and intrepid sailors worked with well-trained horses and by sheer force, dragged each animal into the water. The cattle ships transported passengers as well—an eighteen-hour, noisy, smelly voyage. Later, piers and chutes replaced the cattle swim, one of the most colorful features of Hawai'i's old ranching days, and tugs and barges took the place of cattle boats. [Baker-Van Dyke Collection]

Honolulu Star-Bulletin 1st EXTRA

(Associated Press by Transpacific Telephone)
SAN FRANCISCO, Dec. 7.—President Roosevelt announced this morning that Japanese planes had attacked Manila and Pearl Harbor.

WAR!

OAHU BOMBED BY JAPANESE PLANES

SIX KNOWN DEAD, 21 INJURED, AT EMERGENCY HOSPITAL

Attack Made On Island's Defense Areas

Hundreds See City Bombed

Names of Dead and Injured

Schools Closed

Editorial

Billowing smoke rising from explosions at the Pearl Harbor attack are seen from 'Aiea. [Baker-Van Dyke Collection]

Aircraft destroyed on the ground at Ford Island in Pearl Harbor. In the background are the smoke and flames of giant battleships destroyed at their berths. [U.S. Navy – National Archives]

1940—Hawai'i's population is 420,770 persons.

1940—Hawai'i's first escalator, going up only, begins operating at Mitsukoshi department store at King and Bethel Streets.

1940, November 5—A general election plebiscite favors statehood by a 2 to 1 margin.

1941, December 7—More than 350 Japanese bomber planes attack Pearl Harbor, leading the United States to enter World War II. The attack kills 2,390 U.S. military personnel with another 1,178 wounded. Twenty-one United States ships are sunk or badly damaged, and 323 U.S. planes are destroyed or damaged. In the fiery sinking of the U.S.S. *Arizona* 1,177 men perish.

1941, December 7—At 4:30 p.m. territorial governor Joseph B. Poindexter declares Martial Law which remains in effect until October of 1944.

1942—The movie *Song of the Islands,* starring Betty Grable and Victor Mature, is released. It includes scenes shot on Hawai'i Island. Also starring Hilo Hattie, this is the first all-color feature film using scenes from the Islands.

1942—Approximately 1,300 Americans of Japanese ancestry from the Islands travel to Wisconsin's Camp McCoy for training and then form the 100th Infantry Battalion.

1942, June 4—American fighter pilots and dive bombers sink four carriers of the Japanese naval fleet near Midway Atoll in the Battle of Midway, securing the strategic location for the duration of the war. The following day, U.S. Admiral Nimitz (1885-1966), the commander of the Pacific Fleet, announces victory over the Japanese Fleet at Midway. The Battle of Midway is a turning point of World War II.

The destroyer U.S.S. *Shaw* was moored at the Pearl Harbor dry docks when it was hit during the early-morning attack. Despite heavy damage inflicted by the horrific explosion, by February 1942 the *Shaw* was outfitted with a false bow and sailed to the West Coast for further repairs. [National Archives]

During the first few minutes of the Pearl Harbor attack, the U.S.S. *Arizona* took a hit from a 1,760-pound armor-piercing bomb that slammed through the deck. The forward ammunition magazine instantly exploded with a horrific blast that sent a column of black smoke spiraling from the ship. Within nine minutes, as burning oil turned the ocean into an inferno, the U.S.S. *Arizona* and 1,177 of her crew sank to the bottom of the harbor. [National Archives]

1943, February 1—The U.S. announces the formation of the 442nd Infantry Regimental Combat Team comprised of Nisei (second generation Japanese American) volunteers who want to demonstrate their loyalty to the U.S. despite the harsh racism experienced in the wake of the Pearl Harbor attack. About 10,000 Hawai'i Nisei volunteer within days (compared to just 1,256 from the mainland).

1944, June—The 100th Infantry Battalion joins ranks with the 442nd Regimental Combat Team in Italy, and in October of 1944, the 442nd/100th breaks through German forces to liberate the French towns of Biffontaine and Bruyeres, rescuing about 200 members of the "Lost Battalion" (141st Regiment, 36th Infantry Division) near Bruyeres.

The 442nd/100th eventually becomes the most decorated unit in U.S. history, earning more than 18,000 total awards for their stellar war performance and valorous fighting in numerous battles, despite suffering high casualty rates.

1944, July 19—The Democratic National Convention endorses statehood for Hawai'i.

1945, August 15—Victory over Japan Day ("V-J Day") is declared after the United States drops nuclear bombs on Japan in Hiroshima (August 6) and Nagasaki (August 9). The Japanese officially surrender on the deck of the U.S.S. *Missouri* battleship on September 2, 1945.

1946—Pineapple is the second largest industry in the Islands, with nine companies producing crops valued at $75 million annually.

EXTRA

TIDAL WAVES CRASH HILO

Honolulu Star-Bulletin

LATE NEWS FINAL

20 Dead Reported In The Territory And Toll May Grow

Aleutian Quake Is Blamed

Above, upper: Four long years of wartime deprivations had recently ended for the people of Hawai'i when a natural disaster struck on April 1, 1946. In the early hours, the sea floor on the northern slope of the Aleutian Trench began to move, sending out tremors that lasted only a minute. Although the earthquake was recorded around the world and on seismographs at the University of Hawai'i and the Hawai'i Volcano Observatory, there was, as yet, no early warning system for tsunami. Five hours and two thousand miles later, the waters of Hilo Bay on the windward coast of the island of Hawai'i suddenly began to drain, as hundreds of residents watched in fascination. Moments later, a wave slammed into the town's waterfront with such power that buildings were smashed, railroads and bridges uprooted, and people sucked out to sea. Unaware that more waves were coming, shocked curiosity-seekers rushed to the shoreline to see the destruction as another wave hit. A third and final wave sent residents running for their lives. [Bishop Museum]

Above, lower and left: At nearby Laupāhoehoe, an important settlement in 1880 partly due to its convenience in loading passengers and cargo on awaiting off-shore ships, a school class watched the receding ocean that preceded the immense wave. A crowd ran out to collect exposed fish and shells. Sixteen children and five teachers were killed when the tsunami slammed into the unprotected village. The "April Fools' Day" disaster claimed 159 lives. Only 115 bodies were recovered. This marked the beginning of the decline of the community as a population center. [Hawai'i State Archives]

1946, April 1—An earthquake in the Aleutian Islands generates at least 15 tsunami waves that kill 159 people in Hilo and Laupāhoehoe on Hawai'i Island, as well as hitting Maui and Kaua'i. Five hundred buildings are destroyed in Hilo as water surges up to 56 feet above sea level, causing an estimated $26 million damage, including railroads, bridges, piers and ships.

1946, July 26—Honolulu publisher Rudy Tongg starts Trans-Pacific Airlines (later renamed Aloha Airlines). The first flight carries 21 passengers to Hilo from Honolulu in a war surplus DC-3.

1946, September 1—The "Great Hawai'i Sugar Strike" occurs when 28,000 workers from 33 sugar plantations go on a statewide strike against the Hawai'i Employers Council. The ILWU represents the strikers during the 79 day strike. The union is victorious and ILWU national chief Harry Bridges states that Hawai'i is no longer a feudal colony.

1947—Gabby Pahinui begins recording music. He eventually becomes one of Hawai'i's most influential slack-key guitarists.

1948, February 2—President Harry S. Truman endorses statehood for Hawai'i during his report to Congress.

1949—Scientists at Pōhakuloa on Hawai'i Island begin raising extremely endangered nēnē (Hawaiian geese) in captivity. In 1951 England's Slimbridge Wildfowl Trust also begins raising the birds. The efforts are eventually a great success, with more than 2,000 nēnē raised in captivity between 1960 and 1990 to be released on Kaua'i, Maui, and Hawai'i Island.

1949—The National Memorial Cemetery of the Pacific is dedicated at Pūowaina (Punchbowl) on the fourth anniversary of V-J Day. Today the Cemetery is the final resting place of more than 33,000 military personnel who served in World War II, the Korean War, and the Vietnam War, including 776 victims of the 1941 Pearl Harbor attack.

1949, May 1—The "Great Hawaiian Dock Strike" occurs when the ILWU, led by regional director Jack Hall, strikes against Hawai'i's "Big Five" companies. The strike lasts 157 days crippling the flow of goods and food to Hawai'i, which is almost totally dependent on shipping. The strike bankrupts many small businesses and results in statewide food shortages.

Labor Strife

In the postwar era, another tidal wave of change was about to sweep through the Islands, a tsunami of labor unrest and political protest, which eventually unseated the powers that had ruled Hawai'i for over forty years. During World War II, the firm hand of martial law prevented any efforts by labor leaders to improve conditions on the sugar plantations. However, after the war, the International Longshoremen's and Warehousemen's Union (ILWU), under the leadership of Jack Hall, took aggressive action to organize a united, multicultural front against the "Big Five" oligarchy. In September of 1946, over twenty-one thousand workers on thirty-three plantations went on strike, virtually shutting down the sugar industry. The strike dragged on through October with thousands of pickets, scores of arrests, and threatening accusations that the Islands were controlled by a tyranny of labor unions. Finally, after seventy-nine days, the ILWU was victorious. The plantations' paternal system of providing employees with housing and credit at the company store had ended – workers now earned cash they could spend at their own discretion.

The ILWU's success was followed by active organizing throughout the plantations and on the waterfronts. By 1947, the union had thirty thousand members—more than any other union in the Islands—and significant political clout. The ILWU worked with the once almost defunct Democratic Party to sponsor territorial office candidates with a favorable stance on labor. When charges of communist infiltration surfaced in 1948, the political struggle over economic justice in Hawai'i attracted national attention.

On May 1, 1949, the storm broke when two thousand ILWU dock workers walked off the job and brought Hawai'i's economy to a standstill. Nothing could enter or leave the Islands; thirty-four thousand people were laid off, businesses closed, and household supplies dwindled. Scenes of labor unrest at Pier 32, and at labor rallies in Honolulu, were common as the dock strike continued for 177 days. Finally, the longshoremen won a wage increase. The era of the "Big Five" oligarchy was clearly coming to an end. [Bob Ebert]

MOMENT IN HISTORY

THE DAY OF INFAMY, DECEMBER 7, 1941

Sunday dawned peacefully for most Islanders, who looked forward to another relaxing weekend at the beach or at home. Few knew that in the early morning hours a midget Japanese submarine had been sighted and attacked in the waters off O'ahu. A North Shore radar operator had also detected squadrons of foreign aircraft approaching from the northwest. Many of Honolulu's parks were already filled with amateur baseball games. A handful of civilians heard the drone of planes overhead at Kāne'ohe on the windward side of the island, and on the leeward side at Waialua and Waipahu.

At approximately 7:55 a.m. the first bombs began to fall. Japanese aircraft attacked American ships and military installations at Pearl Harbor, Kāne'ohe Bay, Hickam, Bellows, Wheeler Army Air Corps Base, Schofield Barracks and the Marine airfield at 'Ewa. Military personnel and civilians were caught completely by surprise as two waves of explosions crippled the American fleet at Pearl Harbor. Within minutes, all eight ships moored on Battleship Row along Ford Island had been hit by either bombs or torpedoes. When the assault ended two hours later, twenty-one U.S. ships were sunk or damaged. Over three hundred American aircraft were destroyed or damaged; 2,403 military personnel and 57 civilians died, and 1,178 were wounded. Japanese losses were comparatively light—less than thirty planes. Two hours of hell thrust Hawai'i onto center stage in the greatest conflict in human history.

Damage at King and McCully streets, December 7, 1941. [Hawai'i War Records Depository / University of Hawai'i at Mānoa]

Pearl Harbor

On Dec. 7, 1941, more than 350 Japanese bomber planes attacked Pearl Harbor and other O'ahu military sites. The first planes struck the Mōkapu Peninsula's Pacific Naval Air Base, killing or wounding 84 and damaging 36 seaplanes. Seven minutes later, at 7:55 a.m., the surprise attack on Pearl Harbor began, entering the United States into World War II.

Deaths at Pearl Harbor totaled 2,390 military personnel and 60 civilians with another 1,178 wounded. Eight huge American battleships were sunk or damaged, along with three light cruisers, three destroyers, and four smaller ships. In all, 21 United States ships were sunk or badly damaged and 323 planes were destroyed including planes on Ford Island and at Wheeler Airfield. In total the U.S. suffered 3,566 military casualties along with the deaths of 48 O'ahu residents.

1,177 men perished in the U.S.S. *Arizona* which was at its moorings on Battleship Row when it sank just nine minutes after being hit by a 1,760-pound armor-piercing bomb. The bodies of 945 of the crew members of the U.S.S. *Arizona* were never recovered, remaining entombed in the sunken vessel; 334 crew members survived. The U.S.S. *Oklahoma* was struck by several torpedoes trapping 400 men as the ship rolled completely over.

United States anti-aircraft guns responded to the attack 15 minutes after the start of the bombing and destroyed 29 Japanese planes and sunk five midget submarines. One Japanese pilot crash landed on Ni'ihau. Other sites hit on O'ahu included Hickam, Wheeler, Bellows, and Kāne'ohe airfields as well as 'Ewa Marine Corp Air Station and Schofield Barracks. In total, fifty-five Japanese airmen and 9 submariners were killed along with one captured.

On December 30, 1941, Japanese submarines shelled the ports of Kahului on Maui, Nāwiliwili on Kaua'i, and Hilo on Hawai'i Island. On January 28, 1942, a Japanese submarine torpedoed the Army transport ship *Royal I. Frank* in Hawaiian waters killing 21 people. A lone Japanese plane bombed Honolulu on March 2, 1942. Throughout the Islands there was a general fear of being attacked by Japan.

On September 2, 1945, Japan officially surrendered on the deck of the U.S.S. *Missouri*, now berthed at Pearl Harbor's Battleship Row. Victory ("V-J Day") had been declared on August 15, 1945 after the United States dropped nuclear bombs on Hiroshima (August 6, 1945) and Nagasaki (August 9, 1945) leading to Japan's imminent defeat.

At the outset of the attack, many thought the military was carrying on a maneuver. People gathered on streets to watch. [Hawai'i War Records Depository / University of Hawai'i at Mānoa]

The 422nd/100th

After the 1941 Pearl Harbor attack, the U.S. declared Japanese Americans 4C, non-draftable. The Japanese and Japanese American population of Hawai'i at this time was about 100,000 including 35,000 first generation Japanese. Many of the most influential were detained, including community leaders, ministers, Buddhist priests, and principals of Japanese schools.

Initially Japanese and Japanese Americans detainees were taken to Sand Island, whose use as an internment camp began on December 8, 1941. Less than 1,500 Hawai'i residents were part of about 115,000 Americans of Japanese ancestry interned in ten camps on the U.S. mainland.

Despite the government's suspicions about Hawai'i's Japanese residents and their harsh and often racist treatment after the Pearl Harbor attack, many wished to show their loyalty and join the war effort. In the summer of 1942, 1,300 Americans of Japanese ancestry traveled from Hawai'i to Wisconsin's Camp McCoy for training, and then formed the 100th Infantry Battalion. On February 1, 1943, the government announced the formation of the 442nd Infantry Regimental Combat Team, initially consisting of Nisei (second generation Japanese American) volunteers from Hawai'i.

In June of 1944 in Italy, the 100th Infantry Battalion joined ranks with the 442nd Infantry Regimental Combat Team, and the two units, comprised mostly of Hawai'i's Nisei soldiers, became the most decorated unit in U.S. history, earning more than 18,000 awards for valorous fighting. For their heroic efforts despite heavy losses in Italy, France, and Germany, the 442nd became known as the "Purple Heart Battalion."

The motto of the 442nd was "Go For Broke," a Hawaiian slang term referring to risking everything. In October of 1944 they broke through German forces and liberated the French towns of Biffontaine and Bruyeres rescuing 200 members of the "Lost Battalion" (141st Regiment, 36th Infantry Division) near Bruyeres. The rescue was considered a pivotal battle in the war and resulted, in just one month, in the loss of 800 soldiers of the 442nd, two-thirds of their men.

The actual date these Nisei soldiers were to leave Honolulu for Oakland, California, was a military secret. Several days after the official departure ceremony, they were awakened early and taken by the Oahu Railway to 'A'ala Park. Shouldering their heavy duffel bags from the station to the ship docked at the harbor, they expected a quiet farewell from their beloved Islands. However, all the streets were lined with families and friends who had gotten word of the "secret" departure from the "coconut wireless." This unofficial sendoff was an emotional moment they carried with them halfway around the world. [National Archives/DeSoto Brown Collection]

Right, upper: Hawai'i's 422nd is off to the war in a ceremony at 'Iolani Palace on March 28, 1943. Nisei volunteers in the army spent only a short time at Schofield Barracks' "Tent City" before being shipped out to basic training at Camp Shelby, Mississippi. Recognizing that these young men had family members who wanted to wish them a special aloha before leaving, the military arranged a farewell ceremony at 'Iolani Palace in March of 1943. A huge crowd of friends and relatives watched two thousand new soldiers march smartly down King Street, then assemble on the palace grounds for final speeches, an official photograph, and to receive lei and small envelopes of cash as traditional gifts. The actual date that these soldiers were to leave Honolulu for Oakland, California, was a military secret. Several days after the official departure ceremony, they were awakened early and taken by the Oahu Railway to A'ala Park. As they shouldered their heavy duffel bags from the station to the ship docked at the harbor, they expected a quiet farewell from their beloved Islands. However, all the streets were lined with families and friends who had gotten word of the "secret" departure from the "coconut wireless." [Hawai'i State Archives]

Center: Nisei volunteers in the Army spent only a short time at Schofield Barracks' "Tent City" before being shipped out to basic training at Camp Shelby, Mississippi. Recognizing that these young men had family members who wanted to wish them a special aloha before leaving, the military arranged a farewell ceremony at 'Iolani Palace in March of 1943. A huge crowd of friends and relatives watched 2,000 new soldiers march smartly down King Street (above), then assemble on the palace grounds for final speeches, an official photograph, and receiving lei and small envelopes of cash as traditional gifts. [Hawai'i State Archives]

Lower left: A Japanese family returns from internment on the mainland, December 11, 1946. [Hawai'i War Records Depository / University of Hawai'i at Mānoa]

Lower right: A father and son have an emotional reunion upon the 442nd's return. [Bob Ebert]

During World War II, over a million military personnel passed through the Islands, transforming the social and racial complexion of its population. Soldiers and sailors seemed to be everywhere as downtown Honolulu buses were inundated with men in uniform. During a November 5, 1943 air-raid alert, civilians and servicemen enter a Mānoa Valley bus at the Bishop Street stop in front of the Alexander Young Hotel. [*Honolulu Star-Bulletin*/Hawai'i War Records Depository/University of Hawai'i at Mānoa]

"Loose Lips Sink Ships" was a constant fear for Hawai'i's military government, which attempted to minimize the flow of sensitive information into the civilian population. All letters handled by the U.S. Post office were censored for any mention of ship movements, and indecipherable words were cut out. To encourage the entire population to "Serve in Silence," in 1944 a parade was conducted on downtown Hotel Street. Store display windows were decorated with posters and slogans to remind everyone that "Rumors Delay Victory." [U.S. Army Museum of Hawai'i]

Martial Law

Martial Law was declared in the Islands at 4:30 p.m. on December 7, 1941 by Territorial governor Joseph B. Poindexter which stripped him of his administrative powers. Poindexter turned civilian duties over to Lieutenant General Walter Short who became the military governor.

Under Martial Law, all residents of the Hawaiian Islands were subject to the Uniform Code of Military Justice, and the Territorial constitution was suspended as well as the authority of the Supreme Court and the legislature. Civilian courts were replaced with military judges. 'Iolani Palace was barricaded and trenches were dug around the building for security as the building was used by the military.

Martial Law imposed many restrictions including enforced blackouts from 6 p.m. to 6 a.m., curfews and blackout wardens patrolling neighborhoods. All residents over the age of six were fingerprinted and given personal identification cards that had to be carried at all times. The media and all mail were censored. Food and gas were rationed, alcohol was prohibited, and business hours were restricted. The military was allowed to take whatever land was needed with the Army eventually controlling about one-third of O'ahu including the campus of Punahou School taken over by the Corps of Engineers.

Laws imposed by the military governor were known as General Orders, and any transgressions were dealt with by military tribunals—without appeals. Many of Hawai'i's Japanese population were arrested and interned under suspicion of espionage or sabotage though none were ever found guilty.

In 1943, the Territorial Government regained control of most civilian functions, but Martial Law remained in effect until October 1944. Curfews, censorship and gas rationing ended in 1945. In 1946, the declaration of Martial Law in Hawai'i was determined to be unconstitutional by the U.S. Supreme Court.

World War II affected every aspect of U.S. civilian life, especially in Hawai'i, which was the center of the U.S. armed forces' Pacific theater. From food control and gasoline rationing to "victory gardens," bomb shelters, gas masks and sales of war bonds, the need to organize and arouse the war effort was emphasized by posters displayed throughout the Islands. [Hawai'i War Records Depository/DeSoto Brown Collection]

In an August 10, 1944 meeting that included General Douglas MacArthur, President Franklin D. Roosevelt, and Admiral William Healy at Queen's Surf, then a private residence, Admiral Nimitz points to the Japanese home Islands on a large map of the Western Pacific. Nimitz argued strenuously with maps and intelligence information that fighting the Japanese in the Philippines would be unnecessary. By neutralizing Japan's airbases in the region, the U.S. Navy could instead go on to invade Formosa and launch an attack on Japan. General MacArthur then rose and told President Roosevelt that bypassing the Philippines would be politically and militarily disastrous. "American public opinion will condemn you," he finally stated. "And it will be justified." With a re-election campaign only months away, FDR approved MacArthur's highly publicized "return to the Philippines." [Hawai'i War Records Depository / University of Hawai'i at Mānoa]

1950—Hawai'i's population is 499,794 people, of which 85 percent are U.S. citizens. About one-third of the population is Caucasian, one-third Japanese, twelve percent part Hawaiian, and about ten percent Filipino, with smaller numbers of Chinese, North Koreans, and Puerto Ricans. About two percent are pure Hawaiian.

1950, April 19—The House Un-American Activities Committee holds hearings at 'Iolani Palace to investigate alleged Communist infiltration of the labor movement.

1950, June 25—North Korea invades South Korea beginning the Korean War. The United States sends troops to the conflict including an estimated 17,000 Hawai'i residents, of which 341 are killed and 79 are missing in action. The war ends on July 27, 1953.

1950, August 15-17—Hurricane Hiki hits Kaua'i with winds that reach 68 miles per hour. Extensive flooding occurs at Waimea where more than 52 inches fall in four days, causing $200,000 damage. A farmer in Kohala is killed when he touches wires blown down by strong winds.

1951, August 28—Seven union organizers are indicted for violating the Smith Act, which prohibits advocating the use of force or violence to overthrow the U.S. government.

1952—Three Hawai'i residents win gold medals in the Helsinki Olympics, including William Woolsey (800-meter freestyle relay); Ford Konno (1,500-meter freestyle); and Yoshio Oyakawa (100-meter backstroke).

The military presence in Hawai'i was heightened during World War II, when more than a million servicemen passed through the Islands, and nearly one third of O'ahu was taken over by army and navy personnel. For over three years residents coped with blackouts, food control, fingerprinting, mail censorship, gas-mask and air-raid drills, and martial law. Hollywood captured the spirit of Hawai'i at war in the Academy Award-winning film *From Here to Eternity,* the classic 1954 adaptation of the James Jones novel, starring Ernest Borgnine as "Fats," Burt Lancaster as "Sergeant Warden," and Frank Sinatra as "Maggio." [Luis Reyes Collection/Screen Gems]

1952, December 1—Hawai'i's first regular television programming begins on KGMB-TV.

1953—A new Hawai'i State Archives building is constructed on the grounds of 'Iolani Palace behind the original building, which becomes known as the Old Archives building. In 1959 the Old Archives building is renamed Kana'ina and the new one Kekāuluohi. The new Archives allows public access to important historical documents including genealogical records, manuscripts, photographs, maps, private papers and items from various collections.

1953—*From Here to Eternity*, based on the James Jones novel, is filmed on O'ahu including three weeks at Schofield Barracks. The movie takes place before the Pearl Harbor attack and involves a private who is punished for not boxing on his unit's team.

1953, February 20—President Dwight D. Eisenhower signs an executive order placing Kaho'olawe under the jurisdiction of the Secretary of the Navy.

1953, June 17—Jack Hall and six other defendants are convicted under the anticommunist Smith Act.

1953, November—Samuel Wilder King becomes Hawai'i's first appointed governor of Hawaiian ancestry.

1954—Japanese American veterans from World War II lead a "Democratic Revolution." Many

As the population of O'ahu grew in the 1950s, the suburbs with single-family dwellings began to be developed on the east and windward sides of the island. California developer Henry J. Kaiser, in 1959, initiated a massive development project on the Bishop Estate lands and fishponds of Maunlua Valley, a project he called Hawai'i Kai. Kaiser believed that suburbanites would prefer to live on this side of Honolulu because they could travel to and from work each day without the sun in their eyes. [Camera Hawai'i]

veterans are distinguished members of the renowned 442nd Infantry Regiment.

1955—Mormons establish the Church College of Hawaiʻi in Lāʻie. Dedicated in 1958, the school in 1974 becomes a branch campus of Provo, Utah's Brigham Young University.

1955—Pineapple production in the Islands peaks at 76,700 acres.

1955—The worst air disaster in Hawaiʻi's history occurs when a military transport plane crashes in the Waiʻanae Mountains, killing all 66 passengers.

1956—The Waikīkī Shell opens in Kapiʻolani Park.

1957—The International Marketplace opens in Waikīkī, featuring restaurants, shops, kiosks, and eateries centered around a hundred-year-old banyan tree.

1957, March 9—An earthquake in the Aleutian Islands generates a tsunami that destroys 75 homes on Kauaʻi's northern shore.

1957, May—The first two tunnels of the Nuʻuanu Pali Highway open to one-way traffic providing passage through the Koʻolau Mountains from Nuʻuanu Valley to the windward side of Oʻahu. All four lanes are open to two-way traffic on August 1, 1961. The Pali Highway follows the route of the ancient Pali trail long used by farmers carrying produce from the fertile windward side to Honolulu city. The steep, winding Pali trail was widened and paved with rocks in 1845, widened again in 1862 to accommodate horses, dynamited and paved in 1896 and then widened again in 1900 to accommodate automobiles.

1957—Communist North Vietnam invades South Vietnam, beginning the Vietnam War. The conflict lasts until 1975, claiming 221 Hawaiʻi residents and another 51 war-related deaths. About 13,000 Hawaiʻi residents see action.

After the war, many young Nisei veterans, such as Daniel Inouye and Spark Matsunaga, returned to the Islands with a zeal for political change. With many Japanese Americans having sacrificed their lives in the name of freedom in Europe, the returners were determined to redress the political and economic inequities in Hawai'i, where the "Big Five" was still in control. Revitalizing the Democratic Party and forming important alliances with the local labor movement, these Nisei leaders staged a "Bloodless Revolution" in 1954, seizing control of both houses of the territorial legislature. The domination of the Islands by the sugar oligarchy faded quickly as a new Asian-American middle class emerged with growing political clout. [Family of Spark Matsunaga]

In the late 1950s, the Dillingham Corporation began building a large shopping center on a tract of land near Ala Moana Park. The grounds of the future Sears store at Ala Moana Shopping Center were dedicated by Revered Abraham Akaka in 1958, as the city government braced itself for the enormous impact that the private development would have on sewer lines, water supply, and traffic access. When it was completed, the Ala Moana Shopping Center became the world's largest shopping complex. Within a very short time, many of Fort Street's department and clothing stores would close as downtown Honolulu was no longer the center of Island fashion. [Camera Hawai'i]

During a 1954 visit, James Michener, whose novel Hawai'i would become a worldwide best-selling saga, walks with Donn Beach, aka Don the Beachcomber, one of Waikīkī's early entrepreneurs and restaurateur who helped create Hawai'i's reputation as a visitor destination. [Phoebe Beach Collection]

Honolulu Star-Bulletin

Soviet Planes Airlift Troops in Laos

U.S. Vows to Back South Vietnam As Red Rebels Push Terror Drive

Michener's Racial Blast Stirs Up Storm

Friend Says Wife 'Suffered'

U.S. Jet Downs U.S. Bomber

Heiress to $6 Million Found Dead in Royal Hawaiian Suite

Free Trust Territories, Reds Demand

James Michener autographs *Hawaii* for Albertine Loomis. 1959. [*Honolulu Star-Bulletin*]

1958, August 31—The Matson Navigation Company's cargo ship *Hawaiian Merchant* leaves San Francisco, California for the Hawaiian Islands carrying 20 aluminum deck-top containers, each 24 feet long, ushering in the new era of container shipping that allows

Honolulu Star-Bulletin

Hurricane 'Dot' Batters Kauai; Wind, Flood Damage Is Heavy

mechanization of the loading and unloading process.

1959—The population of the State of Hawai'i is 622,000 people, and the annual visitor count is 240,000.

1959—Kīlauea Iki ("Little Kīlauea") crater in the summit area of Kīlauea Volcano sends fountains of lava erupting to heights of 1,900 feet, the highest ever recorded in the Islands.

1959—Kaiser Hospital opens on O'ahu.

1959—Daniel Inouye is elected to the U.S. House of Representatives, becoming Hawai'i's first Congressman and the first Japanese-American in the U.S. House or Congress.

1959—Construction begins on Maui's Kā'anapali Resort, Hawai'i's first master-planned resort.

1959, July 29—Qantas Empire Airways begins Hawai'i's first commercial jet air service with a Boeing 707 flight connecting Sydney, Nadi, Honolulu, and San Francisco. *The City of Sydney* arrives July 31 becoming the first jet flight into Honolulu and is greeted by the Royal Hawaiian band playing "Waltzing Matilda." Pan American soon offers flights from Tokyo to the west coast of the United States stopping at Honolulu and Wake Island.

1959—At a cost of $28 million, the Ala Moana Shopping Center opens on August 3, 1959, the same year Hawai'i is admitted as the 50th state. The 50-acre shopping center sits on an area that was once marshland three feet underwater and covered with duck farms. In 1931, the City and County of Honolulu cleaned up

STATEHOOD!

House Sends Bill to Ike

Honolulu Star-Bulletin

Sirens, Bells Herald Statehood Arrival

Faubus's Telegram

First Class Citizens Now

the area, which had also been the site of a refuse dump. In 1934 President Franklin Delano Roosevelt dedicated Moana Park, and in 1947 it was renamed Ala Moana. Eventually sand was brought to the beachfront area, and the two-story Ala Moana Shopping Center was built on an adjacent 50 acres of land using coral fill dredged from the offshore reef.

As a result of the 1959 elections, the Republican Party also sent a self-made millionaire by the name of Hiram Fong to Congress. Here, he and his family are greeted at the airport by Governor Quinn and his wife. The U.S. Senate's first Chinese-American, Senator Fong won re-election until his retirement in 1985. [Uprichard Collection/United Airlines]

1959—James Michener publishes the novel *Hawaii*, finishing the best-selling book on the day the U.S. Congress approves Hawaiian statehood.

1959, August 6—Hurricane Dot passes over Kaua'i with winds of more than 100 miles per hour, causing $20 million in damage.

1959, August 21—President Eisenhower signs the Statehood Proclamation, officially admitting Hawai'i as the 50th state. On July 4, 1960, a 50th star is added to the flag of the United States, and Hawai'i's state flag is formally accepted.

MOMENT IN HISTORY

"NOW WE ARE ALL HAOLES"... HAWAI'I BECOMES THE 50TH STATE MARCH 11, 1959

President Dwight David Eisenhower signs the Statehood Act on August 21, 1959. [National Archives]

For nearly three decades Hawai'i's statehood had been a long and hotly debated topic, both in the Islands and the U.S. Congress. The first Congressional hearings in the 1930s focused negatively on Hawai'i's non-American aspects, the loyalty of its large Japanese population, and its minority of white citizens. Many members of Congress also felt that the democracy expected of a state had been subverted by the Territory's powerful sugar industry. The "second-class citizenship" felt by many local residents—especially the Nisei—was especially galling during World War II. This attitude turned to activism after so many young men and women of Asian and Pacific ancestry had sacrificed their lives for the United States. Momentum to recognize Hawai'i as a full and equal partner in the Union grew during the 1950s, backed by local Democratic party leaders who equated statehood with first-class citizenship status for all residents. Petitions were signed by thousands of Islanders a plebiscite in support of statehood returned a vote of overwhelming approval. These efforts culminated on March 11, 1959, when the U.S. Congress passed the Statehood Admission Bill. In the Islands the news was greeted by ringing the bells of Kawaiaha'o Church, with street parties, and with the historic comment of one Islander, "Now we are all haoles."

WITNESS TO HISTORY

THE HOPES AND FEARS OF STATEHOOD, REVEREND ABRAHAM K. AKAKA

There are some of us to whom statehood brings great hopes; and there are some to whom statehood brings silent fears. One might say that the hopes and fears of Hawai'i are met in statehood today. There are fears that statehood will motivate economic greed toward Hawai'i, that it will turn Hawai'i into a great big (as someone has said) spiritual junkyard filled with smashed dreams, worn-out illusions—that it will make us lonely, confused, insecure, empty, anxious, restless, disillusioned—a wistful people.

We need to see statehood as the lifting of the clouds of smoke, and the opportunity to affirm positively the basic Gospel of the Fatherhood of God and the brotherhood of man. We need to see that Hawai'i has potential moral and spiritual contributions to make to our nation and world. The fears Hawai'i may have are to be met by men and women who are living witnesses of what we really are in Hawai'i, of the spirit of aloha...

Reverend Abraham K. Akaka Statehood Service at Kawaiaha'o Church, March 13, 1959

Democratic Revolution

During the first half of the twentieth century, Caucasian, Republican interests connected to the sugar plantation economy dominated politics in Hawai'i then controlled by the "Big Five" companies: Theo H. Davies; American Factors (Amfac); C. Brewer & Co.; Alexander & Baldwin; and Castle & Cooke.

Native Hawaiians as well as the many ethnic groups that came to Hawai'i as contract laborers—Chinese, Japanese, Portuguese, Filipinos, Puerto Ricans, Okinawans, Spanish, Koreans—were largely excluded from political power. In the mid-1950s Hawai'i's political landscape changed rapidly when returning World War II veterans, many distinguished members of the renowned 442nd Infantry Regiment, began to assert their political power.

Japanese Americans led a new political movement forming alliances with other ethnic groups, including Filipinos. These increasingly powerful Democratic ethnic groups won important election victories in what became known as the Democratic Revolution of 1954. Favoring statehood, liberal labor benefits, land reform, and equality in education, they gained a majority in the Territorial House of Representatives and two years later won both Houses.

In 1962, former Honolulu police captain and U.S. Representative John Burns was elected and for the first time Democrats controlled both Hawai'i's executive and legislative branches. Burns served until 1974 and the Democratic Party ruled uninterrupted until the election of Republican Linda Lingle in 2002.

Statehood

A general election plebiscite on November 5, 1940 favored statehood by a 2 to 1 margin. After World War II ended in 1945, the Hawaiian statehood movement grew. From 1945 to 1956, control of Hawai'i's economic, political and social life was dominated by Caucasian and Republican corporate interests buttressed by the powerful "Big Five" firms.

In 1954, proponents of statehood gathered on Bishop Street with 150,000 signatures on a three-mile-long petition written on a roll of blank newsprint. Hawai'i's delegates to Congress—John Burns, Joseph Farrington, and Elizabeth Farrington—pushed for statehood. The United States Senate passed a statehood measure on March 11, 1959, followed by the U.S. House of Representatives on March 12, 1959. President Dwight D. Eisenhower signed the statehood act into law on March 18, 1959 though it required a plebiscite of Hawaiian residents for approval which occurred on June 27, 1959 when Hawai'i's residents voted in favor of statehood, 17 to 1 with only Ni'ihau's residents opposing.

In Hawai'i's first general election held on July 28, 1959 William F. Quinn was elected governor of the State of Hawai'i, Oren E. Long and Hiram L. Fong were elected as Hawai'i's first senators, and Daniel K. Inouye was elected to the House of Representatives.

On August 21, 1959, President Eisenhower signed the Statehood Proclamation and Hawai'i was officially admitted as the 50th state. At this time Hawai'i's population was 622,000, with more than 240,000 annual visitors. On July 4, 1960, a 50th star was added to the flag of the United States, and Hawai'i's state flag was formally accepted. As a result of statehood, 1.8 million acres of ceded lands were transferred to the State of Hawai'i by the United States government to be held in trust for public education, public use, public improvements, farm and home ownership, and the betterment of Native Hawaiians.

Above, upper: The decade of the 1950s was a transitional period, as Hawai'i shifted from rural to urban. Downtown Honolulu, as viewed from Aloha Tower in 1958, still retained the distinctive architectural charm of the Hawaiian style promoted in the early territorial era by C. W. Dickey and Hart Wood. Still visible in this photograph are the domed American Factors building (in the foreground at Fort and Queen Streets), the roof of the nineteenth-century historic courthouse on Queen Street, the Alexander Young Hotel (on Bishop Street between King and Hotel Streets) and the Damon Building (on the makai—Diamond Head corner of King and Bishop Streets). By the end of the century, all these historic structures would be replaced by steel-and-glass skyscrapers. [Camera Hawaii]

Lower: By the 1950s Waikīkī's streams and ponds had been filled in with ground dredged in the making of the Ala Wai Canal. A new municipal golf course had replaced the wetland agriculture, the Moana had added the Surfrider Hotel to its property, and the Royal Hawaiian had just celebrated its silver anniversary. From the agricultural lifestyle and communal living of the ancient Hawaiians, to the starched and proper days of the monarchy and Protestant missionaries, to the loose flappers of the Roaring Twenties, the history and attitudinal changes in Hawai'i have been played out on this stretch of beach. [Baker-Van Dyke Collection]

Above: Inter-island travel increased as Hawaiian Airlines shortened the time of trips and improved the comfort of passengers who once had to take steamships to visit the neighbor Islands. [Hawai'i State Archives]

Left: In the 1950s, many Islanders saw Hawai'i's territorial status as another stigma of a second-class citizenship under the regime of the sugar oligarchy. Statehood, they believed, would allow full and equal rights, including the election of a governor, full representation in Congress, and voting for state judges. To demonstrate popular support, in 1954, a "Statehood Roll of Honor" was spread out on Honolulu's Bishop Street. The three-mile-long roll of newsprint extended between King and Hotel Street, and an estimated one hundred and fifty thousand residents signed the petition, which was then sent to Washington, D.C. [*Honolulu Advertiser*]

1960—Hawai'i's population is 632,772.

1960, February 18—The Hawai'i State Legislature convenes its first regular session.

1960, May 22—A large earthquake near Chile generates a tsunami that arrives in Hawai'i 15 hours later on the morning of May 23. Its bore rushes ashore in Hilo Bay over a four-mile section of the waterfront sending water up to 36 feet above sea level and killing 61 people.

1960—The East-West Center is established at the University of Hawai'i to "strengthen understanding and relations between the United States and the countries of the Asia Pacific region."

1960—Duke Kahanamoku is officially appointed as Hawai'i's "Ambassador of Aloha."

1961, April—Elvis Presley begins filming *Blue Hawaii*, which will become his most commercially successful movie. He sings the "Hawaiian Wedding Song" in the famous wedding scene atop a canoe in the lagoon at Kauai'i's Coco Palms hotel. Other notable Elvis songs in the movie include "Blue Hawaii," "Rock-a-Hula Blues," "Can't Help Falling in Love," and "Aloha 'Oe," written by Lili'uokalani in 1878. Also opening in 1961 is *Gidget Goes Hawaiian*.

Presley examines with interest his picture on the cover of the Star-Bulletin's new Hawaiian Life magazine presented to him by Robert [illegible], right, 11-year-old newsboy from Kailua.—Star-Bulletin Photo by Jack Titchen.

Elvis Sings Up a Storm To Aid Arizona Memorial

By PHIL MAYER

1962—John Burns is elected governor of the State of Hawai'i, and for the first time Democrats control both the executive and legislative branches of the government.

Honolulu Star-Bulletin

Democrats Sweep Nation and Hawaii; Burns in Stunning Victory Over Quinn

Senate Margin Boosted; Little Loss in House

Party Unity Credited by Congress Trio

Win Greatest For One Party In Isle History

New Procedure Slows Vote Count

Elections-at-a-Glance

No Sweeping, Radical Changes Planned by Burns

Some Cuba Missiles Put On Red Ships

Khrushchev Sees No Need For Summit

Defeated Quinn Sings 'Irish Eyes Are Smiling'

DIRECTORY

1962—Singer Don Ho performs at Duke's in Waikīkī from where he will go on to become one of the most widely-known Island musicians. He releases his first album in 1965 and becomes a staple of the Waikīkī music scene for the next 40 years with his renowned hit, "Tiny Bubbles."

1962, May 31—The U.S.S. *Arizona* Memorial is established to honor those who died in the Dec. 7, 1941 Japanese attack on Pearl Harbor.

The 184-foot long Memorial is an open structure positioned directly over the wreck of the U.S.S. *Arizona* where 1,177 died, more than 900 still entombed. The architect of the U.S.S. *Arizona* Memorial is an Austrian named Alfred Preis who fled the Nazis in 1939 and later moved to Hawai'i. President Dwight D. Eisenhower approved the creation of the Memorial in 1958, and it was officially dedicated on Memorial Day, May 31, 1962. An Elvis Presley benefit concert raised about $64,000 toward its $500,000 cost. Designated as a National Historical Landmark in 1989, the U.S.S. *Arizona* Memorial is one

In postwar years, the nation turned its attention to the building of memorials to commemorate the events of the war years and to pay tribute to those who lost their lives. Hawai'i proposed a plan to build a U.S.S. *Arizona* memorial and the Pacific War Memorial Commission was formed. Funds came from the legislature and from donations solicited through the television program "This Is Your Life" hosted by Ralph Edwards; over $64,000 was raised in a sold-out Elvis Presley concert at Block Arena in Pearl Harbor.

The Navy stipulated that the new memorial be a type of bridge, with no part touching any of the sunken ship, and able to accommodate two hundred people. Architect Alfred Preis first submitted a design for a structure that allowed visitors to view the underwater remains of the U.S.S. *Arizona* from a subsurface structure. The navy flatly rejected his proposal. Preis' second concept was approved, and the white marble bridge-like structure was erected above the U.S.S. *Arizona* and dedicated on Memorial Day 1962. The 184-foot U.S.S. *Arizona* Memorial has a shrine room at the back, with names etched in the marble wall of the 1,177 crewmen who lost their lives. Over a million people tour the site each year. [Mutual Publishing]

of Hawai'i's most well-attended attractions with more than 1.6 million people touring the Memorial each year. In 2010 the new Pearl Harbor Visitor Center opened as part of a newly designated World War II Valor in the Pacific National Monument. Other Pacific National Monument sites at Pearl Harbor include the U.S.S. *Arizona*, U.S.S. *Oklahoma*, and U.S.S. *Utah* Memorials. The U.S. Navy's Pearl Harbor Historic Sites include the Battleship *Missouri* Memorial, the Pacific Aviation Museum and the U.S.S. *Bowfin* Submarine Museum and Park.

1962, October 6—The *Sigma 7* spacecraft, after circling Earth six times with Astronaut Walter M. Schirra on board, plunges into the Pacific Ocean 1,300 miles north of Honolulu. The aircraft carrier *Kearsarge* picks up Schirra, who is then flown to O'ahu's Hickam Air Force Base.

1962—A nuclear bomb detonates 800 miles from Hawai'i at Johnston Island lighting up the sky.

1963—John Dominis Holt writes the essay "On Being Hawaiian" considered to be a seminal work that inspired a cultural reawakening known as the "Hawaiian Renaissance." Some of the events associated with this are: the revival of Polynesian canoe culture and navigation; protests against the use of Kaho'olawe by the military for bombing practice; cultural events reviving hula and ancient traditions; an increase in Hawaiian language programs in schools and universities; inspirational works by artists, musicians, composers, and writers; and political activism.

1963, June 9—President Kennedy speaks at the National Conference of Mayors in Honolulu urging the mayors to help calm the civil rights crisis then occurring.

1963, October 12—The Polynesian Cultural Center opens in Lā'ie,

The pride and power of the Hawaiian heritage has in recent years found a new meaning in the celebration of the Merrie Monarch Festival. For the Hawaiian and Hawaiian-at-heart, no event compares to the annual Merrie Monarch Festival, where both men's and women's hālau compete in ancient and modern dancing styles. The first Merrie Monarch Festival was held in 1963 in Hilo, as a celebration of hula in honor of King Kalākaua (nicknamed the "Merrie Monarch"), who was instrumental in restoring this art form to prominence in the late nineteenth century. The idea for a statewide hula competition originated from Hilo residents George Na'ope and Gene Wilheim, who conceived the festival as a way to draw international attention to hula and Hilo town. By 1971, the competition was drawing hālau from around the state that came to dance and be judged on movement, costume, adornments, style, stance, and manner. The annual event at the Edith Kana'ole Stadium is now televised statewide. In this photo, Nina Maxwell's Pukalani hālau hula performs during the 1985 festival. [Boone Morrison]

O'ahu. A significant expansion in 1975 makes the site a major O'ahu attraction with 42 acres and seven theme villages representing the cultures of Polynesia.

1964—Caucasians become Hawai'i's majority for the first time.

1964—The Honolulu International Center, with a sports arena complex, exhibit hall, and auditorium, opens. In 1967 it is renamed "Blaisdell Center."

1964—Premiering as part of the Hilo Festival, the Merrie Monarch Festival becomes an organized hula competition in 1971, quickly becoming the premier and largest hula event in the state. It is named in honor of King David La'amea Kalākaua (1874-1891), who was known as the Merrie Monarch for his revival of hula and other Hawaiian customs. At his coronation ceremony in February of 1883, Hawaiian men chanted and pounded on pā ipu (gourd drums) and women in traditional dress performed hula. Kalākaua encouraged revival of these practices despite the protests of the era's missionaries. The Merrie Monarch Festival starts each year on Easter Sunday. Stringent guidelines require contestants to present the judges with fact sheets detailing the research and rationale of their performance. Costumes are required to fit the time portrayed in the chant or dance.

1964—One of North America's largest earthquakes ever recorded occurs in Alaska. It registers a magnitude of 8.4 on the Richter scale and generates tsunami waves that cause flooding in Kahului, Maui, and Hilo.

1966—William S. Richardson is appointed Chief Justice of the Hawai'i Supreme Court by Governor John Burns. Holding the post until 1982, Richardson leads an activist court that significantly expands native Hawaiian rights as well as public access to beaches and state waters.

The growth of tourism during the 1950s was the result of pervasive affluence in postwar America, which allowed vacations to such tropical paradises as Hawai'i. At the same time, the Hawai'i Visitors Bureau did an effective job of marketing a very accessible image of the Islands to middle-class families. The colorful mu'umu'u became a popular tourist fashion, along with the famed "aloha shirt." Acclaimed Hawai'i-born singer Alfred Apaka helped to popularize Hawaiian music around the world, while the 'ukulele became synonymous with hapa-haole music and fun on the beach at Waikīkī. Through all of the hoopla of the new postwar tourism, one figure remained beloved—Duke Kahanamoku, who embodied the spirit of the Islands as he danced a hula for friends on his birthday in 1950 at the Outrigger Canoe Club. [Bob Ebert]

Frank Fasi

[Honolulu Star-Bulletin]

Frank Francis Fasi (August 27, 1920–February 3, 2010) was the longest serving mayor of Honolulu, Hawai`i and is credited for having built the foundations of today's Honolulu.

In 1958, he won his first race for the senate of the then Territory of Hawai'i. His term was cut short when Hawai'i achieved statehood and the territorial legislature dissolved. He again ran for office in 1965 winning a seat on the Honolulu City Council where he served as a councilman through 1968.

By the late 1960s, he had gained a colorful reputation. The newspapers used the words "firebrand," "trailblazer" and "maverick" to describe him. In 1969, he was elected Mayor of Honolulu and served until 1981 when he was defeated for the first time for re-election. He defeated May Eileen Anderson in the 1984 election and served as mayor until 1994, when he resigned to seek the governorship. In all, he served 22 years as the mayor of Honolulu.

There are many legacies of the Fasi era. He opened the Neal S. Blaisdell Center. He established TheBus, the Satellite City Hall system, and the nation's largest elected neighborhood board systems. He pushed for the construction of the H-POWER waste-to-energy plant. He created the popular Summer Fun program and the annual Honolulu City Lights winter festival. He popularized the shaka hand sign when he ordered it to become the city's signature logo and printed on all city signs and publications. Fasi is also credited with transforming the Capitol District by bulldozing massive parking structures near the State Capitol, 'Iolani Palace and Kawaiaha'o Church to create large parcels of green space known as the Honolulu Civic Center, where he built a central office building to house the city's departments.

1966—The "Lani Bird" satellite, officially known as "Intelsat 2," broadcasts the Islands' first live television show from the U.S. mainland.

1966—There are fewer than 1,000 humpbacks left from a pre-whaling population of 200,000 whales.

1967—The State of Hawai'i's annual visitor count exceeds one million for the first time.

1968, January 22—Duke Kahanamoku—Olympic champion, movie star, sheriff, and Hawai'i's official "Ambassador of Aloha"—passes away at the age of 77. Thousands attend his "Beachboy" funeral

Fasi says 'the little people' made him Honolulu's mayor

Mayor-elect Frank F. Fasi

Democrats sweep State

Only 18 voting

ceremony, where his ashes are scattered in the waters off Waikīkī.

1968—Hawai'i Democrats establish the nation's first right-to-strike law for public-employee unions, strengthening a powerful union lobby that begins to significantly influence political change.

1968—Frank F. Fasi is elected as Mayor of the City and County of Honolulu, eventually serving five consecutive terms.

1969, March 15—Governor Burns dedicates the new State Capitol Building in Honolulu. Costing $28 million, the building includes a central rotunda, the nation's only open-air Capitol.

1969, July 26—The *Apollo 11* "Columbia" space capsule splashes down in the Pacific Ocean after returning from the first human visit to the moon. The craft carries U.S. astronauts Neil A. Armstrong, Michael Collins, and Edwin E. (Buzz) Aldrin, Jr., who are picked up by the carrier U.S.S. *Hornet* and brought to Pearl Harbor where they are greeted by an estimated 25,000 people. The astronauts are able to see the crowds only through the windows of their isolation trailer. They are kept at Pearl Harbor's Ford Island for three days before being flown to Houston with the space capsule.

1969—Statues of Kamehameha I and Father Damien are placed in Washington D.C.'s National Statuary Hall to honor the two men as being among the greatest of United States' heroes.

1969—The Bank of Bishop & Co. Ltd. is renamed First Hawaiian Bank, and remains today as the state's oldest financial institution.

In January 1960, Kapoho Village was declared a disaster area as a spectacular eruption poured out lava, consuming farmlands, homes and businesses. When the lava reached the sea, only a few homes and the Kumukahi Lighthouse had been miraculously spared. By the time the devastation ended, Kapoho Village was gone and Hawai'i Island had gained a square mile of new land. [Bishop Museum]

A slight drizzle provides the traditional Hawaiian blessing as Governor John A. Burns and other officials conduct the ground-breaking ceremonies of the State Capitol on the former site of ʻIolani Barracks. November 10, 1965. [*Honolulu Star-Bulletin*]

Elvis Presley's big 1961 concert in Hawaiʻi was a fundraiser for the memorial to the men of the battleship U.S.S. *Arizona*, sunk with heavy loss of life on Pearl Harbor Day, December 7, 1941. [*Honolulu Advertiser*]

In 1968 when *Hawaii Five-O* debuted on CBS, few knew that twelve years and 284 episodes later, it would be the longest-running police show in media history. Part of the recipe for the series' popularity was the on-location filming against the beautiful and exotic scenery of Hawaiʻi, against which crime stories unfolded with local personalities often featured in cameo roles. The other reason for its success was its star and producer, Jack Lord, who, as gruff Steve McGarrett, fought a relentless battle against evil. His customary signature ending, "Book 'em, Danno," was viewed in eighty countries, with a weekly audience estimated at more than three hundred million. The show did more to boost Island tourism than any advertising campaign could ever hope to achieve. [*Hawaii Five-O*]

Honolulu Star-Bulletin

Planes Airlift Troops In Laos

U.S. Vows to Back South Vietnam As Red Rebels Push Terror Drive

Michener's Racial Blast Stirs Up Storm

Author of 'Hawaii' Says Discrimination Drove Him Out

Friend Says Wife 'Suffered'

Gabby Pahinui was a genuine folk hero whose slack-key guitar stylings in the 1970s became one of the most influential sounds of the Hawaiian Renaissance. Born in Honolulu in 1921, at the age of twelve he was playing professionally. In 1963 he and Eddie Kamae formed the Sons of Hawai'i. Their 1971 album was a top-seller, and he became the favorite star of the local Hawaiian concert scene. A modest man of humble means, often appearing in overalls or with a grandchild on his knees, the genius of his artistry was described by an observer as "his uncanny ability to bring out the very soul of the music he plays." [*Hawai'i Observer*]

1970—Hawai'i's population is 769,913 people.

1970, October 9—Two thousand hotel workers, represented by the ILWU, strike.

1971—The first annual Pipeline Masters surf contest is held on O'ahu's north shore.

1971, January 1—Transit workers represented by Hawai'i Teamsters Local 996 strike against the Honolulu Rapid Transit Company. The strike lasts for two months, inconveniencing 70,000 commuters and leading to the creation of a city transportation system.

1971, July 1—A major strike by West Coast and Hawai'i dockworkers begins with 15,000 members stopping work until October of 1971 when President Nixon halts the strike for 90 days. The strike resumes the day after Christmas and continues until February.

1972—The annual visitor count of the Hawaiian Islands exceeds two million.

1973—Elvis Presley performs at O'ahu's Honolulu International Center in his "Aloha From Hawai'i" concert, broadcast live via satellite to an estimated 1.5 billion people worldwide.

When Governor Burns died in office in 1973, Lt. Governor George Ariyoshi took over the reins of the Democratic Party and the State of Hawai'i. Often described as "quiet but effective," Governor Ariyoshi won the 1974 election, becoming Hawai'i's first chief executive of Japanese-American ancestry. The Democrats continued to consolidate their power base when he won re-election in 1978 and 1982. At one point, the party machine was so strong some islanders wondered if a Republican Party was even necessary. While the Ariyoshi administration responded to growing criticism about development with a platform of "selective growth" and "diversification," economic dependency on tourism intensified. Trends in Asia soon launched the Islands on a roller-coaster ride of Japanese investment. [Hawai'i State Archives]

1973—The first Honolulu Marathon is held.

1973, April 26—An earthquake in Hilo causes an estimated $1 million in damage.

1974—George Ariyoshi is elected as governor, becoming the first U.S. governor of Japanese-American ancestry. Formerly an attorney, Ariyoshi had been elected to the Territorial Legislature in 1954 before serving as John Burns' lieutenant governor, and then as acting governor when Burns became ill in 1973.

1975—Commercial whale-watching trips to view humpback whales begin in Hawaiian waters, first off Maui and then eventually around all the major Islands.

1975, March 8—The *Hōkūle'a* voyaging canoe, built to show that migrating Polynesians could have sailed east against the prevailing winds, is launched and completes its first voyage to Tahiti in 1976.

1975, September 12—Aloha Stadium, hosting baseball and football games as well as concerts, opens. The first game in the ten-story-tall stadium takes place on September 13, 1975 when 32,247 fans watch the University of Hawai'i Warriors play Texas A&I.

1975, November 29—Two strong earthquakes shake the southeast region of Hawai'i Island, generating a localized tsunami that kills two people.

1975—The National Guard is called to restore order at Hawai'i State Prison after a prisoner takeover.

Of all the recent manifestations of the Hawaiian Renaissance, no one event has had a more dramatic effect than the 1976 voyage of the *Hōkūle'a*, a sixty-foot-long replica of the ancient double-hulled migration canoe that brought the first Polynesians to Hawai'i a thousand years ago. One of the members of the early *Hōkūle'a* voyages was Clay Bertelmann, a cowboy at Parker Ranch in Waimea. In 1993, Bertelmann founded Na Kālai Wa'a Moku o Hawai'i, a Big Island voyaging program. Along with Mau Piailug, the Micronesian navigator who mentored the crew of the *Hōkūle'a*, Bertelmann built the Big Island's own voyaging canoe, the fifty-four-foot Makali'i, whose maiden voyage came in February, 1995. The Makali'i voyaging program continues as one of the Islands' most important platforms to reconnect Hawaiian youths with their heritage, roots, and traditions. After Bertelmann's death in January, 2004, the voyaging 'ohana pledged to build a voyaging canoe for Mau Piailug and the people of Micronesia as a symbol of gratitude and unity. The *Alingano Maisu* was built in Kawaihae and given to Mau in 2007. Today, Na Kālai Wa'a continues its educational and cultural programs from its home in Māhukona. [Alexis Higdon]

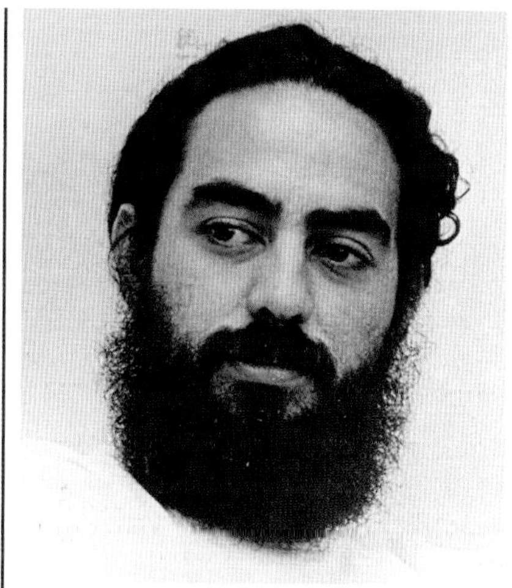

George Helm, talented Hawaiian musician/singer who became passionately involved with the issues of "Aloha 'Āina" (love for the land) and the misuse of Kaho'olawe. He disappeared at sea while returning from Kaho'olawe to Maui on a surfboard after having searched for other activists whom he feared were marooned. He was a sensitive, articulate, and gentle man, deeply concerned about Hawai'i's future. [Alexis Higdon]

1975—The Sugar Act expires, leading to the end of quotas and tariffs originally enacted to maintain prices of United States sugar. It eventually causes Hawai'i's plantations to shut down.

1976, January 4—Hawaiians organize a grass-roots protest movement known as the Protect Kaho'olawe 'Ohana. The group leads the first protest occupation of Kaho'olawe in an effort to stop the use of the island as a military bombing target. Seven of the nine protesters occupying the island are arrested within hours, but two protesters are not caught and remain on the island for three days.

1977—The southwest O'ahu region of Kapolei is envisioned as a second major metropolitan center of O'ahu by city planners and the Campbell Estate, owners of the former sugarcane land. Today Kapolei is one of the island's fastest growing areas with commercial, resort, and residential projects.

1977—George Jarrett Helm Jr. and James "Kimo" Mitchell disappear during their attempt to reclaim the island of Kaho'olawe for native Hawaiians.

1978—During a State Constitutional Convention, the Office of Hawaiian Affairs is created, and Hawaiian is also declared an official language of the State of Hawai'i.

1978—The Nā Hōkū Hanohano Awards are established to recognize excellence in the recording arts in Hawai'i by the Hawaiian Academy of Recording Arts (HARA).

1978, February 18—The first Ironman Triathlon competition includes a 2.4-mile ocean swim, 112-mile bike race, and 26.2 mile marathon. Twelve of the fifteen entrants complete the race. Today the event is known as the Ironman Triathlon World Championship and 50,000 people from 50 countries compete in qualifying races to become one of up to 2,000 entrants allowed in the Championship held each year in Kona on Hawai'i Island. Tens of thousands of spectators line the route to watch the race, which is also televised.

MOMENT IN HISTORY

THE LAUNCHING OF THE *HŌKŪLEʻA*
MARCH 8, 1975

Thousands gathered at the sacred beach of Kualoa on Oʻahu's windward side for a truly momentous event: the launching of the first voyaging canoe in hundreds of years to leave Hawaiʻi for Tahiti. Distinguished Native Hawaiian chanters presided over traditional religious ceremonies. Christian blessings were also offered as the *Hōkūleʻa* began its historic journey.

The construction of an ocean-going canoe in the ancient style was the vision of members of the Polynesian Voyaging Society. In 1975, they successfully completed a sixty-two-foot, two-masted, double-hulled vessel with eight ʻiako, or crossbeams, joining the hull. A pola, or platform, was lashed to the crossbeams. Society members intended to demonstrate that ancient Polynesians did not settle the Hawaiian Islands by accident. Scholars had argued that regular travel in the Pacific over thousands of miles was impossible without a compass or sextant, but the builders of the *Hōkuleʻa* were convinced it could be done using only the ancient method of studying the stars, the currents, cloud formations, and other clues of nature.

A year later, the *Hōkūleʻa* and her crew successfully completed their first voyage to and from Tahiti, relying solely on traditional forms of navigation. A resurgence of pride in the accomplishments of ancient Hawaiian civilization poured forth. The *Hōkūleʻa* went on to sail throughout the Pacific, and Native Hawaiians shrugged off scholars' theories about their history and continued to reclaim their cultural inheritance.

1978, March 17—The *Hōkūleʻa* voyaging canoe capsizes in large swells and gale-force winds twelve miles off the island of Lānaʻi, forcing the crew's 15 members to cling to the canoe's overturned hull. Eddie Aikau volunteers to paddle his surfboard toward Lānaʻi for help and is never seen again. His unselfish act becomes known as "Eddie Would Go."

1978, November—Jean King becomes Hawaiʻi's first female lieutenant governor.

1979—The annual visitor count of the Hawaiian Islands exceeds four million people.

Honolulu Star-Bulletin
Home ★★★★
Festive End for an Odyssey

Honolulu Star-Bulletin
Home
Ariyoshi Calls Emergency; Gas Rules Start Monday
Ethics Panel Clears Mayor
Gas Czar Evinces Optimism
Rationing Might Be Necessary

Honolulu Star-Bulletin
Tenants Burn It
Waiahole Gets Eviction Order
Farmers, Supporters Dig In
FBI Agents Will Escape Prosecution for Corruption

The *Hōkūle'a* Voyaging Canoe—Rediscovering the Past

In the 1970s, members of the Polynesian Voyaging Society constructed a voyaging canoe called the *Hōkūle'a* (hōkū means "star" and le'a means "happiness," or "joy"), to show that migrating Polynesians could have sailed east against the prevailing winds. Launched on March 8, 1975, the *Hōkūle'a* completed its first voyage to Tahiti in 1976.

Still sailing today, the *Hōkūle'a* has two 62-foot long kuamo'o (hulls), eight 'iako (crossbeams) joining the two hulls, two kia (masts), and pola (decking). Weighing about eight tons, the canoe can reach speeds up to twelve knots and can carry more than five tons including a crew of twelve to sixteen and supplies.

When in 1980 Nainoa Thompson led the original crew that sailed to Tahiti, he became the first Hawaiian in centuries to navigate a voyaging canoe. Many more *Hōkūle'a* voyages took place, including a 1995 voyage to the Marquesas. When the *Hōkūle'a* crew sailed around the Hawaiian Islands in 1996–1997, it allowed thousands of school children to visit or sail. The canoe has now sailed over 100,000 nautical miles, including six major continental and Pan-Pacific voyages.

Eddie Would Go

In 1978, the *Hōkūle'a* voyaging canoe capsized off Moloka'i. Crew member Eddie Aikau, a respected lifeguard, surfer, and Hawaiian waterman, paddled a surfboard toward land to get help, but was never seen again. The rest of the crew was eventually rescued.

Eddie, the third of six children, was the son of Solomon "Pops" Aikau and his wife Henrietta. Born May 4, 1946 in Kahului, Maui, he was a full-blooded Hawaiian. His father often took the family surfing with a classic 75-pound surfboard.

In 1967, Eddie surfed 15-foot Sunset Beach waves and on November 19 of that year he startled Hawai'i's top surfers by taking off on an estimated 40-foot set wave at Waimea Bay. That same year he took sixth place in his first major surf contest, the Duke Kahanamoku Classic.

In 1968, Eddie became Waimea Bay's first lifeguard and went on to save many people. He was voted Lifeguard of the Year in 1971, and later appeared in surf movies. Also a talented musician, he wrote songs and was proficient at slack-key guitar.

In 1978, Eddie was chosen to be one of the 16-member crew invited to sail on the *Hōkūle'a*. On the night of March 16, 1978 the *Hōkūle'a* capsized in large swells and gale-force winds twelve miles off the island of Lāna'i forcing the 15 crew members to cling to the canoe's overturned hull. Eddie Aikau volunteered to paddle his twelve-foot tandem surfboard toward Lāna'i for help. As he stroked away from the capsized *Hōkūle'a*, Eddie stopped and tossed off his life preserver which was hampering his paddling. As he rose to the peak of a swell he turned and gave the crew a final wave goodbye and paddled into the distance never to be seen again.

A Hawaiian Airlines plane later saw a flare shot up by the *Hōkūle'a* and a Coast Guard helicopter arrived and tossed a metal cage down to rescue the stranded crew. An intensive five day air-sea search and rescue effort was unable to find Eddie.

In 1987, a surf contest was initiated in honor of Eddie. Officially known as the Quiksilver in Memory of Eddie Aikau, the contest became known locally as "The Eddie," pitting the world's best big wave surfers against each other. The contest only commences if waves reach the 20 to 30 foot heights considered worthy of his name. The second Eddie was won by Clyde Aikau, his brother.

Eddie Aikau was known for his humility, never seeking thanks or praise for his many heroic deeds. Today the saying "Eddie Would Go" is frequently seen on local bumper stickers and heard throughout the Islands, recalling Eddie Aikau's selflessness and bravery.

1980–1989

1980—Hawai'i's population reaches 964,691.

1980—Protect Kaho'olawe 'Ohana enters into an agreement with the U.S. Navy that authorizes an archeological survey, goat eradication, and clearance of weapons materials from the island's surface. Work begins even though military training on Kaho'olawe continues.

1980—The CBS television series *Hawaii Five-O,* starring Jack Lord as Steve McGarrett, ends after twelve seasons. It was the first network series to be filmed only in Hawai'i, and the longest-running TV crime drama.

1981, March 18—Kaho'olawe is placed on the National Register of Historic Places.

1982—The population of Hawai'i exceeds 1 million.

1982-83—The University of Hawai'i Rainbow Wahine women's volleyball team wins back-to-back NCAA championships.

1982, November 3—Hurricane 'Iwa passes between Kaua'i and Ni'ihau with gusts of wind exceeding 100 miles per hour and causing $239 million damage.

1983, January 3—A flank eruption on the East Rift Zone of Kīlauea Volcano at Nāpau Crater sends up 250-foot fountains of lava. The activity moves to Pu'u 'Ō'ō Vent in June with lava fountains 1,400 feet high. Lava flows eventually reach the Royal Gardens subdivision, burying or burning 16 homes.

1983, August—In one of Hawai'i's most famous corporate scandals, the investment firm of Bishop, Baldwin, Rewald, Dillingham and Wong collapses financially due to the manipulations of Ron Rewald, who deceives a large number of people by purporting to have many local connections, throwing lavish parties, and staging polo matches. Rewald's activities result in a loss of about $20 million by 418 investors. In 1985, Rewald is convicted of 94 counts of tax evasion, perjury, and fraud, and sentenced to 18 years in federal prison. He is released in 1995 due to a back injury.

1983—A flank eruption on the East Rift Zone of Kīlauea Volcano begins, and has continued almost uninterrupted to the present day, making it the longest continuously erupting volcano on Earth today. Since 1983, Kīlauea Volcano has released more than 67 billion cubic feet of lava that has covered more than 40 square miles, increasing the size of Hawai'i Island by more than 535 acres.

Wednesday **Honolulu Star-Bulletin**

A Gannett Newspaper

Islands Assess Damag

Two Storm-Relat Deaths Are Listec

A Minute-by-Minute Monitoring of Hurricane Iw

Rainbow Wahines—They're Incredible!!!

Pull Off Miracle Comeback for NCAA Volleyball Crown

USC's Clark MVP

Star-Bulletin SPORTS Section D

Hurricane 'Iwa struck O'ahu and Kaua'i in November of 1982, resulting in one death and $250 million in damage. During this natural disaster, islanders braced themselves against sustained winds clocked at 65 mph, with gusts up to 117 mph. *[Honolulu Advertiser]*

Ellison S. Onizuka became Hawai'i's first astronaut, representing the hopes and aspirations of all young Islanders who yearned to reach for the stars. Born in Kona, Hawai'i and educated in the public schools, Onizuka was selected by NASA to be a member of the crew of the *Challenger* Flight SI-L. The tragic explosion of the *Challenger* space shuttle on January 28, 1986 stunned the nation and cast the Islands into mourning for a native son. [Rod Thompson/*Honolulu Star-Bulletin*]

STOCKS | SPORTS | INDEX

HOME EDITION

TUESDAY

Honolulu Star-Bulletin

A GANNETT NEWSPAPER

Space Shuttle Explodes; All 7 Aboard Are Killed

Tragedy Claims McAuliffe and Big Island's Onizuka

UH Regent Tells of Shock, Grief, Tears After Blast

Stunned President Reagan Defends NASA Safety Record

STOCKS | FOOD | TODAY | INDEX

Honolulu Star-Bulletin

Feb. 26, 1986

Marcos Arrives in Isles

Exiled Dictator, Family to Stay at Hickam Base

Marcos' Restrained Arrival Here a Sharp Contrast to Other Visits

Aquino Picks Cabinet; Amnesty Planned

1983—C. Brewer & Co. becomes the world's largest producer of macadamia nuts.

1985—Businessman David H. Murdock, chief executive of the "Big Five" company Castle & Cooke, purchases ninety-eight percent of the island of Lāna'i. He ends pineapple production and initiates the construction of two new luxury resorts, the Mānele Bay Hotel, and the Lodge at Kō'ele, as well as expensive townhouses.

1985—The Quiksilver In Memory of Eddie Aikau surf contest is initiated matching the world's best big wave surfers in the biggest of waves. The first "Eddie" is won by Denton Miyamura. In 1986, Clyde Aikau, Eddie Aikau's brother, is the winner.

1986, January 28—Ellison Onizuka, the first Hawai'i-born astronaut and the first Japanese-American to fly in space, dies along with the crew of the space shuttle *Challenger* when it explodes after takeoff from Florida's Kennedy Space Center. Major Onizuka initially flew into space aboard the space shuttle *Discovery* in 1985.

1986, February 25—Ousted Philippines dictator Ferdinand Marcos arrives in exile aboard a U.S. Air Force transport plane with his wife Imelda and 89 relatives, friends and assistants as well as $8 million in cash and jewels. He lives lavishly for the next three and a half years before succumbing to illness on September 28, 1989.

1986—John D. Waihe'e is elected governor becoming the first elected U.S. governor of Hawaiian ancestry. He serves until 1994.

Wow! Robin still gets 'em
Batman's sidekick scores as a financial whiz
Noriega will resign defense post
Leading indicators shoot up 0.8%
UH spikers advance to regional finals

Honolulu Star-Bulletin
THE PULSE OF PARADISE
FRIDAY, APRIL 29, 1988 — 35 CENTS

Miracle over Maui: Blast spares 94

The Honorable John Waihe'e, shown here with First Lady Lynne Waihe'e strolling across the grounds of 'Iolani Palace, was inaugurated on December 1, 1986. As the first elected Hawaiian governor, Waihe'e said, "I clearly understand that I am a symbol of Hawaiian pride in what we are in the present and what we can become in the future." [Ken Sakamoto / *Honolulu Star-Bulletin*]

1986—The State of Hawai'i annual visitor count exceeds five million. Tourism continues as the driving force of Hawai'i's economy.

1986—Mary Kawena Pūku'i, one of Hawai'i's most revered scholars of Hawaiian culture, passes away at the age of 91.

1988, April 28—Aloha Airlines Flight 243 is en route from Hilo to Honolulu when a large chunk of the jet's roof and walls are suddenly torn from the plane's cabin. A flight attendant standing at seat row five disappears through the hole in the left side of the fuselage. Another flight attendant is hit in the head by the windstorm of debris and suffers head lacerations and a concussion. Sixty-five unspecified injuries are sustained, eight of which are considered "serious." The $5 million dollar Aloha Airlines Boeing 737 airplane is safely landed but sustains major damage and has to be dismantled and sold for parts and scrap.

1988—The *Magnum P.I.* television series, starring Tom Selleck and filmed in Hawai'i, ends after eight seasons.

1988—The tourist industry represents 32 percent of the state's economy, up from 3 percent in the 1950s. Japanese investment capital, which drives Hawai'i's economy along with tourism, decreases significantly in the 1990s contributing to an economic downturn.

The 1980s increase in Japanese visitors to the Islands was a driving force behind the upscale services and products sold in Waikīkī. While their length of stay was far less than the U.S. mainland visitor, the daily amount of money spent was remarkably higher due to the weak U.S. dollar and the Japanese custom of omiyage, or souvenir gift-giving. To capitalize on these free-spending consumers, exclusive stores proliferated. [Charles Okamura/*The Honolulu Advertiser*]

1989—Shortly after taking off from Honolulu Airport, a United Airlines 747 flying to Sydney, Australia experiences an electrical short that causes a cargo door to open resulting in an explosive decompression and loss of power in two engines. Nine passengers are sucked out of the plane over the ocean. The plane lands safely.

270 Maui students to attend school year-round in state test/A-3

Honolulu Star-Bulletin
THE PULSE OF PARADISE
SATURDAY, APRIL 30, 1988 — 35 CENTS

Flight of terror: Weak hull hinted

McGarrett Books 'Em for the Last Time

By Jerry Buck, Associated Press

Lord's 5-0 badge

Lord when he started the series in 1968.

Lord as he will finish the series next month.

Star-Bulletin Today Features Entertainment

Left: By the 1980s, Honolulu no longer offered cheap and simple living but had grown into an expansive freeway-culture city. [*Honolulu Advertiser*]

Below: The traveler's nightmare: late in the 1980s aging passenger jets start coming apart in midair. The finger of tragic bad luck points at Hawai'i, not once but twice: Aloha Airlines Flight 243, Hilo-Honolulu, April 28, 1988 (pictured) and United Airlines Flight 811 departing Honolulu for Sydney, February 24, 1989. [*Honolulu Advertiser*]

1990—Hawai'i's population is now 1,108,228.

1990—Daniel Akaka becomes the first U.S. Senator of Native Hawaiian ancestry.

1990—Lava flows from Kīlauea Volcano destroy numerous homes in and around Kalapana Gardens along with the country store and the Mauna Kea Congregational Church. By the end of 1990 the destruction totals 181 homes, and the black sand beach on crescent-shaped Kaimū Bay is filled with lava.

EXTRA
Bone-marrow advocate Tamashiro dies
Simpson wins the Shoot-out at Waialae
Honolulu Star-Bulletin
WAR!
U.S. launches Desert Storm

1990, January 17—Operation Desert Storm begins in response to Iraq's invasion of Kuwait on August 2, 1989. More than 7,000 troops based in Kāne'ohe serve.

1991, August—Hawai'i Regional Cuisine, Inc. is developed on Maui by twelve Island chefs who form the association to develop a world-class cuisine.

Hawai'i's chefs achieved national and international fame in the 1990s with the creation and export of Hawai'i Regional Cuisine. [Steven Minkowski]

Bows' Santiago might leave QB corps
Honolulu Star-Bulletin
Bush halts Kahoolawe bombing
Oil prices plunge on peace talk
Rounding up the stray calf

1990, October 22—President George Bush ends the use of Kaho'olawe for bombing practice and creates a congressional commission to return the island to the Hawaiian people.

1992—The Keck Telescope, the largest optical-infrared telescope in the world, becomes operable atop Mauna Kea. In 1996, Keck II becomes operable, and in March of 2001 the light-gathering powers of the two Keck telescopes are combined.

1992, September 11—Hurricane 'Iniki directly hits Kaua'i, damaging 14,000 homes, causing $1.8 billion in damage and shutting down 90 percent of the island's vacation accommodations.

1992, November 4—A large area around the Hawaiian Islands is designated as the Hawaiian Islands Humpback Whale National Marine Sanctuary. Governor Benjamin Cayetano approves the

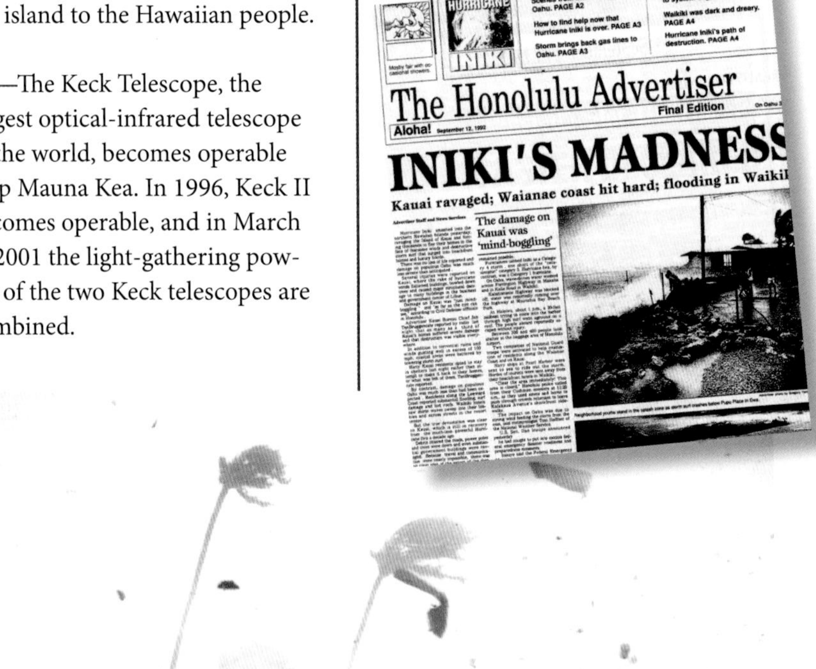

HURRICANE INIKI
The Honolulu Advertiser
Final Edition
Aloha!
INIKI'S MADNESS
Kauai ravaged; Waianae coast hit hard; flooding in Waikiki
The damage on Kauai was 'mind-boggling'

Hurricane 'Iniki was an unexpected visitor that brought death and destruction in September of 1992 as it surged over the Leeward Coast of O'ahu and slammed head-on into Kaua'i with sustained winds of 130-160 mph and gusts up to an extraordinary 217 mph. Four people were killed, and over a hundred injured in the most devastating storm of the century. Total damage was estimated at $1.8 billion, crippling Kaua'i's economy for years. [Bruce Asato / *Honolulu Advertiser*]

Hawai'i's sumotori—Akebono (Chad Rowan of Waimanalo) (shown); Musashimaru (Fiamalu Penitani of Wai'anae); and Konishiki (Salevaa Atisanoe)—achieved recognition and acclaim for both the Islands and themselves with their athletic performances and personal popularity. [Mutual Publishing]

Sanctuary in State of Hawai'i waters on June 5, 1997.

1992, December—Ground is broken on the University of Hawai'i's $32.24 million Special Events Arena, (later renamed the Stan Sheriff Center in 1998), built to hold 10,031 people. On October 21, 1994, a UH Rainbow Wahine volleyball game becomes its first athletic event.

1993, January 13–18—The 'Onipa'a Centennial Observance of the 100th anniversary of the overthrow of the Hawaiian monarchy takes place in downtown Honolulu including a pro-sovereignty march from Aloha Tower to 'Iolani Palace.

1993, January 27—At the age of 23, Hawai'i-born Akebono (Chad Rowan) becomes the first sumo wrestler not born in Japan to achieve the esteemed sumo rank of Yokozuna (Grand Champion). He retires in 2001 at the age of 31 with a record of 566-198 including 11 championships.

Hurricane 'Iniki Devastates Kaua'i

On September 11, 1992, Hurricane 'Iniki directly hit the island of Kaua'i causing more than $1.8 billion in property damage and damaging more than 70 percent of Kaua'i's homes including 1,421 that were completely destroyed. Kaua'i residents endured ferocious winds as they huddled in shelters. Airborne debris crashed violently into buildings and smashed windows. Whole roofs detached and broke apart, and were lifted upward to disappear into the vortices of wind. Entire houses were blown off their foundations. Then suddenly the wind stopped. It was still cloudy, but there was now pure blue sky above the clouds, a welcome sight amidst all the destruction. The hurricane had not passed, however, but instead was actually directly overhead! Within minutes, as the hurricane's eye moved past, the full force of the hurricane was again felt, this time all at once as devastating winds exceeded 100 miles per hour. With the wind now going in the opposite direction, structures that had been weakened to the collapsing point by the first half of the hurricane were now quickly finished off. One ferocious gust of wind within the hurricane was clocked at 217 miles per hour.

In 1992, Benjamin Cayetano became Hawai'i's first governor of Filipino ancestry. He immediately faced a declining economy due to tourism slumping and the depletion of state revenues. During his 1998 re-election campaign, the Democratic Party, which had been in power for decades, came under fire from within and without. A rejuvenated Republican Party mounted a strong challenge, and Cayetano won by only a narrow margin of votes. [George Kodama / Governor's Office]

'Onipa'a Centennial Observance

From January 13th to January 18th of 1993, the 'Onipa'a Centennial Observance of the 100th anniversary of the overthrow of the Hawaiian monarchy was held in downtown Honolulu. On January 17, the day of the anniversary of the overthrow, a procession of 10,000 pro-sovereignty supporters marched from Aloha Tower to 'Iolani Palace. Governor John Waihee ordered the American flag lowered and the Hawaiian flag raised on government buildings in the Capitol District area while Native Hawaiians and their supporters called for the restoration of Hawaiian sovereignty, declaring the overthrow of the monarchy an illegal act. 'Onipa'a meaning "Stand firm," was the motto of Lili'uokalani.

Above, upper: During 'Onipa'a, over ten thousand kanaka maoli and their supporters gathered at 'Iolani Palace to lament the overthrow of a nation and celebrate the possibility of a restoration of sovereignty and self-determination. Thousands of marchers approached 'Iolani Palace while their Ka Lāhui Hawai'i supporters lined the streets. [Bruce Asato / *Honolulu Advertiser*]

Lower: Over four days in January of 1993, thousands of Native Hawaiians and their supporters of all ages and backgrounds gathered at 'Iolani Palace to relive the overthrow of the monarchy and voice concerns about injustices committed against the Hawaiian nation. This historic "'Onipa'a" commemoration included a group of Roosevelt High School students who entered the Palace grounds with a greeting chant in honor of Queen Lili'uokalani. ['Onipa'a Committee]

WITNESS TO HISTORY

ʻONIPAʻA...THE DAWN OF A NEW HAWAIIAN NATION JANUARY 17, 1993

For several days the capitol district in downtown Honolulu was filled with thousands of Native Hawaiians and their supporters of all races, gathered in memory of events a century earlier, when the Hawaiian monarchy had been overthrown. The ceremonies were named in honor of Liliʻuokalani, whose motto "ʻOnipaʻa" means "steadfast." Activities ranged from official speeches and floral offerings at the queen's statue to sovereignty rallies to a "living history" reenactment of scenes from 1893 when the monarch was illegally overthrown.

The ceremonies culminated with a torchlight procession through the streets of downtown Honolulu on the evening of January 17, 1993, ending at the steps of ʻIolani Palace. The solemn mood was intensified by a master chanter who repeatedly intoned "auwē!," or "alas!" during a mele kanikau, or chant of mourning. Following speeches by the American Samoan delegate to Congress and two Hawaiʻi State Senators, "The Queen Prayer" was sung. This affecting piece had been composed by Liliʻuokalani during her imprisonment in the palace. Finally, all torches were extinguished except for two placed at the statue of the queen.

One participant noted that these events marked the "dawn of a new Hawaiian nation." What form that nation will take, and its ramifications for all the people of Hawaiʻi, is the greatest challenge of the next millennium.

Hawaiians, friends and sympathizers gathered at ʻIolani Palace to recognize and protest the 100th anniversary of Hawaiʻi's Annexation by the United States ins 1898. Here a hula hālau chants a mele of protest. [Ed Greevy]

On August 29, 1992, the Hālawa Coalition, a group of mostly Hawaiian women, blocked access to concrete delivery trucks heading toward a major concrete pour during the H-3 freeway construction. The Coalition was resisting deconstruction of a newly discovered women's heiau, Hale O Papa. The freeway was rerouted because of concerns raised by the Coalition and others. [Ed Greevy]

The *Hawai'iloa* Voyaging Canoe

Launched in 1993, the 57-foot-long *Hawai'iloa* voyaging canoe was the first voyaging canoes to be built almost entirely out of traditional materials. It was modified and launched again in 1994, making its first voyage in 1995. With no navigational instruments, its crew sailed more than 6,000 miles, from the Hawaiian Islands to Tahiti and the Marquesas and then back to Hawai'i.

The *Hawai'iloa* was named after an ancient voyager who, according to legend, was the first discoverer of the Hawaiian Islands. For the ship's two hulls, old growth Sitka spruce trees were acquired from southeast Alaska as there were no longer any large Hawaiian koa trees available. The use of Sitka spruce may be considered traditional since ancient Hawaiians sometimes used drift logs, possibly from Alaska, to make canoes.

Traditional materials and tools were used whenever possible. Every attempt was made to build an accurate replica of a traditional voyaging canoe with different native trees to create the canoe's various components. Traditional tools used to construct voyaging canoes and their various parts before Western contact included the stone adze and the bone gouge. Coral files were also used, as well as sharkskin for sanding.

1993, November 23—Acknowledging the 100th anniversary of the overthrow of the Hawaiian monarchy, United States President William J. Clinton signs Public Law 103-150, an apology to native Hawaiians on behalf of the United States, written as a Joint Resolution of Congress.

1994—Aloha Tower Marketplace is built at Honolulu Harbor's Piers 8, 9, 10 and 11. The architects are Burno D'Agostino and Edward R. Aotani & Associates.

1994—Benjamin Cayetano, lieutenant governor under John D. Waihee, is elected governor of Hawai'i, becoming the first United States governor of Filipino-American descent. He serves until 2002.

1994—Under a congressional appropriations act and presidential order, the island of Kaho'olawe is returned to the State of Hawai'i.

1995—The *Hawai'iloa* voyaging canoe built almost entirely out of traditional materials makes its first voyage.

1995, June 4—Pope John Paul II beatifies Father Damien in Brussels, Belgium, bringing him one step closer to sainthood. Father Damien had ministered to Hansen's disease patients at Kalaupapa, Moloka'i from 1873 until his death in 1889.

1996—The First Hawaiian Center is dedicated in downtown Honolulu, becoming Hawai'i's tallest building at over 428 feet.

1997, June 26—Renowned Hawaiian musician Israel Ka'ano'i Kamakawiwo'ole passes away at age 38 and is memorialized by thousands at the State Capitol Rotunda.

Bruddah Iz (1959–1997)

A pure-blooded Hawaiian, Israel Ka'ano'i Kamakawiwo'ole was born on May 20, 1959 and lived in O'ahu's Pālolo Valley until the age of ten when his family moved to Mākaha. The next year he and his brother Skippy began playing music, and a few years later they joined Louis "Moon" Kauakahi, Sam Gray, and Jerome Koko to form the Mākaha Sons of Ni'ihau.

During the next 15 years. The Mākaha Sons released ten albums, toured the United States, and won numerous Nā Hōkū Hanohano awards. They also hosted the annual Mākaha Bash on Memorial Day at the Waikīkī Shell.

In 1982 Israel's brother, Skippy Kamakawiwo'ole, passed away. That same year Israel married his childhood sweetheart, Marlene Ku'upua Ah Lo, with whom he had a daughter, Ceslieanne Wehekealake'alekupuna "Wehi" Kamakawiwo'ole.

Iz began his solo career in 1993 with the album Facing Future, and quickly became Hawai'i's most popular entertainer and singer. The album N DIS LIFE released in 1997 won four Nā Hōkū Hanohano awards: Male Vocalist; Island Contemporary; Album Graphics; and Favorite Entertainer of the Year.

Israel passed away of respiratory failure at age 38 on June 26, 1997. He was memorialized by thousands at the State Capitol Rotunda, and his ashes were scattered off Mākua Beach. In 2001 a new CD, Alone in IZ World, was released and immediately became a top seller.

1997, August 9—An article titled "Broken Trust," written by prominent community members including a former Kamehameha Schools principal, calls for Bishop Estate reforms. Three days later, the governor asks State Attorney General Margery Bronster to investigate the matter eventually leading to the removal of the trustees.

1997, December 12—Opening ceremonies are held for the H-3 "Trans-Ko'olau" freeway connecting Honolulu to Kailua and Kāne'ohe on O'ahu's Windward side. The 16.1-mile-long freeway took 30 years to complete due to legal battles, design changes, and controversy about intruding on

The music of Israel "Bruddah Iz" Kamakawiwo'ole captured the hearts of thousands of Islanders and carried the message of Hawaiian pride around the world. In 1997, the untimely death of "Bruddah Iz," whose haunting melodies such as "E Ala Ē" and "N Dis Life" endeared him to his people, was deeply mourned. His body lay in state at the State Capitol before his ashes were scattered at sea off Mākua Valley. [Mountain Apple]

The Bishop Estate Scandal

On August 9, 1997, the *Honolulu Star-Bulletin* published an article titled "Broken Trust," written by a former Kamehameha Schools principal and three other prominent community members, calling for reform. Three days later, the governor asked State Attorney General Margery Bronster to investigate the matter.

On May 6, 1999, Circuit Judge Bambi Weil removed Lokelani Lindsey from her position as a Trustee of Bishop Estate due to "poor judgment...creation of a climate of fear...misappropriation of trust assets to her own benefit," and "breaches of loyalty and trust," a decision resulting from a lawsuit filed by fellow trustees Oswald Stender and Gerard Jervis. The next day judge Kevin Chang removed four of the five trustees: Richard Wong, Lokelani Lindsey, Henry Peters, and Gerard Jervis, and accepted the resignation of the fifth trustee, Oswald Stender.

NIGHT FINAL

Honolulu Star-Bulletin

Y2K bug threatens party plans

Broken trust, broken lives

Bishop's 'bizarre' problems deepen

exclusive

After a tragic death, a husband describes a warm, caring wife and a happy marriage

The seeds of major new economic and population centers for the twenty-first century were planted in the 1990s at Kapolei on O'ahu (pictured) and Kīhei on Maui. [Douglas Peebles]

the culturally significant Hālawa and Ha'ikū valleys. The freeway cost $1.3 billion making it the most expensive public works project in Hawai'i's history with 26 bridges, two long viaducts, and two sets of tunnels—4,890-feet-long in the Kāne'ohe-bound direction and 5,165 feet in the Hālawa-bound direction.

1998—Rell Kapolioka'ehukai Sunn, the "Queen of Mākaha," passes away due

Rell Sunn, affectionately known as the Queen of Mākaha, excelled not only at surfing, but also at bodysurfing, outrigger canoe paddling, and spearfishing. An all around waterwoman, she was Hawai'i's first female lifeguard, an international surfing champion, and founder of the Women's Professional Surfing Association, which, in the 1970s, helped develop the first women's pro surfing tour.

In 1982, she was ranked number one in the world in women's longboard surfing. Her middle name, Kapolioka'ehukai, given to her by her grandmother, means *"Heart of the sea."* [*Honolulu Star-Bulletin*]

U.S.S *Missouri* Battleship and U.S.S. *Bowfin* Submarine

Japan officially surrendered on September 2, 1945 on the deck of the U.S.S. *Missouri* battleship, the "Mighty Mo." Originally launched in 1944, the U.S.S. *Missouri* was permanently decommissioned on March 31, 1992. On January 29, 1999, the 58,000-ton ship docked at Pearl Harbor's Battleship Row, just a few hundred yards from the U.S.S. *Arizona* Memorial. The U.S.S. *Missouri* had a 50-year career serving in World War II (in the battles of Iwo Jima and Okinawa), Korea, and Operation Desert Storm in the Persian Gulf.

Also located at Pearl Harbor is the U.S.S. *Bowfin* submarine, which was first launched one year after the 1941 Pearl Harbor attack. The submarine known as the "Pearl Harbor Avenger," carried a crew of 80 and sunk 44 ships in the Pacific Ocean. A memorial on board honors the 3,500 submariners who were lost during the war along with 52 U.S. submarines.

to cancer. Three thousand people attend her funeral at Mākaha.

1998, July 1—The four-story, 1.4-million-square-foot Hawai'i Convention Center opens to host major conventions and international events. The Center features a roof-top tropical garden, glass-encased meeting rooms, and outdoor palm-lined areas. It houses a $2 million permanent Hawaiian art collection.

1998—University of Hawai'i postdoctoral student Teruhiko Wakayama develops a new cloning technique that produces, from adult cells, three generations of genetically identical cloned mice.

1999, January 29—The 58,000-ton U.S.S. *Missouri* battleship opens as a tourist attraction at Pearl Harbor.

1999, May 9—A landslide at the popular O'ahu waterfall and swimming hole in Sacred Falls State Park kills eight people. Falling debris and boulders injure at least 42 others.

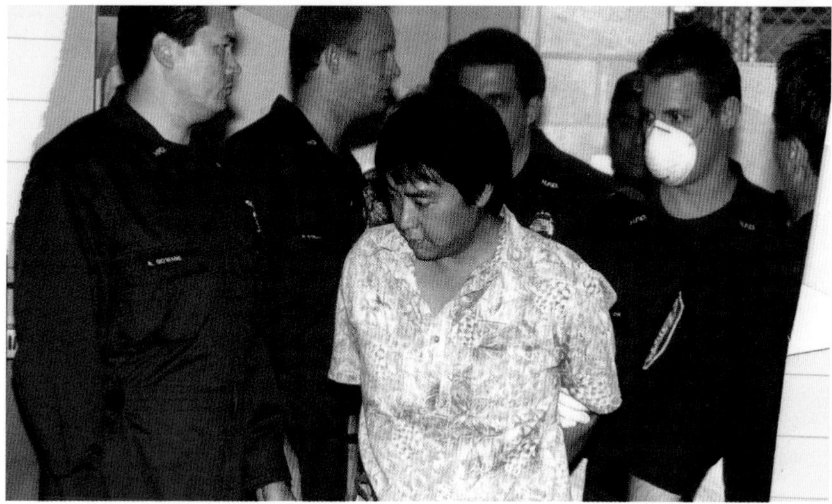

Xerox gunman Byran Uyesugi is brought into the receiving desk of the Honolulu Police Department following a six-hour standoff in Honolulu Park. [*Honolulu Star-Bulletin*]

1999—About 370,000 people go on whale-watching trips in Hawaiian waters, up 25 percent from a decade earlier. The ocean surrounding the Islands are the breeding and birthing waters of more than 4,000 humpback whales that arrive around October and stay as late as May.

1999, November 2—The worst mass murder in Hawai'i's history occurs when O'ahu Xerox worker Byron Uyesugi shoots seven co-workers. He surrenders to police after a five-hour standoff.

As Honolulu enters the second decade of the twenty-first century, the city is experiencing a condominium boom. More high rises are being built or are on the drawing boards particularly for Kapiʻolani Blvd., Kakaʻako and Waikīkī. With Honolulu's urban skyline becoming more dense, there is renewed concern about open space, congestion and environmental impact. Honolulu is a major urban center hosting millions of visitors every year, with rural areas now needing preservation more than ever. [Doug Peebles]

21ST CENTURY

2000— Hawai'i's population is 1,211,537 people, including 239,655 of Hawaiian ancestry. Twenty-one percent of the 1.21 million residents identify their ancestry as Japanese; 17.7 percent, Filipino; 16.3 percent, Hawaiian; 8.3 percent, Chinese. Visitor arrivals total 6,948,595, and visitor expenditures total $10.9 billion

2000, February—In the legal case *Rice vs. Cayetano,* the U.S. Supreme Court rules seven to two that Hawaiians-only voting in elections for trustees of the Office of Hawaiian Affairs (OHA) violates the 15th Amendment's ban on race-based voting restrictions. The court ruling is the result of a lawsuit against the state by Hawai'i Island rancher Harold "Freddy"

ONLINE EDITION

Honolulu Star-Bulletin

Top court backs Rice in OHA vote challenge

What happens with OHA trustees?

Rice, a fifth-generation kama'āina (born in Hawai'i) who was barred from voting in an OHA election.

2000, July—U.S. Senator Daniel Akaka introduces the Native Hawaiian Reorganization Act, known as the Akaka Bill, to provide federal recognition to native Hawaiians and protect federal funding of Hawaiian entitlements

ONLINE EDITION

Honolulu Star-Bulletin

U.S. nuke sub hits Japanese training vessel

EPHEDRINE

Hawaii specialists may visit Tibet sites

jeopardized by the recent U.S. Supreme Court decision in *Rice v. Cayetano*. Various versions of the bill have continued to stall in Congress, lacking the votes to pass.

2001, February 9—The fast-attack submarine U.S.S. *Greeneville* is engaged in a rapid-ascent surfacing drill nine miles south of Diamond Head when it crashes into the *Ehime Maru*, a fishing boat on a training expedition with Japan's Uwajima Fisheries High School. The submarine rips open the trawler's bulkheads and fuel tanks, killing four students, two teachers, and three of the *Ehime Maru*'s crew members and sinking the ship. In 2003, the Navy pays $13 million to the families of the victims.

2001, March—Engineers and scientists at the Keck telescopes atop Mauna Kea succeed in combining the light-gathering powers of the two 10-meter Keck telescopes, forming the world's largest optical interferometer. In 2002, they break the record for sighting the most distant objects ever seen by viewing a galaxy 15.5 billion light years away.

2001, April 5—Public education in the state is shut down by two major strikes involving 3,000 University of Hawai'i faculty and 10,000 public school teachers, the state's first combined upper and lower education strike.

Honolulu Star-Bulletin

SPRING DRILL

STEPS DOWN

GIVING UP

State, teachers far apart

Bulletin faces more challenges in future

Crew lauds Greeneville and its skipper

2001, September 11—Terrorists hijack four passenger jets, flying two into the World Trade Center towers in New York, crashing one into the Pentagon building in Arlington, Virginia, and crashing one jet in a Pennsylvania field. The attacks kill nearly 3,000 people, including more than 2,600 Americans, and at least nine with Hawai'i ties. Immediately after the attack, tourism in the Hawaiian Islands drops more than 30 percent.

2001—In a test flight from the Navy's Pacific Missile Range Facility on Kaua'i, NASA's solar-powered plane *Helios* soars to a height of 96,500 feet, setting a new record for solar-powered flight for a

SATURDAY ★ EDITION
Honolulu Star-Bulletin
Wahine win
Rep. Patsy Mink dies
Lockout expected to delay isle cargo

winged aircraft. The plane crashes during a flight on June 26, 2003 when its 247-foot wingspan suddenly begins bending and flapping, tearing the skin of the fragile craft and sending it plunging into the sea about ten miles offshore.

Although Republican Linda Lingle, mayor of the County of Maui, narrowly lost her 1998 bid for governor, Island politics were entering an era of new political alliances. In 2002, she became the first Republican governor in forty years and the first female Hawai'i governor. She was easily re-elected in 2006. [*Honolulu Star-Bulletin*]

2002, August 24—A United States postage stamp featuring Duke Kahanamoku is dedicated on the 112th anniversary of his birth.

2002, September 29—Representative Patsy Mink, who in 1964 became the first Asian-American woman elected to the U.S. Congress, passes away.

2002, November 5—Linda Lingle, the former mayor of Maui County, is elected governor of the State of Hawai'i, becoming the state's first ever female governor and the first Republican governor in 40 years.

2003, March 9—The Pearl Harbor-based submarine U.S.S. *Cheyenne* launches the first Tomahawk missile to begin the Iraq War. The target is a bunker believed to be the location of Iraqi President Saddam Hussein.

2003—Federal spending in the State of Hawai'i totals $11.27 billion, including $4.84 billion of defense spending. Compared to other states, Hawai'i ranks sixth in federal spending and second in per-capita defense spending.

2004, January—The Vatican's Congregation for the Causes of Saints affirms Mother Marianne's "heroic virtue," a step toward canonization and sainthood.

2004, June 15—The University of Hawai'i Board of Regents fires UH President Evan Dobelle "for cause," which the contract defines as corruption, mental illness, or criminal behavior. On July 29, after arbitration, the Regents rescind their decision. Dobelle is given a resignation severance worth $3.2 million and absolved of any wrongdoing.

2004—Mufi Hannemann is elected mayor of Honolulu.

2004, August 18—Hiram Fong, who became the first elected Asian-American U.S. Senator in 1959, passes away at the age of 97.

2005—The Grammy Awards adds a Hawaiian music category, Best Hawaiian Music Album, and the Grammy goes to the album *Slack Key Guitar, Volume II* that includes ten different slack key artists. (In 2011 the Hawaiian category is eliminated.)

2005—The U.S. Fish & Wildlife Service reports that 317 species in Hawai'i are either threatened or endangered, including 273 plants.

2005, Aug. 2—A federal appeals court rules that the Kamehameha Schools policy of admitting only native Hawaiians to the school is racial discrimination, resulting in a protest march and rally on the grounds of 'Iolani Palace attracting more than 10,000 participants. In December, 2012, the court decision against the admissions policy is reversed.

Sept. 11 mastermind wanted to attack 10 sites in U.S.
NIGHT FINAL
Honolulu ★ Star-Bulletin
STONS RULE!
In Sports: Detroit shocks L.A. to win NBA title. B1 • U.S. Open golf preview. B7
UH regents fire Dobelle
The UH regents announce that the president "no longer has our trust"
Dobelle is sacked "for cause," which means he won't be paid $2.26 million
Record 'Idol' viewership balloons local Fox ratings

2005, Sept. 2—The Hawaiian group Hui Malama I Na Kupuna O Hawai'i Nei is ordered by United States District Judge David Ezra to return 83 rare Hawaiian artifacts to the Bishop Museum. The group had placed the objects in a sealed cave on Hawai'i Island. Eddie Ayau, the leader of the group, is jailed on December 27, 2005 for refusing to disclose the location.

2005, October—Fifteen-year-old golfing phenomenon Michelle Wie turns professional and signs major endorsement deals, making her the world's highest-paid female golfer and the third highest-paid female in any sport.

GOOD MORNING

EXTRA!

NEWSPAPER CELEBRATES FIFTH YEAR SINCE ITS REBIRTH

EXTRA!

SPECIAL SECTION INSIDE

Star ☆ Bulletin

CRISIS ON KAUAI

2006, March 14—In northern Kaua'i just east of Kīlauea town, an 1890s-era dam breaks during a period of heavy rains. A flood of water and mud surges down the mountain valley killing seven people and wiping out the only road to the north shore.

2006, June 15—Papahānaumokuākea Marine National Monument is established by Presidential Proclamation to protect an array of cultural and natural resources including 7,000 marine species. It is the largest U.S. conservation area encompassing 139,797 square miles in the Northwestern Hawaiian Islands.

2006, June 23—The Office of Hawaiian Affairs trustees approve a plan of action called Ho'oulu Lāhui Aloha to develop a Native Hawaiian registry known as Kau Inoa. It is to serve as the voting base in forming a new entity that will seek self-government rights, including the right to form a "nation-within-a-nation" Hawaiians-only government that will attempt to negotiate with the state and federal governments over money, land, and other assets. By April 2007, more than 61,000 were registered.

The 2006 earthquake was a reminder of the vulnerability of Hawai'i Island to the forces of Mother Nature. The Big Island remains an isolated mass of land in the cradle of the world's biggest ocean, subject to lava flows that destroy homes and property, hurricanes, tsunamis, and earthquakes. 2006. [Kucera Design]

2006, October 15—An earthquake on Hawai'i Island causes an estimated $100 million damage, knocking out power and causing landslides. The initial earthquake hits at 7:07 am, followed by numerous aftershocks.

2006, December 22—Honolulu's City Council votes to approve a proposed 28-mile mass transit system that will cost an estimated $5 billion.

2007, March 8—A tour helicopter crash on Kaua'i kills four people and critically injures three others. Three days later another Kaua'i tour helicopter crashes killing one person.

2007, April 14—Legendary singer and entertainer Don Ho dies at age 76 of a heart attack.

2007, June 9—The Hawaiian voyaging canoe *Hōkūle'a* reaches the Japanese port of Yokohama after a five-month journey covering 8,500 miles across the Pacific.

2007, August 26—The Hawai'i Superferry makes its maiden run, a 3-hour trip from Honolulu to Maui, amidst protests by environmentalists. When the Hawai'i Supreme Court later rules as unconstitutional a state law which had allowed

FOOD & MOOD

RESEARCH SHOWS THAT WHAT WE EAT DIRECTLY AFFECTS HOW WE FEEL --TODAY

The Rainbows hold on to beat the Huskers. B1

Star ☆ Bulletin

MASS TRANSIT: THE CITY COUNCIL APPROVES A PLAN FOR A FIXED GUIDEWAY

ALL ABOARD!

The decision leaves open the possibility for rail or buses

Thousands gather at Waikīkī Beach for a concert that followed the memorial services for entertainer Don Ho, May 5, 2007. [Richard Walker/*Honolulu Star-Bulletin*]

the Superferry to operate without a complete environmental impact statement, the Hawai'i Superferry is forced to cease operations on March 16, 2009.

2007, December—The University of Hawai'i football team completes an undefeated regular season and wins their first outright WAC title in twenty-nine years, earning them a spot in the Sugar Bowl in New Orleans where they lose to the Georgia Bulldogs. In January, head coach June Jones leaves for Southern Methodist University.

2008, February 26—Renowned Island entertainer and teacher Genoa Leilani Keawe dies at the age of 89.

2008, March 25—Moloka'i Ranch abandons operations.

2008, March 31—Aloha Airlines ends its passenger service citing rising fuel prices and competition.

2008, October 31—A public statement by Hawai'i Health Department Director Dr. Fukino confirms that she has "personally seen and verified that the Hawai'i State Department of Health has Senator Obama's original birth certificate.

The Hawaii Superferry, *Alakai*, approaches Honolulu Harbor for the first time. The 350-foot vessel could carry up to four hundred passengers and 110 vehicles. [*Honolulu Star-Advertiser*]

Auntie Genoa Keawe, one of the greats of Hawaiian music, was famed for her falsetto renditions of the old classics and the sensitivity of her interpretations of Hawai'i's songs. [Alexis Higdon]

2008, December 6—The University of Hawai'i activates the Panoramic Survey Telescope & Rapid Response System (PSI) which is designed to search for dangerous asteroids.

Star Bulletin

Wednesday

2008

OBAMA WINS

Hawaii Democrats give him 76% of the vote to Clinton's 24%

Morning Digest

Military jury gets case

2009, January 20—Punahou alumnus Barack Hussein Obama II takes office as the 44th President of the United States.

2009, March 19—A report by the U.S. Interior Department states that one third of the nation's endangered birds are in Hawai'i. The birds are threatened by destruction of habitat, feral animals and insect-borne diseases.

2009, June 1—Governor Linda Lingle orders three days of unpaid furloughs each month for 14,500 state employees due to a $729 million budget shortfall that she terms a "fiscal emergency."

2009, Oct. 11—Pope Benedict XVI canonizes five new saints including Father Damien who worked with Hansen's Disease (leprosy) patients on Moloka'i.

2010, May 28—Hawai'i becomes the first state in the U.S. to ban the sale or possession of shark fins, a popular Chinese food delicacy.

2010—W. S. (William Stanley) Merwin, a Hawai'i resident of Maui since 1976, is named the seventeenth United States Poet Laureate by the Library of Congress. Hawai'i becomes the only state ever to have concurrently a U.S. President, a saint, and a poet laureate.

2010, July—The U.S. Fish and Wildlife Service designates two species of Hawaiian damselflies as endangered.

2010, September 20—A "re-imagined" *Hawaii Five-O* television series premiers in the U.S. on CBS, 42 years to the day after the premier of the original show. By 2013, *Hawaii Five-O* has a worldwide audience of more than 20 million. The "Five-O Effect" is credited with boosting Hawai'i tourism and stimulating Hawai'i's film industry.

2010, November—Neil Abercrombie is elected governor of Hawai'i

2011—North Pacific Humpback whales now number over 20,000, about half of which visit Hawaiian waters.

Governor Neil Abercrombie had served in Hawai'i's House of Representatives and Senate before serving in the U.S. Congress where he was re-elected ten times. In 2010, he easily won Hawai'i's gubernatorial election. [Ted Morita / Governor's Office]

2011—Governor Neil Abercrombie signs Act 195 creating the Native Hawaiian Roll Commission that recognizes Native Hawaiians as the only indigenous people of Hawai'i who exercise sovereignty as a people, thus granting them status as a political entity and not just as a racial preference.

2011, March 11—A 9.0 magnitude earthquake off Japan's coastline causes a tragic natural disaster with massive damage and loss of life in Japan. Damages to Hawai'i ports, roads and homes from the tsunami surges total in the tens of millions of dollars. Five days later Hawai'i business leaders, government and citizens launch "Aloha for Japan," a statewide effort to collect donations and provide relief for the Japan tsunami victims.

2011, July 9—In what is called the "Wonder Blunder" the University of Hawai'i is duped by a concert promoter claiming to represent Stevie Wonder to whom they paid $200,000 and sold $200,000 worth of tickets to the public.

2011, August—China Eastern Airlines launches the first direct, regular airline flights from China to Hawai'i with twice weekly flights from Honolulu to Shanghai leading Chinese tourist numbers to grow rapidly.

2011, November—The Occupy Movement encamps at Thomas Square. They add "de" to their name to show solidarity with the Hawaiian sovereignty movement which claims that Hawai'i has been occupied since the 1893 overthrow of Queen Lili'uokalani. In April 2013, they move their tents to the Blaisdell Concert Hall area when

Privately owned Lāna'i, known as The Pineapple Island, has a land area of 140.5 square miles. Its population of over 3,000 live mostly in Lāna'i City. [Douglas Peebles]

Honolulu Mayor Kirk Caldwell uses a newly enacted sidewalk nuisance law to prevent their camping at Thomas Square.

2011, November—*The Descendants,* based on the novel by local writer Kaui Hart Hemmings and filmed in Hawai'i, premiers in the US. The movie wins an Academy Award for Writing Adapted Screenplay and Golden Globe Awards for Best Drama Film and Best Actor (George Clooney).

2012—Hawai'i's 7.89 million visitors tops the previous 2006 record of 7.6 million in 2006. Spending also reaches new highs with $13.9 billion in direct visitor expenditures. The recovering strong tourist industry helps the slumping state economy rebound.

2012, August—A project to build Waikīkī's first oceanfront high rise hotel in more than three decades is cleared to move forward by the Honolulu Zoning Board of Appeals. It is part of a more than $700 million Waikīkī redevelopment project by Kyo-ya Hotels, owners of the Sheraton Waikiki, the Royal Hawaiian, Moana Surfrider, and Sheraton Princess Kaiulani. The plan to build a 26-story luxury, beachfront high-rise had been held up for more than two years by a zoning variance appeal filed by environmental and community groups who argued that the high rise structure would be too close to the beach.

2012, May—Chicago-based General Growth Properties Inc. announces expansion plans for Ala Moana Shopping Center including finding a substitute tenant for Sears' 2014 departure.

2012, June—Mainland billionaire Larry Ellison purchases the island of Lāna'i from Castle & Cooke, Inc. owner David Murdoch for an undisclosed price estimated at more than $500 million. The sale includes 88,000 acres of land (98 percent of the island), two luxury resort hotels managed by Four Seasons Resort, and two championship golf courses.

2012, June 25—John Kapualani Koko, popular and charismatic bassist of the musical trio, "The Makaha Sons," passes away at only fifty-one years of age.

2012, October 27—Waikīkī heeds a tsunami warning reminding Hawai'i again of its vulnerability to acts of nature.

2012, November—A 206-unit, luxury 17-story tower called One Ala Moana atop Nordstrom's six story parking garage at Ala Moana Center quickly sells out at record high prices.

2012, December 26—Lt. Gov. Brian Schatz is appointed by Governor Neil Abercrombie to fill the U.S. Senate seat vacated by the passing of Daniel Inouye who had asked Governor Abercrombie to appoint Congresswoman Colleen Hanabusa to fill out the term. In April of 2013 Hanabusa announces her intention to run for the seat in 2014 and is immediately endorsed by Inouye's widow, Irene Hirano Inouye.

2012, December 27—O'ahu's $5.6 billion, 20-mile-long elevated-rail mass-transit project is allowed to proceed after prevailing in a federal lawsuit brought by former Governor Ben Cayetano and others attempting to halt the project.

2013—Homelessness continues to grow (4.7 percent) from the previous year including those living on the streets instead of in shelters particularly in Honolulu's Waikīkī and Chinatown areas. With its many faces and no easy remedy, it strains social services

Daniel Inouye

Born on September 7, 1924, Daniel Inouye was the first of four children of Hyotaro and Kame Inouye. He attended Honolulu's McKinley High School and worked at various jobs including parking cars at Honolulu Stadium. In 1943, at the age of 18, he enlisted in the Army, and from 1944 to 1947 served in the renowned 442nd Infantry Regiment.

As a Sergeant, he fought in the Italian campaign where he became a combat platoon leader. Fighting in the French Vosges Mountains in the fall of 1944, he won a Bronze Star when he helped rescue "The Lost Battalion," a Texas Battalion (141st Regiment, 36th Infantry Division) surrounded by German forces. He also was promoted to Second Lieutenant.

During an attack on a well-defended hill in Italy, a bullet tore through his abdomen and came out his back just missing his spine. As platoon leader, he alone continued to advance, and threw two hand grenades at the machine gun position that had pinned down his unit. Then a German rifle grenade hit him from close range tearing up his right arm. With his left hand, he threw his last grenade and then fired his submachine gun before finally being stopped when he was hit yet again by a bullet in the leg.

After nearly two years in the hospital, Inouye returned home in 1947 with the second highest award for military valor, the Distinguished Service Cross, later upgraded to a Medal of Honor. He also earned a Purple Heart with cluster and a Bronze Star along with a dozen other citations and medals.

After attending the University of Hawai'i (1950) and George Washington University Law School (1952), he became in 1954 Honolulu's Deputy Public Prosecutor. He was elected to the Territory of Hawai'i's House of Representatives in 1954, re-elected in 1956, and in 1958 elected to the Territorial Senate. When Inouye was elected to the U.S. House of Representatives in 1959 after Hawai'i became the 50th state, he became Hawai'i's first Congressman and the first Japanese American to serve in the U.S. Congress.

[Senator Inouye's Office]

Inouye was re-elected to the House in 1960, elected to the U.S. Senate in 1962, and then repeatedly re-elected to the Senate. In 1968, he served as the Keynote Speaker at the Democratic National Convention.

At the time of his death on December 17, 2012, Inouye was the most senior U.S. Senator, the Chairman of the U.S. Senate Committee on Appropriations as well as its Subcommittee on Defense, and the second longest serving senator in U.S. history. Due to his extensive influence, over his long political career hundreds of millions of federal dollars have been allocated to programs in Hawai'i.

providers and the Honolulu Police Department. On any given night on O'ahu as many as 1,300 people live on the streets.

2013, May—The Hawai'i Community Development Authority, the state agency guiding development of Honolulu's Kaka'ako area, announces a draft of rules that will allow historic change to the area by the construction of high rise towers.

Following spread: **William Ellis, an early English missionary and historian, identified the kahuna Pa'ao as a Roman Catholic priest. [Hawai'i State Archives]**

Hawai'i's Native Species: Peril and Hope

Human settlement brought vast changes to Hawai'i's landscape beginning with the first Polynesians, and then more rapidly after Western contact. The result was endangerment and extinction for many of Hawai'i's native species.

The rich biodiversity in the Islands today includes plants, birds, mammals, reptiles, marine life and insects that adapted to a wide variety of ecosystems of varying rainfall and topography located along shorelines to mountain peaks.

The Islands have a remarkably high percentage of native species that are also endemic, i.e., found naturally nowhere else, largely due to the extreme isolation of the archipelago in the middle of the Pacific Ocean, 2,400 miles from the nearest continental land mass. This results in an exceptionally high rate of extinct and endangered species - more per square mile than anywhere else on Earth—making Hawai'i the "endangered species capital of the world." Only two tenths of one percent of the size of the U.S., Hawai'i accounts for 70 percent of historically documented plant and animal extinctions.

Human Settlement Affects Native Species Populations

The first Polynesians brought dozens of plant species to the Islands, from taro and breadfruit to wauke to make kapa barkcloth. They farmed and fished, hunted birds for food and feathers, and utilized resources from the land and sea.

Western contact brought new pressures on Hawai'i's native species. In 1790, the sandalwood trade with China stripped forests of trees. In 1819, whaling began, peaking in 1846 with 596 whaling ships arriving. The humpback whale became all but extinct before protective laws were enacted.

Native species were affected in many ways. The Hawaiian monk seal was hunted for its oil and pelts. Commercial and residential development encroached on native habitats, as did agriculture.

Introduced species—livestock, horses, deer, donkeys—competed with or preyed on Hawaiian species. The Indian mongoose, which was brought in 1883 to control rats plaguing the sugar plantations, decimated bird populations and were ineffective as rats are nocturnal while mongoose are diurnal (inactive at night).

Native Bird Populations Decline Over Time

When Captain Cook arrived in Hawai'i, at least 35 bird species were already extinct due to hunting, predation by the pigs and dogs brought by the Polynesians as well as the rats that hitched canoe rides. Particularly vulnerable were ground-nesting birds.

According to fossil evidence along with DNA studies, since Cook arrived in 1778, at least 24 native Hawaiian land bird species or subspecies became extinct and dozens more endangered. Many of Hawai'i's unique birds, from forest to water and seabirds, have suffered from hunting, parasites and foreign diseases as well as being preyed upon by introduced species who compete for food and habitat.

The high demand for woods such as koa reduced forest habitats for birds and other native species. Avian malaria carried by mosquitoes devastated many native bird populations. The last of several critically-endangered forest bird species now survive only in mosquito-free high forests.

There have been success stories. Hawai'i's state bird, the nēnē, was on the verge of extinction in the 1940s when scientists began raising them in captivity and have since released thousands back into the wild.

Continuing Challenges for Native Species

Today more than 360 native Hawaiian species are listed as threatened or endangered by the U.S. Fish and Wildlife Service. One third of all federally listed plants and animals are Hawaiian.

Concerted efforts have helped protect Hawai'i's biodiversity. From the nēnē bird to the albatross and even to the humpback whales, many native Hawaiian species have grown in numbers giving hope that the trend of endangerment and extinction can be reversed.

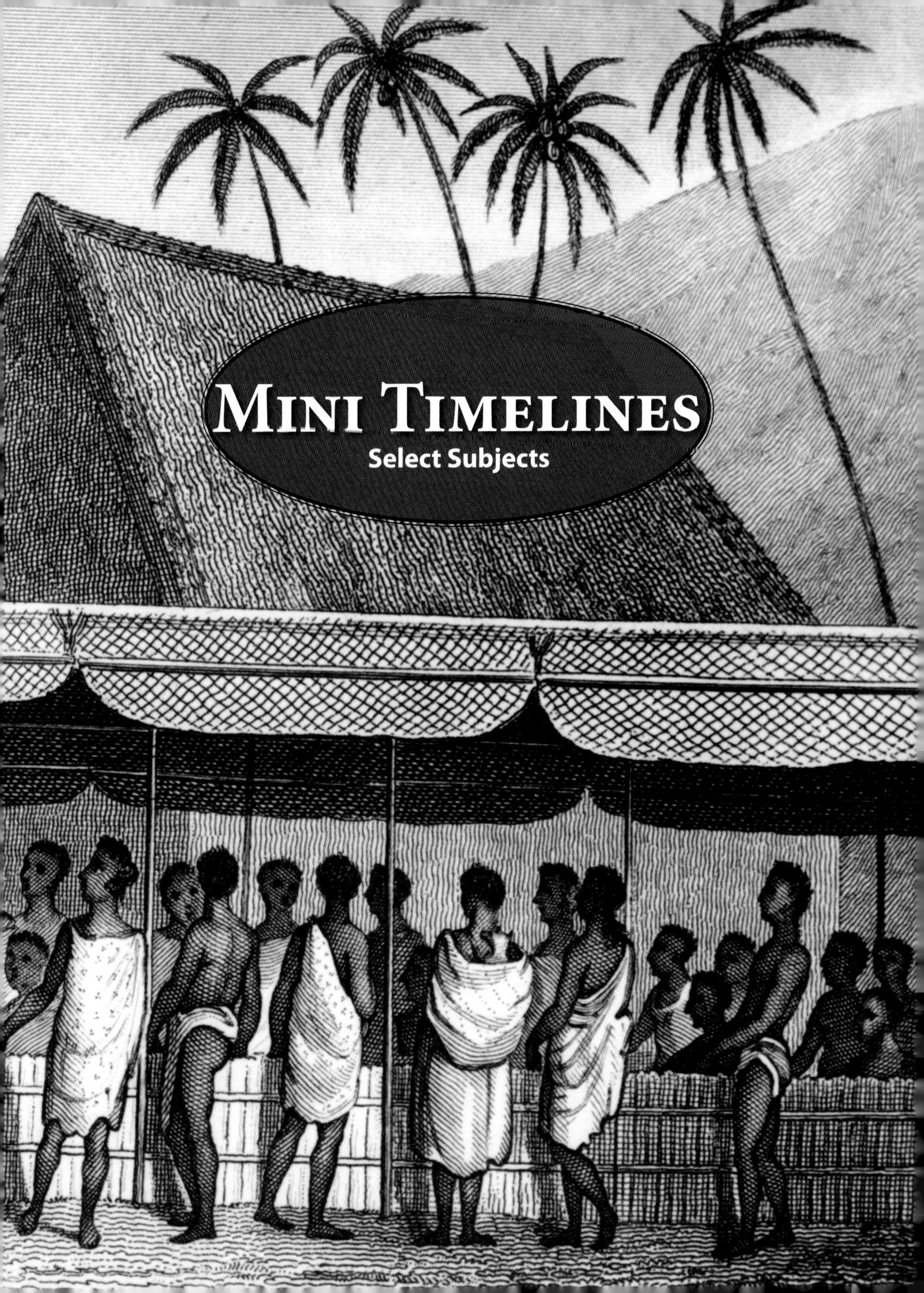
MINI TIMELINES
Select Subjects

NOTABLE WARS AND BATTLES OF EARLY HAWAIʻI

from *A Military History of Sovereign Hawaiʻi* by Neil Bernard Dukas

War	Description	Protagonists	Notable Battles/ Campaigns
Kalaunuiohua's War, or Kaweleweleiwi War ca. 1480-1500	Kalaunuiohua of Hawaiʻi defeats Maui, Molokaʻi and West Oʻahu before being stopped by Kukona of Kauaʻi	Kalaunuiohua (Hawaiʻi) vs. Kamaluohua (Maui), Kahokuohua (Molokaʻi), Huapoleilei (West Oʻahu), and Kukona (Kauaʻi)	Battle of Kōloa (Kauaʻi)—Kalaunuiohua defeated by Kukona of Kauaʻi; chiefs of Maui, Molokaʻi and West Oʻahu restored
ʻUmi a Līloa Rebellion ca. 1600	Overthrow of Hākau of Hawaiʻi—Hilo and Kohala districts gain independence	Hākau (Hawaiʻi) vs. ʻUmi (Hawaiʻi)	Battle of Waipiʻo (Waipiʻo, Hawaiʻi)—Hākau defeated
ʻUmi's War ca. 1600-1620	ʻUmi a Līloa conquers the Island of Hawaiʻi	ʻUmi (Hawaiʻi) vs. Hawaiʻi chiefs	Battle of Kuolo (Keaʻau, Hawaiʻi)—ʻUmi subdues Puna district
Piʻilani's Sons' War before 1620	War of succession on Maui	Lono a Piʻilani (Maui) vs. younger brother, Kiha a Piʻilani (Oʻahu) allied with ʻUmi (Hawaiʻi)	Battle of Hāna (Maui)—Lono defeated
Umi's Sons' War ca. 1625	War of succession on Hawaiʻi	Keawenui a ʻUmi (Hawaiʻi) vs. supporters of Kūkaʻilani (Hawaiʻi)	Battle of Puʻumaneo (Kohala, Hawaiʻi)—Kūkaʻilani's forces defeated
Kanaloakuaʻana Rebellion or Umi's Grandsons' Rebellion ca. 1645	Rebellion on Hawaiʻi against rule of Lonoikamakahiki	Lono (Hawaiʻi) vs. his brothers Kanaloakuaʻana, Kanaloakapulehu and Kanaloakuakawaiea	Battles of Kawaluna, Kaiʻōpae and Kaiʻopihi (Kohala, Hawaiʻi)—rebels defeated
Kamalālāwalu's War or First Hawaiʻi-Maui War ca. 1650	Kamalālāwalu of Maui invades Hawaiʻi	Lono (Hawaiʻi) vs. Hilo district allied with Kamalālāwalu (Maui)	Battles of Puʻuoaoaka and Hōkuʻula (Waimea, Hawaiʻi)— Kamalālāwalu defeated
ca. 1758	Kapiʻi o Hokalani of Oʻahu invades Molokaʻi	Kapiʻi (Oʻahu) vs. Molokaʻi chiefs allied with Alapaʻi (Hawaiʻi)	Battle of Kawela (Kapulei and Kamaloʻo, Molokaʻi)—Kapiʻi defeated (Hawaiʻi attains military stature equal to that of its rival, Oʻahu)
Kauhiʻaimoku Rebellion ca. 1758	Kauhiʻaimoku o Kama, son of Kekaulike, rebels against rule of Kamehamehanui of Maui	Kamehamehanui (Maui) vs. Kauhiʻa (Maui)	Maui—Kamehamehanui defeated; takes refuge with Alapaʻi
ca. 1758-1759	Alapaʻi invades Maui for second time	Alapaʻi (Hawaiʻi) allied with Kamehamehanui (Maui) vs. Kauhiʻa (Maui) allied with Peleiōhōlani (Oʻahu and Kauaʻi)	Battle of Keawawa (Honokōwai and Puʻu Nēnē, Maui)—Alapaʻi sues for peace with Peleiōhōlani; Kamehamehanui restored; Kauhiʻa defeated (famous last stand, Kaʻanapali, Maui)
Kalaniʻōpuʻu Rebellion ca. 1759	Kalaniʻōpuʻu, grandson of Keawe (previous ruler of Hawaiʻi), rebels against rule of Alapaʻi of Hawaiʻi	Alapaʻi (Hawaiʻi) vs. Kalaniʻōpuʻu (Hawaiʻi)	Running battles near Hilo— Kalaniʻōpuʻu rules at Kaʻū and West Puna (Hawaiʻi)

War	Description	Protagonists	Notable Battles/ Campaigns
Kalaniʻōpuʻuʻs War ca. 1760	War of succession on Hawaiʻi—Keaweʻōpala succeeds rule upon death of Alapaʻi	Kalaniʻōpuʻu (Hawaiʻi) vs. Keawe (Hawaiʻi)	Battles of Keʻei and Hōnaunau (Hawaiʻi)—Keawe defeated
ca. 1765	Hawaiʻi invasion of East Maui	Kalaniʻōpuʻu (Hawaiʻi) vs. Kamehamehanui (Maui)	Hāna and Kīpahulu (Maui) fall to Hawaiian forces
Kapalipilo War ca. 1765	Kamehamehanui attempts to force Hawaiians from Hāna, Maui	Kamehamehanui (Maui) vs. Hawaiian chiefs at Hāna, Maui	Battle of Makaolehua (Hāna Maui)—Hawaiians defeated but hold onto stronghold of Kaʻuiki (eventually retaken by siege)
Oʻahu Rebellion ca. 1773	Overthrow of Kumahana on Oʻahu	Oʻahu chiefs vs. Kumahana (Oʻahu)	Kahahana selected by Oʻahu chiefs to succeed Kumahana
Oʻahu-Molokaʻi War ca. 1773	Kahahana of Oʻahu conquers Molokaʻi	Kahahana (Oʻahu) vs. chiefs of Molokaʻi	Molokaʻi
Third Hawaiʻi-Maui War ca. 1775-1779	Kalaniʻōpuʻu invades Maui to retake stronghold of Kaʻuiki (Hāna)	Kalaniʻōpuʻu (Hawaiʻi) vs. Kahekili (Maui)	Battle of Kalaehohea (Puʻumaneone, near Kaupō, Maui)—Kalaniʻōpuʻu routed by Kahekili, withdraws to Hawaiʻi
ca. 1776	Kalaniʻōpuʻu returns to Maui—fights two major engagements known as the Kakanilua battles	Kalaniʻōpuʻu (Hawaiʻi) vs. Kahekili (Maui)	First Battle of Wailuku (Kakanilua) at Kalua, Wailuku, Maui—slaughter of the ʻĀlapa (Hawaiian forces)
ca. 1776	The Kakanilua battles	Kalaniʻōpuʻu (Hawaiʻi) vs. Kahekili (Maui)	Second Battle of Wailuku (Kakanilua) at Wailuku, Maui—Kalaniʻōpuʻu routed by Kahekili; hostilities ended by intercession of kapu chief, Kīwalaʻō
ca. 1778	Kalaniʻōpuʻu invades Lānaʻi—Battle for control of stronghold of Hoʻokiʻo	Kalaniʻōpuʻu (Hawaiʻi) vs. chiefs of Lānaʻi	Battle of Kamokuhi (near Maunalei, Lānaʻi)—annihilation of Lānaʻi chiefs; Kalaniʻōpuʻu ʻs army suffers from shortages; withdraws to Maui
ca. 1778-1779	Kalaniʻōpuʻu returns to Maui and invades Kahoʻolawe	Kalaniʻōpuʻu (Hawaiʻi) vs. Kahekili (Maui) allied with Kahahana (Oʻahu)	Battle of Haleili (stronghold of Kāhili at Paʻupaʻu, Maui, near Lahaina)—Kalaniʻōpuʻu ceases operations against Maui in connection with arrival of Cook Expedition at Kealakekua, January 1779

War	Description	Protagonists	Notable Battles/ Campaigns
Kealakekua Bay February 14, 1779	Skirmish results in death of British navigator Captain James Cook, and others	James Cook (HMS *Resolution*) and Charles Clerke (HMS *Discovery*) vs. Kalani'ōpu'u (Hawai')	Skirmish at Ka'awaloa (Kealakekua Bay, South Kona, Hawai'i)—death of Cook; Clerke fires on Ka'awaloa but soon establishes peaceful relations
O'ahu-Maui War ca. 1780-1783	Maui invasion of O'ahu	Kahekili (Maui) vs. O'ahu chiefs under Kahahana	Battle of Kahe'iki or Punchbowl (1783)—Kahekili annihilates O'ahu ali'i
'Īmakakoloa Rebellion ca. 1781	'Īmakakoloa rebels against rule of Kalani'ōpu'u on Hawai'i	Kalani'ōpu'u (Hawai'i) vs. 'Īmakakoloa (Hawai'i)	Puna district, Hawai'i—'Īmakakoloa defeated
The War of Succession ca. 1782-1791	War of succession following death of Kalani'ōpu'u (Apr. 1782)—transitions into a war of unification under Kamehameha of Kohala, Hawai'i	Kamehameha (Hawai'i) vs. Kīwala'ō (Hawai'i) allied with Keōua (Hawai'i)	Battle of Moku'ōhai (1782, between Hōnaunau and Ke'ei, Hawai'i)—Kīwala'ō defeated, Keōua escapes
ca. 1783-1784	Kamehameha attacks Hilo and Ka'ū districts on Hawai'i	Kamehameha (Hawai'i) vs. Keawema'uhili (Hilo, Hawai'i) and Keōua (Ka'ū, Hawai'i) allied with Kahekili (Maui)	Battle of Kama'ino or Kaua Awa (Pua'aloa, near Pana'ewa, Hilo, Hawai'i)—Kamehameha defeated
ca. 1785	Kamehameha attacks Hilo district on Hawai'i	Hilo and Maui chiefs vs. Kamehameha (Hawai'i)	Battle of Hāpu'u Bay (Hālawa shoreline, Hawai'i)—Kamehameha achieves limited success; withdraws
ca. 1785	Kamehameha attacks Laupāhoehoe, Hawai'i	Kamehameha (Hawai'i) vs. Keawe (Hilo, Hawai'i)	Second Battle of Laupāhoehoe (Hilo district, Hawai'i)—Kamehameha temporarily retakes stronghold at Laupāhoehoe
East Maui War ca. 1786	War for control of Kīpahulu and Hāna, Maui	Kalanimālokuloku (Kamehameha's younger brother) vs. Kamohomoho allied with Kalanikūpule (Maui)	Battles of Ka'ahu'ula and Ma'ulili (near Kīpahulu, Maui)—Hawaiians defeated
Olowalu Massacre early 1790	Massacre of Maui natives at Olowalu by American merchant seaman, Captain Simon Metcalfe	Simon Metcalfe of the MV *Eleanora* vs. inhabitants of Olowalu (Maui)	Ambush and massacre of unarmed natives in retribution for the abduction and murder of a crew member
The War of Unification ca. 1790-1804	Kamehameha lands a large force at Hāna, Maui	Kamehameha (Hawai'i) vs. Kapakahili (Maui)	Battle of Kawa'anui or Hoalua Bay, 1790 (near Huelo, Hāmākualoa, Maui)—Maui forces defeated

War	Description	Protagonists	Notable Battles/ Campaigns
ca. 1790	Kamehameha effectively subdues Maui	Kamehameha (Hawai'i) vs. Kalanikūpule (Maui) allied with Kaua'i and O'ahu chiefs	Battle of Kapaniwai or 'Uwa 'u Pali or Kokomo ('Īao Valley, Wailuku, Maui)—Maui forces defeated, withdraw to O'ahu, truce established with Kahekili
ca. 1790	Ka'ū district attacks Hilo district on Hawai'i	Keōua (Ka'ū district, Hawai'i) vs. Keawe (Hilo district, Hawai'i)	Battle of 'Alae ('Alae, Hawai'i)—Keawe defeated
ca. 1790	Kamehameha attacks Hilo district on Hawai'i	Kamehameha (Hawai'i) vs. Keōua (Hawai'i)	Battles of Pā'auhau and Koapāpa'a or Ne'e Kaua ki Hakaka, at Pā'auhau (near Honoka'a, Hawai'i) and Koapāpa'a (near Pa'auilo, Hāmākua, Hawai'i)—first known use of Western weapons in quantity; ends in a draw
ca. 1790	Kamehameha attacks Ka'ū district on Hawai'i	Keōua (Hawai'i) vs. Ka'iana (Hawai'i)	Battles of Ka Lae (Ka'ū district, Hawai'i) and Pu'uakoki (Puna district, Hawai'i)—Ka'iana defeated
March 1791	Combined Kaua'i and Maui fleet (sent from O'ahu) against Kamehameha	Kā'eokulani (Kaua'i and O'ahu) and Kahekili (Maui) vs. Kamehameha (Hawai'i)	Battle of Kepuwaha'ula'ula (off Waimanu, Hawai'i)—famous use of cannon at sea; Kā'eo and Kahekili withdraw to Maui
1791	Skirmish results in the death and sacrifice of Keōua of Hawai'i—effectively ends The War of Succession	Kamehameha vs. Keōua	Skirmish at Kawaihae, Hawai'i—Keōua defeated
The Kuki'iahu War Nov.-Dec. 1794	War of succession on O'ahu and Kaua'i following the death of Kahekili	Kalanikūpule (O'ahu and Maui) vs. Kā'eo (Kaua'i) allied with O'ahu chiefs from Wai'anae and Waialua	Battle of Aiea or Kalauao (Aiea, O'ahu)—Kā'eo defeated; (George) Kaumuali'i assumes rule on Kaua'i
May 1795	Kamehameha conquers O'ahu—Hawaiian Islands (less Kaua'i) united under Kamehameha I	Kamehameha (Hawai'i) vs. Kalanikūpule (O'ahu and Maui) allied with Kona and Ko'olaupoko chiefs (O'ahu), Kaua'i chiefs, and Ka'iana (Hawai'i)	Battle of Nu'uanu or Ka'uwa 'u Pali or Kaleleka'anae (Nu'uanu Valley, O'ahu)—allied O'ahu forces defeated
Nāmakehā Rebellion Aug.-Sept. 1796	Last major battle of The War of Unification	Kamehameha (Hawai'i) vs. Nāmakehā (Hawai'i)	Battle of Kaipalaoa (South Hilo, Hawai'i)—Nāmakehā defeated
Invasion of Kaua'i Apr. 1796	Abortive invasion of Kaua'i	Kamehameha (Hawai'i) vs. Kaumuali'i (Kaua'i)	Kaua'i Channel—Hawaiian naval disaster

THE MONARCHS OF HAWAIʻI

KAMEHAMEHA I

Born circa 1758,
Ascended circa 1795,
Died May 8, 1819

Kamehameha I was born in the Kohala region in the northernmost corner of Hawaiʻi Island during a time when one century differed little, if at all, from previous centuries. When he died, Hawaiʻi's ancient culture had almost vanished and western ways and ideas were changing the Islands.

Kamehameha was the nephew of Kalaniʻōpuʻu, king of Hawaiʻi Island (and the Hāna district of eastern Maui). At that time each major island had its own ruler. Numerous attempts to unite the entire island chain were unsuccessful.

When Kalaniʻopuʻu died, Kamehameha defeated his successor Kīwalaʻo and proceeded to establish his rule over Hawaiʻi Island. Then he conquered Maui, Lānaʻi, and Molokaʻi, and later Oʻahu at the battle at Nuʻuanu Pali. The conquest of Oʻahu effectively established him as king of all Hawaiʻi uniting a people that had never before been a nation and keeping the nation together in the face of foreign influences and threats.

During his reign Hawaiʻi underwent unprecedented changes with the ancient way of life suffering devastating blows. Foreign ships arriving in increasing numbers to trade brought venereal and other diseases, alcohol, and firearms. With little immunity to new diseases, Hawaiians died in alarming numbers.

Kamehameha was an old-style autocrat. He was conservative in religious matters maintaining the rites, ceremonies, and kapus. Though his people began to question their religion as they witnessed foreign ways, they dared not disrespect their traditional gods while he lived.

Kamehameha brought Hawaiʻi into the modern world as a nation ready to deal with other nations. The end of his reign was characterized by long years of peace and stability previously unknown in the Islands. This accomplishment alone has bestowed on him the fitting title, Kamehameha the Great.

KAMEHAMEHA II

Born circa November 1797,
Ascended May 20, 1819,
Died July 14, 1824

Raised during long years of peace, Liholiho succeeded his father Kamehameha I at age twenty-two with no military or ruling experience. He shared his power with the kuhina nui, or Prime Minister, Kaʻahumanu, the politically influential widow of his father.

Pressured by Kaʻahumanu and the Council of Chiefs, in 1819 Liholiho ordered the destruction of heiau and religious idols thereby ending the state religion and its kapu system. The kapu system of sacred prohibitions and restrictions had been the only law in the nation for many centuries. With its overthrow, laws would be ordained directly by the monarch.

During Kamehameha II's brief reign, the sandalwood trade flourished, the whaling industry grew and American Protestant missionaries began to arrive. As the foreign population grew, the Hawaiian population declined drastically, falling to 135,000 by 1823.

While on a trip to Great Britain in 1874 to visit King George IV, both Kamehameha II and his wife Kamāmalu died in London after contracting measles.

KAMEHAMEHA III

Born August 11, 1814,
Ascended June 6, 1825,
Died December 16, 1854

Kauikeaouli, the last son of Kamehameha the Great to rule, ascended the throne when he was ten years old upon the death of his older brother Liholiho (Kamehameha II).

He served as king during one of the most difficult periods in Hawaiʻi's history as the influx of large numbers of foreign residents brought problems concerning trade, credit, land titles, and complications unknown to a few generations earlier. As well the prevailing lawlessness of foreigners provoked tensions with foreign powers, particularly Great Britain.

Nevertheless, Kamehameha III brought his kingdom safely through a long reign full of difficulties. Although he yearned for a return to the old ways, he instituted progressive measures. In 1839, he proclaimed Hawaiʻi's Declaration of Rights, also known as the Hawaiian Magna Carta. A year later he promulgated the kingdom's first constitution.

Despite his important role in Hawaiʻi moving from autocracy toward democracy, Kamehameha III is mostly remembered by the 1848 Māhele, which divided Hawaiian land among the king, government, aliʻi, and public. By instituting the Kuleana Act in 1850, the king took great strides in allowing foreigners to become naturalized citizens who could own land.

Kamehameha III died in Honolulu on December 15, 1854, after having named his nephew, Alexander Liholiho, as successor. He had served Hawaiʻi for twenty-nine years. That he was beloved by his people is his epitaph in Hawaiian history.

KAMEHAMEHA IV

Born February 9, 1834,
Ascended January 16, 1855,
Died November 30, 1863

Alexander Liholiho succeeded his uncle, Kamehameha III, on January 16, 1855, assuming the title of Kamehameha IV. He was the first grandson of Kamehameha the Great to become king of Hawaiʻi.

During his reign and that of his successor, there was growing agitation by the sugar planters for annexation to the United States so as to secure a dependable market for island cane. In stark contrast the Hawaiian monarchs sought to strengthen their own power and carry out a policy of "Hawaiʻi for the Hawaiians." Within the Hawaiian government there was continuous wrangling between those who were interested in strengthening the power of the throne and those who wished to limit it. Many foreign residents did not wish to become citizens of Hawaiʻi but wanted to be able to vote to safeguard their interests and preferred that the common Hawaiian remain without suffrage.

As a fifteen-year-old prince, Alexander traveled with his brother Lot and Finance Minister Gerrit Judd to Europe to further their education as future monarchs and to settle differences that had soured relations between France and the Hawaiian Kingdom. While in France the young princes were entertained by the highest elements of society and met with Emperor Louis Napoleon.

In 1856, Kamehameha IV married the beautiful Emma Rooke, a part-European descendant of Hawaiian chieftains. Cultivated and witty, Alexander and Emma symbolized all that was elegant, stylish, and artistic. Together they made steady advancements toward the betterment of Hawaiian health establishing the Queen's Hospital in 1859. Though they brought many non-Hawaiian advisors into the government, they were careful to limit missionary participation. Kamehameha IV was one of the most anti-American of all Hawaiʻi's monarchs being pro-British from an early age.

The royal pair became the proud parents of Prince Albert, a bright and handsome little boy who was the apple of their eye and the hope of the Kamehameha dynasty. Unfortunately, he died when only four years old and the king never recovered from this shattering blow to his love and hopes. Fifteen months later, on November 30, 1863, he succumbed. After his death, Emma attempted to become monarch when in 1874, the Hawaiian Legislature considered her candidacy for queen, but ultimately elected David Kalākaua.

KAMEHAMEHA V

Born December 11, 1830,
Ascended November 30, 1863,
Died December 11, 1872

Lot Kamehameha, who became Kamehameha V, was the last direct descendant of Kamehameha I to sit on Hawaiʻi's throne.

Throughout his reign he opposed any erosion of royal power, overseeing the adoption of a new constitution designed to strengthen the monarchy. He was a more truly Hawaiian king than his younger brother Alexander, Kamehameha IV. Where Alexander had been worldly and witty, graceful and elegant, Lot was stolid, and more of a nativist in every respect.

Problems with the United States continued as they had during his brother's reign. Agitation by elements favoring annexation by the U.S. threatened Hawaiʻi's independence. The king, in an effort to improve relations between the two countries, promoted a treaty of reciprocity that would allow Hawaiian sugar to enter the American market duty-free. Until this time, Hawaiʻi had depended heavily on whaling as a source of export income but by the end of the 1850s whaling was no longer a strong economic force.

Racial tensions increased during Lot's reign due to suspicions that Westerners were trying to take over the Hawaiian Kingdom. In 1866 a fist-fight broke out in the racially divided legislature where white legislators refused to speak Hawaiian, the kingdom's official language, and Native Hawaiian members refused to speak English.

Lot was in bad health for several years before his death. For some unknown reason, he never discussed the important matter of succession. On his deathbed, his counselors and advisors mentioned at least five high-ranking successors. He died on December 1, 1872, his forty-second birthday, without naming a successor ending the dynasty begun by Kamehameha the Great. From then on, Hawaiʻi's monarchs would be elected.

LUNALILO

Born January 31, 1835,
Ascended January 8, 1873,
Died February 3, 1874

After an informal popular vote, the Hawaiian Legislature confirmed William Lunalilo as the new king of Hawaiʻi, and on January 12, 1873 he took his oath of office at Kawaiahaʻo Church.

Lunalilo had a taste for music, literature, and the arts. He was also more liberal than Lot, and made serious efforts to democratize the constitution. Once again during his short reign the question of a treaty of reciprocity with the United States arose. The Hawaiian sugar industry needed the U.S. market to absorb its increasing production. This time a proposed treaty was linked to ceding Pearl Harbor to the United States.

Even though Lot had thought this an unwise accommodation, Lunalilo endorsed the ceding. When the news reached the Hawaiian public, they were outraged. While they understood that a reciprocity treaty would benefit the kingdom, they objected to the ceding of land to a foreign power. Widespread disapproval of the idea forced its eventual abandonment.

An embarrassing event during Lunalilo's short reign was the mutiny of the Royal Household Troops, a small body of Hawaiian soldiers that had long served as the monarchy's standing army. Under Lunalilo's reign the troops struggled with the excessively harsh discipline of their white senior officers. A mutiny was barely prevented by a plea from the king who guaranteed amnesty for all participants.

This difficult moment demonstrated all too clearly the eroding power of Hawaiʻi's monarchy. Soon after, the Royal Household Troops were disbanded, leaving the kingdom without a standing army that would later help contribute to the monarchy's overthrow.

After contracting tuberculosis in August of 1873, Lunalilo died on February 3, reigning for only slightly more than a year. Like his predecessor he failed to name an heir, leaving the 1874 Legislature to choose his successor.

KALĀKAUA

Born November 16, 1836,
Ascended February 12, 1874
Died January 20, 1891

David Kalākaua was elected king by the 1874 Hawaiian Legislature amid scenes of violence and indignity. His rival for the throne was the dowager Queen Emma whose followers made up for their lack of numbers by their willingness to start trouble.

Kalākaua was primarily concerned for the well-being of his people. He maintained a policy of filling administrative posts with Hawaiians wherever possible, a practice that scared the American businessmen who had supported him against Emma, although Kalākaua repeatedly and sincerely insisted that there was room in Hawaiʻi for all people.

The new king soon proved himself an unpredictable individualist. He fired cabinet members and ministers when they disagreed with him. He envisioned himself a Polynesian emperor dreaming of a Federation of Pacific Islands with Hawaiʻi at its head and himself at the helm. He meddled in the affairs of Samoa, going so far as to obtain the signature of the Samoan King (Malietoa) on an agreement of federation, at a time when Samoa was fending off German, American, and British imperialism. In 1881, Kalākaua embarked on an across-the-world trip making him the first monarch in history to circle the globe.

In late 1882 when the new ʻIolani Palace which he had commissioned was completed, Kalākaua decided that such a magnificent stage deserved an equally magnificent performance. On February 12, 1883, he held a coronation ceremony during which he crowned himself king. Though much of the ceremony was borrowed from European protocol, Kalākaua blended it with Hawaiian traditions including the ancient sacred hula.

Toward the end of his reign, Kalākaua suffered various setbacks to his power. His cabinet was overthrown, a new constitution that deprived him of almost all his power was written, and in July 1889, there was an ill-fated insurrection to replace him with his sister Princess Liliʻuokalani. In November 1890 and in declining health, Kalākaua traveled to San Francisco, California, leaving Liliʻuokalani as regent. There he suffered a fatal stroke and died on January 20, 1891 at fifty-four.

Monarch photographs [Hawaiʻi State Archives]

LILI'UOKALANI

Born September 2, 1838,
Ascended January 29, 1891,
Died November 11, 1917

Lili'uokalani was already leading the nation as regent when King Kalākaua died in San Francisco. When she became queen, the political and economic climate of Hawai'i was extremely complicated. Rivalry was intense between the white businessmen who dominated the economy and the native politicians who still retained power.

The possibility of annexation to the United States was openly discussed by a small group of businessmen and wealthy foreigners. Though the annexationists were badly outnumbered, they were not intimidated by their lack of popular support. They considered the Hawaiians incapable of self-government and saw the monarchy as too inept to safeguard business interests.

Tension grew when the queen announced her intention to promulgate a new constitution to restore the power of the monarchy, much of which had been lost in 1887 under a constitution signed by King Kalākaua. Even members of her own cabinet were alarmed and disapproving, fearing that it would give the annexationists the ammunition they sought.

The annexationists reacted by forming a Committee of Public Safety, and then creating a provisional government and a militia. The queen could have declared martial law and arrested the conspirators, but she felt that this would lead to armed conflict costing the innocent lives of her people. Then under the command of Captain G. C. Wiltse, an open supporter of the provisional government, marines and sailors from the U.S.S. *Boston* landed to keep order in Honolulu. A day later the Committee of Public Safety sent armed companies of militia to take over government buildings and offices. The queen was stripped of her power.

She sent a plea to the U.S. minister, asking him to support her sovereignty. He replied that the provisional government was now Hawai'i's only recognized government. Just after sunset on January 17, 1893, the queen surrendered under protest. On January 31, Minister Stevens, at the request of the provisional government's advisory council, raised the U.S. flag over Honolulu believing annexation would soon follow. However, in March 1893 President Cleveland sent a special investigator to Hawai'i to determine the chain of events that led to the raising of the American flag. After the investigation it was concluded that the monarchy had been overthrown by force with the complicity of the U.S. minister.

The provisional government refused to step down. President Cleveland refused to annex Hawai'i. The Provisionals, though disheartened by Washington's rejection, boldly established the Republic of Hawai'i on July 4, 1894 with Sanford Dole as president.

In 1895, Hawaiians loyal to the queen staged a revolt to restore Lili'uokalani to the throne. It was crushed and the queen placed under house arrest in an apartment in 'Iolani Palace. As a condition to obtain amnesty for the Hawaiian rebels she was forced to relinquish any claim to the throne.

The Spanish-American War in 1898 precipitated the US's reconsideration of its position on Hawai'i. The U.S. had taken over the Philippines and Hawai'i's strategic value was now obvious. President McKinley signed the resolution of annexation on July 7, 1898, a happy day for the new rulers. For the royalists and most common Hawaiians, it was a day of misery, as they gathered quietly at both the homes of deposed Lili'uokalani and Crown Princess Ka'iulani to console them and pay homage to the last monarch of the lost kingdom. On June 14, 1900, Hawai'i formally became a U.S. territory under the Organic Act and Sanford Dole, who had served as president of the Hawaiian Republic, was sworn in as Hawai'i's first territorial governor.

After the overthrow of her government until her death in 1917, Lili'uokalani resided at Washington Place, a home just behind 'Iolani Palace that she had inherited from her late husband John Dominis.

Though she was legally known as Lydia Dominis after her forced abdication, the people of Hawai'i still called her Queen Lili'uokalani, and even to this day she is still referred to by this title.

KAMEHAMEHA THE GREAT

ca. 1758—Pai'ea Kamehameha is born in North Kohala on Hawai'i Island to Keōuanui and Keku'iapoiwa. This infant child will one day become the ruler of the Hawaiian Kingdom as King Kamehameha I.

1775—Kamehameha overturns the Naha Stone. A high priestess had predicted that whoever can move the stone will conquer all the Hawaiian Islands.

1778 November—As a young chief, Kamehameha goes aboard Captain Cook's HMS *Resolution* with his uncle Kalani'ōpu'u, ruler of Hawai'i Island, and six other chiefs.

1779 January—Along with Kalani'ōpu'u, Kamehameha again meets Cook.

1780—Hawai'i Island ruler Kalani'ōpu'u tells his chiefs that upon his death, his oldest son Kīwala'ō will be the new ruler, his son Keōua will get land, and Kamehameha will become chief of Kohala on land that was his by inheritance. Kamehameha is also responsible for the family's war god Kūkā'ilimoku.

1782 April—When Kalani'ōpu'u, Kamehameha's uncle, dies. Kamehameha and other Big Island chiefs are slighted by the redivision of

Hawai'i Island which takes away areas formerly under their rule.

1782—At the Battle of Moku'ōhai Kamehameha defeats Kīwala'ō who had given large parts of land to rivals. Kīwala'ō is killed and his famed feather cloak becomes the property of Kamehameha. (Cloak is now in the Bishop Museum.)

1785—Kamehameha marries Ka'ahumanu who will later serves as kuhina nui (regent) of the Hawaiian kingdom.

1790—Kamehameha invades Maui. Using Western weaponry at the Battle of Kepaniwai he defeats Kahekili, and the island of Maui comes under Kamehameha's rule. Bodies of warriors killed in 'Īao Valley were said to have blocked the river giving the battle its name Kepaniwai *(The water dam).*

1790, March—Kamehameha takes a cannon from a captured American trading vessel *Fair American* and receives help using Western weaponry from former crew member Isaac Davis along with John Young. Davis and Young become Kamehameha's supporters and advisers, manning large guns in future battles.

1791—Kamehameha begins construction a large heiau known as Pu'ukoholā dedicated to his war god. The respected kahuna (priest) Kapoukahi had told Kamehameha he would rule over all the Islands if this heiau was built.

1791—Kamehameha is victorious on Maui at the battle known as Kepūwaha'ula'ula *(The War of the Red Mouthed Cannon)*, preventing Kahekili from attacking the heiau site. This is the first Hawaiian sea battle in which both sides are armed with foreign gunners and cannons.

1791, Summer—Pu'ukoholā Heiau is dedicated. Keōua, chief of Puna and Ka'ū, arrives as an invited guest and he and many of his chiefs are slain, and their bodies are sacrificed on the altar of the heiau. Kamehameha now controls Hawai'i Island.

1794, February 25—Kamehameha grants British Captain George Vancouver an informal treaty of cession assuring Hawai'i will be under British protection, though the agreement was never ratified by British Parliament. Vancouver's carpenters help Kamehameha construct the 36-foot *Britannia,* the first foreign designed ship built in the Islands.

1795, April—Kamehameha's troops invade O'ahu determined to defeat its ruler Kalanikūpule. In the Battle of Nu'uanu the O'ahu warriors are overpowered and retreat up into Nu'uanu Valley where many are either driven over the edge of the pali (cliff) or jumped rather than surrender. Kamehameha's victory gives him control of all the Islands except for Kaua'i and Ni'ihau.

1795—Kamehameha marries 17-year-old Keōpūolani who becomes his highest-ranking wife, and from whom two future kings are born, Liholiho (1797) and Kauikeaouli (1814), as well as Princess Nāhi'ena'ena (1815).

1796, April—Kamehameha attempts to invade Kaua'i when his warriors, numbering about 8,000 in at least 800 canoes, are forced to turn back due to a storm and rough seas.

1796, September—In Kamehameha's last battle his forces put down an uprising on Hawai'i Island known as Nāmakaehā's rebellion. Kamehameha remains in Hilo, the capital of the kingdom, for the next six years.

1797—Kamehameha forgives a fisherman who 12 years earlier had hit him with a paddle. He passes what came to be known as Kānāwai Māmalahoe, or *Law of the Splintered Paddle* with the intent of protecting weak people from injustices imposed by those who are stronger. This was the first law meant to protect commoners.

1801—Hawai'i Island's Hualālai Volcano erupts and Kamehameha is told by a kāula (prophet) that the volcano goddess Pele is angry. Kamehameha throws offerings and then his hair into the volcano's eruption to stop its flow and soon the lava ceases.

1802—Kamehameha and Kalākua give birth to Kamāmalu, a future queen as wife of Kamehameha II.

1803—Kamehameha moves the kingdom's capital to Lahaina, and then the following year to Honolulu.

1804—An epidemic thought to be cholera delays a second attempt of Kamehameha to conquer Kaua'i. In a renewed effort for a large-scale attack, Kamehameha began assembling an armada of sailing ships in Waikīkī.

1810—Kamehameha meets the Kaua'i ruler Kaumuali'i in Honolulu where Kaua'i is ceded peacefully to Kamehameha. With this act, all the Hawaiian Islands are finally united under one ruler, fulfilling the prophecy of the Naha Stone. Kamehameha declares Hawai'i to be one nation.

1812—Kamehameha returns to Hawai'i Island to live in Kailua-Kona at his home called Kamakahonu *(Eye of the Turtle).*

1819, May 8—Kamehameha dies at his Kailua-Kona home and his remains are buried secretly as is the custom. Known as Kamehameha the Great, he was Hawai'i's most famous warrior and the first to unite the Islands under one rule.

THE HAWAIIAN MONARCHY

1795—Kamehameha and his men travel to O'ahu, where they attempt to gain control of the island. The fighting ends in Nu'uanu Valley, where many of O'ahu's warriors perish over the Pali Cliff.

1804—Kamehameha continues planning to attack Kaua'i but an epidemic of ma'i 'ōku'u (likely cholera) infects his warriors, killing thousands including high chiefs Ke'eaumoku and Pāpa'iaheahe and delaying for the second time a Kaua'i invasion. Kamehameha renews his attack plans constructing with the help of foreigners an armada of ships in Waikīkī.

1810—Kaua'i's King Kaumuali'i acknowledges Kamehameha's sovereignty and agrees to place Kaua'i and Ni'ihau under his control. Kaumuali'i is allowed to remain as Kaua'i's vassal ruler. Kamehameha declares the Hawaiian Islands to be one nation.

1812—Kamehameha returns to Hawai'i Island to live in Kailua-Kona.

1819, May 8—Kamehameha dies at his Kamakahonu ("Eye of the turtle") Kailua-Kona home. Ulumāheihei (Hoapili) is entrusted with hiding his bones.

1819, May 20—King Kamehameha's 24-year-old son Liholiho takes the throne as Kamehameha II. Within months he eats food in public with the dowager queens Ka'ahumanu and Keōpūolani breaking the kapu (prohibition) against men and women eating together. This begins a process that erodes away at traditional Hawaiian religious beliefs and eventually leads to the complete overturning of the kapu system.

1819—Kekuaokalani, the son of Kamehameha I's younger brother and the keeper of Kamehameha I's renowned war god Kūkā'ilimoku, rebels against Kamehameha II's abolishment of the eating kapu. At the Battle of Kuamo'o on Hawai'i Island Kekuaokalani and his wife are killed, and the revolt is defeated. Another rebellion is later defeated in Hāmākua.

1821, July 21—Kamehameha II sails to Waimea, Kaua'i on the royal yacht *Ha'aheo o Hawai'i (Pride of Hawai'i)* to meet with Kaua'i's vassal ruler Kaumuali'i who pledges his allegiance to the king and accepts his sovereignty. Kamehameha II completes a 42-day tour of Kaua'i and anchors in Waimea Bay on September 16 inviting Kaumuali'i to come aboard where he is taken to O 'ahu as a prisoner. The powerful kuhina nui (premier) Ka'ahumanu, the former queen and wife of Kamehameha I, later marries Kaumuali'i to ensure the monarchy's control over Kaua'i. Kaumuali'i passes away on O'ahu in 1824.

1823, September 16— Keōpūolani, the sacred wife of Kamehameha I, becomes the first native Hawaiian to receive the Protestant rite of baptism, when missionary William Ellis administers the sacrament to her an hour before she dies.

1823, November 27—Kamehameha II and Kamāmalu leave for England on the whaler *L'aigle with* Ka'ahumanu left in charge of the government.

1824—Kamāmalu (July 8) and Kamehameha II (July 14) die of measles in London, England.

1825, May 3—The bodies of Kamehameha II and Kamāmalu arrive from London aboard the Navy frigate *Blonde* commanded by Lord George Anson Byron who later writes *Voyage of H.M.S. "Blonde" to the Sandwich Islands, 1824-25.*

1825, June 6—Liholiho's brother, Kauikeaouli, becomes Kamehameha III, reigning for the next 30 years.

1825, December 4—Ka'ahumanu, former wife of Kamehameha I and Queen Regent for Kamehameha II and III, is baptized along with her cousin Kalanimoku, his son, Leleiohoku, her sister Pi'ia, Deborah Kapule, and Gideon La'anui.

1832, June 5—Ka'ahumanu passes away at her Mānoa Valley home Puka'ōma'o, "Green opening" (the home had green shutters). Ka'ahumanu had served as kuhina nui (premier or regent) after the death of Kamehameha I, co-ruling from 1819 to 1832 with Kamehameha II and Kamehameha III during their reigns.

1836, December 30—Nāhi'ena'ena, daughter of Kamehameha I and Keopuolani, passes away. Before her death, Nāhi'ena'ena was deeply in love with and almost married her brother Kauikeaouli, who went on to become Kamehameha III.

1837, February 14—Kamehameha II marries Kalama in a ceremony performed by Reverend Hiram Bingham.

1839—Kamehameha III proclaims Hawai'i's Declaration of Rights, also known as the Hawaiian Magna Carta.

1840, October 8—Kamehameha III and kuhina nui (premier) Kekāuluohi (Miriam 'Auhea) change Hawai'i to a constitutional monarchy using Hawai'i's first constitution drafted in Hawaiian in 1839. The new government follows the American and British political models and provides for a Supreme Court (that includes the king), an Executive, a Legislative body of fifteen hereditary nobles, and seven representatives elected by the people. It also guarantees freedom of religious worship.

1843, July 31—Kamehameha III recites what will become Hawai'i's national motto as part of his Restoration Day speech: Ua mau ke ea o ka 'āina i ka pono – The life of the land is perpetuated in righteousness.

1846, March—Kamehameha III passes the First Organic Act, establishing an executive branch of government as well as a Privy Council. The Second Organic Act is enacted on April 27, 1846, establishing a new system of land ownership. The Third Organic Act is enacted on January 10, 1848, reforming Hawai'i's judicial system.

1848, January 27—Kamehameha III begins the Great Māhele which divides Hawaiian land between the king and 245 chiefs and replaces Hawai'i's traditional land use practices with a new system of private property ownership. The Māhele ("Division") is completed on March 7, and on the following day the king divides the remaining land between the king and the government. The end result is that about 24 percent of Hawai'i's land is owned by the king (Crown lands); 37 percent is owned by the government; and 38 percent is given to the ruling ali'i (chiefs).

1854—Alexander Liholiho ascends to the throne as Kamehameha IV immediately after Kamehameha III's death and encourages the development of plantation agriculture (the sugar industry).

1854, December 15—The death of King Kamehameha III ends his 30-year reign. Prince Alexander Liholiho, the 21-year-old grandson of Kamehameha I, comes to the throne as Kamehameha IV.

1856, June 19—Kamehameha IV marries Emma Na'ea Rooke at Kawaiaha'o Church.

1858, May 20—Prince Albert Edward Kauikeaouli, son of Kamehameha IV and Queen Emma, is born.

1860, July 15—Construction begins on Emma and Kamehameha IV's Queen's Hospital.

1860— Emma and Kamehameha IV visit Kaua'i with their son, Crown Prince Albert. They stay at the large Hanalei Valley sugar plantation estate of Robert Crichton Wyllie, the Hawaiian Kingdom's Foreign Minister. To honor the young prince, Wyllie changes the name of his estate to Princeville Plantation. Tragically, Prince Albert dies in 1862 at the age of four.

1862—Lydia Kamaka'eha Pākī, the future Queen Lili'uokalani, marries John Owen Dominis.

1863, Nov. 30—Kamehameha IV dies, and is succeeded by his brother, Prince Lot Kapuāiwa Kamehameha who becomes Kamehameha V. With the approval of kuhina nui (premier) Victoria Ka'ahumanu Kamāmalu and the Privy Council, Prince Lot proclaims himself king without opposition but he angers American interests and businessmen when he refuses to take an oath to uphold the Constitution of 1852. On August 20, 1864, he proclaims a new constitution that gives greater power to the king but less control to the Privy Council and Legislative Assembly limiting their voting powers.

1865—The Royal Mausoleum is built in Nu'uanu at Mauna 'Ala ("Fragrant mountain"). It was planned by Kamehameha IV and Emma for their deceased son Prince Albert and designed by Theodore Heuck, Honolulu's first resident architect. Other deceased royalty are later transferred there from the 'Iolani Palace mausoleum. It now holds the remains of King Kamehameha II through V as well as Kalākaua, Lili'uokalani and other important nobles of Hawai'i's past.

1866, May 29—Princess Victoria Kamāmalu, granddaughter of Kamehameha, dies at age 27.

1870, September 20— Kalama, wife of Kamehameha III, dies at age 53.

1871, June 11—Kamehameha V proclaims a holiday in memory of his grandfather, Kamehameha I that becomes known as Kamehameha Day. The first King Kamehameha Day (later known just as Kamehameha Day) takes place on June 11, 1872.

1872, December 11—Kamehameha V dies.

1873, January 8—The Hawaiian legislature selects William Charles Lunalilo as king making him Hawai'i's first elected king.

1874, February 12—After the death of Lunalilo on February 3, 1874, David La'amea Kalākaua is elected king by a Legislative vote of 39 to 6 causing supporters of Emma to ransack the courthouse and attack legislators leaving many injured and one dead. Marines from American and British warships restore order and Kalākaua takes an oath of allegiance to Kamehameha V's 1864 Constitution.

1874, February 14—Kalākaua names his younger brother Prince William Pitt Leleiōhoku his successor. Two new princesses are designated—Princess Kamaka'eha Dominis (the future Queen Lili'uokalani) and Princess Likelike.

1874, November 17—Kalākaua and a royal party leave for San Francisco on the steamer *Benicia* for a goodwill tour of the United States including Washington D.C to promote the Reciprocity Treaty, which had been repeatedly delayed. Kalākaua is the first Hawaiian king to visit the U.S. He arrives back on the U.S.S. *Pensacola* on February 15, 1875.

1875, October 16—Princess Victoria Ka'iulani, daughter of A.S. Cleghorn and Princess Miriam Likelike, is born.

1877, April 19—Prince Leleiohoku dies at twenty-two years of age and Princess Lili'uokalani is proclaimed heir to the throne.

1879, December 31—The cornerstone is laid for 'Iolani Palace in midtown Honolulu. Completed in 1882, it serves first as a royal palace and later as the capitol building of the Republic, the Territory, and then the State of Hawai'i.

1881—Kalākaua leaves on an around-the-world journey calling on eleven heads of state including leaders of the United States, Japan and Great Britain. He is the first ruler of any country to circumnavigate the world.

1883—Princess Ruth Ke'elikōlani, the granddaughter of King Kamehameha I, passes away. Her will bequeaths to Princess Bernice Pauahi Bishop 353,000 acres of Kamehameha lands—nearly nine percent of all land in the Islands.

1883, February 14—A coronation ceremony takes place for Kalākaua and Kapi'olani, and includes the unveiling of a statue of King Kamehameha I in front of Ali'iōlani Hale.

1884—Princess Pauahi dies, leaving 434,000 acres of land in perpetual trust to assist in the establishment of schools bearing the Kamehameha name. Kamehameha School for Boys opens on October 4, 1887, and Kamehameha School for Girls opens on December 19, 1894.

1885, April 25—The Dowager Queen Emma dies at age 49.

1886, November—King Kalākaua's 50th birthday jubilee is held at 'Iolani Palace.

1887— Kapi'olani attends the jubilee of Great Britain's Queen Victoria in England, and later visits President Grover Cleveland.

1890, November 25—Kalākaua departs for San Francisco on the U.S.S. *Charleston.*

1891, January 20—Kalākaua dies in San Francisco.

1891, January 29—Princess Lili'uokalani becomes queen. Under pressure from her cabinet Lili'uokalani takes the oath of office and unwillingly pledges allegiance to the Bayonet Constitution. During the next two years Lili'uokalani works to promulgate a new constitution that restores autonomy of her kingdom by setting aside provisions of the Bayonet Constitution that had limited the power of the monarch. Opposing her is the Hawaiian League with its stated goals of deposing the queen, overthrowing the monarchy and annexing Hawai'i to the United States.

1893, January 17— Lili'uokalani is dethroned and a provisional government is established.

Hawai'i's Royal Family. [Baker-Van Dyke Collection]

1893, October 18—The Blount Report blames the overthrow of the monarchy on U.S. Minister Stevens and suggests restoring the Hawaiian government. President Cleveland denounces the overthrow as lawless and achieved under "false pretexts."

1893, November 4—President Cleveland gives orders to restore the power of Lili'uokalani. He also sends word that he regretted the "unauthorized intervention" that took away the queen's sovereignty.

1894, January 4—The Republic of Hawai'i is established. Six months later, Sanford B. Dole is named president of the Republic of Hawai'i.

1895, January 24— Lili'uokalani is forced to abdicate the throne. She signs a formal abdication calling for the recognition of the Republic of Hawai'i as the lawful government. She later claims that the abdication was invalid due to coercion and that she signed the document only to spare the lives of her supporters.

1897—President McKinley succeeds President Cleveland. Lili'uokalani visits Washington D.C. to petition McKinley to restore the rights of the Hawaiian people, but her petition is not acted upon.

1897, June 16—President McKinley sends an annexation treaty to the Senate.

1897, July 14 - Refusing President Grover Cleveland's demand that the Hawai'i Provisional Government return authority to Lili'uokalani, the Republic of Hawai'i is formally established. The plan is to wait for the election of a president sympathetic to their goal.

1898, August— President McKinley declares that Hawai'i is to become part of the U.S.

1899, March 6—Princess Ka'iulani, the niece of Lili'uokalani and King Kalākaua, passes away at the young age of 23. Though her death is attributed to a fever, many believe she died of a broken heart as the last Hawaiian princess and heiress to a vanished throne.

THE TWELVE COMPANIES OF AMERICAN MISSIONARIES

Reverend Dwight Baldwin. [Hawai'i State Archives]

1820, March 31—From the 1820s to the 1860s, a steady stream of missionaries arrived in the Hawaiian Islands, first converting the ali'i (chiefs) and then the maka'āinana (commoners) to Christianity. The First Company of American missionaries arrives on March 31, 1820 on the brig *Thaddeus,* after leaving Boston on August 31, 1819 under the command of Andrew Blanchard. The missionaries arrived at Kailua-Kona on April 4, 1820.

Sereno Edwards Bishop, the first missionary born in Hawai'i. [Hawai'i State Archives]

1823, April 27—The *Thames,* under the command of Reuben Clasby arrives carrying the Second Company of American missionaries.

1828, March 30—The *Parthian,* under the command of Richard D. Blinn, arrives with the Third Company of American missionaries that includes Gerrit Parmele Judd (1803-1873), a medical doctor who spends a lifetime of service in the Islands including serving as a minister and adviser of Kamehameha III. In 1845 Judd becomes Hawai'i's Secretary of State for Foreign Affairs.

Reverend Samuel Cheney Damon, Julia Mills Damon (wife), and Samuel Mills Damon (son). [Bishop Museum]

1831, June 7—The *New England,* under the command of Avery F. Parker, arrives carrying the Fourth Company of American missionaries.

1831—More than 1,100 missionary schools are operating, with a total enrollment of more than 50,000 students, mostly adults.

1832, May 17—The whale ship *Averick,* under the command of Captain Swain, arrives carrying the Fifth Company of American missionaries.

1833—The *Mentor,* under the command of Captain Rice, arrives carrying the Sixth Company of American missionaries. Aboard is Reverend John Diell (1808-1841), who opens the Seamen's Bethel in Honolulu (1837), and is first chaplain of the American Seamen's Friend Society. He later organizes the O'ahu Bethel Church.

1834, December 5—The *Hellespont,* under the command of Captain Henry, arrives carrying the Seventh Company of American missionaries.

1836—David and Sarah Lyman establish the Hilo Boy's Boarding School.

1837, April 9—The barque *Mary Frazier,* under the command of Charles Sumner, arrives carrying the Eighth Company of American missionaries.

1838-1840—During an evangelical crusade led by Titus Coan (1801–1882) more than 20,000 Hawaiians are converted to Protestantism and become members of the Congregational Church. This event later becomes known as "The Great Revival."

1840s—At least 17 mission stations exist throughout the Hawaiian Islands.

1841, May 21—The *Gloucester,* under the command of Captain Easterbrook, arrives carrying the Ninth Company of American missionaries.

1842—Kawaiaha'o Church is dedicated in Honolulu.

1842, September 21—The brig *Sarah Abigail,* under the command of Captain Doane, arrives carrying the Tenth Company of American missionaries.

1844, July 15—The brig *Globe,* under the command of Captain Doane, arrives carrying the Eleventh Company.

1848, February 26—The bark *Samoset,* under the command of Captain Hollis, arrives carrying the Twelfth (and final) Company.

THE WHALING ERA

Herman Melville (1819-1891), one of the foremost American authors writing about the Pacific, went to sea as a whaler and was discharged (for the third time) at Lahaina Maui in May, 1843. After working a short while in a Honolulu bowling alley, he returned home to New York City where he wrote the classic *Moby Dick* and other works of fiction. [Hawai'i State Archives]

1819, September 29—Hawai'i's whaling era begins when two New England whalers, the *Equator* and the *Balena* arrive. While anchored in Kealakekua Bay, the *Balena* harpoons a large sperm whale that yields more than 100 barrels of oil.

1820—The Nantucket whaling ship *Maro,* under the command of Joseph Allen, becomes the first whaling ship to enter Honolulu Harbor. Allen later discovers rich whaling waters off Japan, and soon hundreds of whaling ships head for the area to exploit the bountiful sperm whale resource. Hawai'i, being centrally located between the American west coast and Japan, quickly develops into a major staging area for ships going to and from the newly discovered whaling area. The main whaling ports are in Honolulu and Lahaina, and thousands of Hawaiians are recruited to work on the ships.

1822—About 60 whaling ships patrol Hawaiian waters, and the number continues to grow as a shore-based fishery in Hawai'i develops specifically to hunt whales.

1823, May 1—The *Globe,* a Nantucket whaling ship under the command of Thomas Worth, arrives in Honolulu, and is later involved in whaling history's worst mutiny, led by Samuel Comstock.

1824—More than 100 whaling vessels arrive.

1825, October—The Lahaina home of Reverend William Richards is attacked by the crew of the British whaling ship *Daniel* angry at restrictions enacted due to missionary influences.

1827, October—The sailors of the British whale ship *John Palmer,* under the command of captain Elisha Clarke fire a cannon at a Lahaina missionary house.

1828—A total of 159 whaling ships arrive in Hawaiian ports including 112 in Honolulu and 47 in Lahaina.

1832—The whaling industry continues to grow with a total of 198 whaling ships stopping in Hawaiian ports, including 118 in Honolulu and 80 in Lahaina. Honolulu merchant Henry A. Peirce outfits the *Denmark Hill,* the first whaling ship to sail under the Hawaiian flag.

1834—The whaling ship *Helvetius* wrecks on the reef off Diamond Head with 1,400 barrels of whale oil on board. Kamehameha III sends men to assist salvaging about 500 barrels.

1840s—Several companies in the Islands are hunting local whales. Sperm whale oil sells for $1 per gallon and whale blubber sells for 30 cents per gallon. Oil from sperm whales fuels the Industrial Revolution.

1846—The peak year for whaling ship arrivals at Hawaiian ports with at least 596 arrivals including at least 429 at Lahaina and 167 at Honolulu.

1852, November 8—The death of imprisoned whaler Henry Burns leads to a riot by thousands of sailors who set fire to the Honolulu police station.

1859—Approximately 549 whaling ships visit Hawaiian ports.

1859—Oil is discovered in Titusville, Pennsylvania and becomes the new source of industrial lubricants thus beginning the end of the whaling industry. Whales are also rapidly disappearing due to over-harvesting.

1868—About 600,000 pounds of whalebone (baleen) and 775,000 pounds of whale oil are transshipped from the Islands. Baleen, before plastic is invented, is in demand for use in women's corsets, hoop skirts, umbrellas, and a variety of other products that require strong, flexible material.

1871—An early Arctic freeze north of the Bering Strait destroys the North Pacific whaling fleet including seven Hawai'i-owned ships.

1966—Humpback whales are near extinction when the International Whaling Commission prohibits all hunting of humpback whales in the North Pacific Ocean.

1992—Congress creates the Hawaiian Islands Humpback Whale National Marine Sanctuary to protect the shallow warm waters surrounding the Hawaiian Islands. The National Oceanic and Atmospheric Administration and the State of Hawai'i jointly manage the sanctuary.

As the sandalwood trade waned, whaling became Hawaii's economic mainstay. Each season the crews of the American whaling fleets descended like locusts on the ports of Honolulu and Lahaina, seeking provisions and sailors' traditional pleasures. It took boldness and strength to be a whaleman. Many lost their lives when the giant sea mammals smashed the tiny boats of their persecutors. [Hawai'i State Archives]

FRENCH/CATHOLICS

1786, May 30—The *Boussole* and the *Astrolabe,* two 500-ton armed naval frigates under the command of French navigator Count de la Pérouse, arrive on at what is now known as La Pérouse Bay (Kalepolepo).

1791, October—The *Solide,* under the command of Etienne Marchand, becomes the first French trading ship to reach the Hawaiian Islands.

1819, August 8—The French corvette *Uraine,* under the command of French Navy captain Louis de Freycinet (1779-1842), arrives. Kamāʻuleʻule (Boki), the future governor of Oʻahu, is baptized aboard the ship. The ship's draftsman, Jacques Arago (1790-1855), writes an account of the visit, that includes his numerous illustrations of Hawaiian life.

1827, July 7—The *Comète,* under Captain Plassard, arrives carrying three Roman Catholic missionaries from Bordeaux France: Alexis Bachelot, Patrick Short, and Abraham Armand.

1827, July 14—(Bastille Day) Reverend Alexis Bachelot leads Hawaiʻi's first Catholic Mass.

1827, November 30—The first baptism of a foreigner child is performed on a child of Spaniard Francisco de Paula Marín (1774-1837), who served Kamehameha I as a physician, adviser, accountant, and rum supplier.

1828—Hawaiʻi's first Catholic chapel opens in Honolulu on land granted by Kamehameha III.

1829—Protestant convert and kuhina nui (premier) Kaʻahumanu orders that practicing Catholics be punished and sent to the island of Kahoʻolawe, which becomes a penal colony.

1831—Kaʻahumanu expels Catholic priests from the Islands, including Reverends Bachelot and Short, and strongly discourages believers in the Catholic religion. Reverend Bachelot will return to the Islands in 1837.

In 1830, after complaining to Kaʻahumanu about an unauthorized search of his home, Father Bachelot was forbidden to teach the Catholic religion in any form. A church facility in Makiki was named after him. [Archives, Diocese of Honolulu]

1837, December 18—At the urging of Protestant missionaries, Kamehameha III issues an ordinance rejecting the Catholic religion leading to a controversy with France.

1837, July 8—The British Royal Navy ship *Sulphur* arrives in Honolulu. The French naval vessel *Venus* also arrives. A controversy regarding Catholic priests in the Islands results in a treaty assuring equal treatment for French residents.

1839, June 7—Kamehameha III issues a Declaration of Rights (the Hawaiian Magna Carta). The document is a predecessor to Hawaiʻi's first formal constitution in 1840 and serves as that constitution's preamble. On June 17, the king issues an Edict of Toleration regarding religious differences reversing his earlier stance banning the practice and teaching of Catholicism.

1839, July 9—The French Navy frigate *L'Artémise* arrives under the command of Cyrille Pierre Théodore Laplace, who is commissioned by the French government to demand rights for French citizens staying in Hawaiʻi. Laplace threatens war unless his demands—freedom of worship, a site for a Catholic Church, and $20,000 in reparations—are met.

1839, July 17—Kamehameha III and Laplace sign the Convention of 1839 granting numerous protections to French citizens in Hawaiʻi. Officials of other countries become alarmed when Laplace makes additional demands, leading to official recognition of Hawaiian independence by France, Great Britain, and the United States.

1840, May—Bishop Rouchouze, the vicar apostolic of the Pacific, arrives along with three other Catholic priests including the exiled Father Maigret.

1840—Under the protection of the French, a permanent Catholic mission is established.

Cathedral of Our Lady of Peace located in central Honolulu, was built on land obtained by the first French clerics from Boki in 1841. [Archives, Diocese of Honolulu]

1842—The French sloop-of-war *Embuscade* arrives under the command of Captain S. Mallet to seek assurances that Catholic priests be allowed to worship, and that French wines may be freely imported.

1843—About 100 Catholic Mission schools with about 3,000 students operate in the Islands.

1843, August 15—Our Lady of Peace Cathedral is blessed and dedicated on Bishop Street, to serve Honolulu's Roman Catholic Diocese.

1846, March 22—The French naval frigate *Virginie* arrives under the command of Rear Admiral Hamelin, who repays the $20,000 demanded by Captain Laplace in 1839.

1846—Father Louis Desire Maigret (1804-1882), who first arrived in 1837, is named Vicar Apostolic to the Sandwich Islands (Hawai'i) and serves until his death in 1882.

1848, April—The French Navy frigate *Poursuivante* and steam-corvette *Gassendi* arrive under the command of Rear Admiral Legoarant de Tromelin who presents ten demands, including equality of worship. He engages in reprisals that include taking over government buildings, damaging the fort in Honolulu, and seizing Kamehameha III's yacht. Tromelin departs ten days later taking with him Guillaume Patrice Dillon, the French consul whose complaints initiated Tromelin's actions.

1848—A full-length portrait of Louis Philippe, painted by renowned portraitist Franz-Xavier Winterhalter, arrives as a gift from France to King Kamehameha III.

1851—Kamehameha III signs a secret agreement with the United States assuring protection in the event of further French interference.

1864—Father Damien is ordained as a Roman Catholic priest at Honolulu's Cathedral of Our Lady of Peace, and in 1873 he begins his service at Kalaupapa.

MORMONS IN HAWAI'I—THE POLYNESIAN CULTURAL CENTER

Mormon missionary Walter Murray Gibson arrived in Honolulu on July 4, 1861. Thereafter he played a dramatic role in Hawaii for twenty-six years. He was especially concerned with the development of the island of Lānai, where a small Mormon colony had grown up. When an investigating committee of Mormon elders discovered that Gibson had diverted church funds to purchase half the island and put the property in his own name he was excommunicated. He became a naturalized citizen of Hawai'i in 1866, moved to Honolulu in 1872 and entered politics.

1850, December 12—Ten Mormons arrive from the California gold camps to become Hawai'i's first Mormon missionaries. One of them, George Q. Cannon, is a leader in the effort to translate the *Book of Mormon* into Hawaiian.

1851, August 8—The first branch of the Church of Jesus Christ of Latter-day Saints is established at Kealakou, Maui.

1855—Cannon publishes *Ka Buke a Moramona*, the Hawaiian translation of the *Book of Mormon.*

1861, July 4—Walter Murray Gibson (1822-1888) arrives after becoming a Mormon missionary. With the approval of Brigham Young to convert Pacific Islanders, Gibson leads a colony of Mormons on Lāna'i. Mormon church elders later find out that Gibson has used church funds to purchase about half of Lāna'i in his own name.

1864—Gibson is excommunicated.

1865—Mormons from Lāna'i purchase 6,000 acres of land in the Lā'ie region at the base of O'ahu's Ko'olau Mountains.

1919—Volcanic rocks and crushed coral are used to build a smaller version of the Salt Lake City temple. Costing $500,000, the temple is dedicated on November 27, 1919 and is the first Mormon temple built outside of the continental United States.

1955—Mormons establish the Latter-day Saints Church College of Hawai'i in Lā'ie, which is dedicated in 1958.

1963, October 12—The success of Polynesian shows put on by the college in the 1950s leads to the construction of the Polynesian Cultural Center, which opens on October 12, 1963 and is run by the college and staffed by students.

1971—Church College has 1,300 students, many from the Pacific Islands.

1974—The school becomes a branch campus of Provo, Utah's Brigham Young University, and is a four-year college with an enrollment of about 2,000 undergraduates. The Mormon temple is considered the "cornerstone" of the college.

1975—A significant expansion makes the Lā'ie site a major O'ahu attraction. Today the Polynesian Cultural Center encompasses 42 acres, including seven theme villages arranged around lagoons representing the Marquesas, Samoa, Fiji, New Zealand, Tahiti, Tonga, and Hawai'i. About 900,000 people visit the Polynesian Cultural Center each year, making it O'ahu's second most visited attraction after the U.S.S. *Arizona* Memorial.

Mormon Temple. [Douglas Peebles]

HEROES OF KALAUPAPA—FATHER DAMIEN

Damien at the dormitories—one of his unending responsibilities. [The Hawaiian Historical Society]

1859—Belgian priest Joseph Damien DeVeuster joins the Sacred Hearts Congregation at Louvain.

1864—DeVeuster is ordained as a priest in Honolulu's Cathedral of Our Lady of Peace, becoming Father Damien.

1865—Hawai'i's first victims of Hansen's disease (leprosy) arrive at remote Kalawao on Moloka'i's Kalaupapa Peninsula beginning the practice of segregating patients from the general population. (The disease is caused by the slow-growing bacterium Mycobacterium leprae.) Over the following decades, nearly 9,000 infected persons will be quarantined here. Kalaupapa Peninsula, located along Moloka'i's north-central coast, is surrounded on three sides by ocean and on the remaining side by 2,000 to 3,000 foot high cliffs. Archaeological sites indicate that Kalaupapa was an important place in ancient Hawai'i, and well populated before Western contact in 1778.

1873—Father Damien volunteers to minister to the needy at Kalaupapa.

1874—Damien builds Our Lady of Sorrows Catholic Church at Kalua'aha, Moloka'i on the site of Moloka'i's first Christian mission and oversees the construction of a home for boys and a home for girls.

1875—Six chapels have been built.

1889, April 15—At only 49 years of age Father Damien dies of Hansen's disease.

1936—Father Damien's body is exhumed on Moloka'i and sent to Belgium. Bones from his hand are reinterred on Moloka'i.

1969, April 15—Eighty years after Father Damien's death he is honored by the unveiling of a statue designed by New York sculptor Marisol Escobar in the Capitol Rotunda in Washington D.C., a gift to the National Statuary Hall along with a statue of Kamehameha I. A second Damien statue is placed in front of Hawai'i's State Capitol Building.

After becoming established in the colony at Kalaupapa, on Moloka'i, Father Damien posed with a group of patients. Believing the disease to have come to the Islands with Chinese immigrants, Hawaiians called the terrible affliction Ma'i Pākē, the Chinese sickness. [Hawai'i State Archives]

One June 13, 1992, Pope John Paul II officially approved the "real miracle" attributed to Damien's intercession (Sister Simplicia's overnight cure from a seven-month-long, grave intestinal disease in 1895. She had been praying for a cure through Damien's intercession)/ On June 4, 1995, Pope John Paul II beatified Father Damien in a Pontifical Mass in Brussels, Belgium, in recognition of a life of extraordinary holiness and heroic virtue. Beatification is the next-to-last formal step in the canonization process. This photograph was taken a few weeks before he died in 1889. [Hawai'i State Archives]

1977—Pope Paul VI declares Father Damien to be venerable, the first of the three steps to canonization (sainthood).

1995, June 4—Pope John Paul II beatifies Father Damien in Brussels, Belgium.

2009, Oct. 11—Father Damien is canonized in a ceremony at the Vatican, becoming Saint Damien. President Barack Obama issues a statement affirming his deep admiration for the life of Saint Damien who "challenged the stigmatizing effects of disease, giving voice to the voiceless and ultimately sacrificing his own life to bring dignity to so many." Father Damien is fondly known as the "Martyr of Moloka'i."

HEROES OF KALAUPAPA—MOTHER MARIANNE

Mother Marianne Cope at the time she was elected Mother Provincial in 1877. [*Pilgrimage and Exile*]

Sister M. Rosalia McLaughlin, Sister M. Martha Kaiser, Sister M. Leopoldina Burns, Walter Murray Gibson (Prime Minister of the Hawaiian Kingdom), Sister M. Charles Hoffman, Sister M. Cresentia Eilers, Mother Marianne Cope. [*Pilgrimage and Exile*]

1862—Barbara Koob, born in Germany, takes the name Marianne upon joining the Sisters of the Third Order of St. Francis in New York. As Mother Marianne Cope she will minister to Kalaupapa's Hansen disease (leprosy) patients.

1888—Mother Marianne moves to Kalaupapa in 1888 to supervise a new girls' home. She later runs a home for boys and girls. She works alongside Father Damien.

1918—Mother Marianne passes away at the age of 80 after ministering to Kalaupapa's needy for 30 years. Known for her uplifting attitude, she helped patients in many small but meaningful ways, such as planting flowers and trees, organizing picnics, sewing their clothes, and playing piano for sing alongs. She also founded Maui's first hospital now known as Maui Memorial Hospital. Kalākaua honored Mother Marianne with royal decorations and famed author Robert Louis Stevenson wrote of her.

2004, January—The Vatican's Congregation for the Causes of Saints affirms Mother Marianne's "heroic virtue," a step toward canonization and sainthood.

2004, April 19—Mother Marianne is declared venerable in a papal decree issued by Pope John Paul II.

2005, January—Mother Marianne's bones are exhumed to be enshrined in the headquarters of the Sisters of St. Francis in Syracuse, New York.

2005, May 14—Pope Benedict XVI announces that Mother Marianne is beatified–the last formal step before sainthood.

2011, December 19—Pope Benedict XVI signs and approves the promulgation of the decree for the sainthood of Mother Marianne. She is canonized on October 21, 2012, and is now named Saint Marianne Cope as well as Saint Marianne of Moloka'i.

Mother Marianne a few days before her death in August 1918 with a few patients and nuns from C.R. Bishop Home at Moloka'i. [*Pilgrimage and Exile*]

SCHOLARS AND EARLY PUBLICATIONS

Many of Hawai'i's early historical writings were the product of interviews with Hawaiian elders and were written in the Hawaiian language. Particularly notable was the voluminous amount of research done by students of Maui's Lahainaluna Seminary founded in 1831 by American Protestant missionaries as a seminary of advanced education for young Hawaiian men.

1784—The first published chart of the Hawaiian Islands is included in the official account of Captain James Cook's third voyage.

1788—George Dixon's *A Voyage Round the World,* including drawings and written descriptions of the Hawaiian Islands, is published.

1824—*Memoires du Capitaine Peron sur ses Voyages* is published by Pierre Francois Peron and includes late 1700s descriptions of Kamehameha I and Hawai'i.

1825—Lord George Anson Byron returns the bodies of King Kamehameha II and Kamāmalu back from London on the frigate *Blonde.* He later publishes *Voyage of H.M.S. "Blonde" to the Sandwich Islands, 1824-25.*

1826—William Ellis publishes both *Hawaiian Tour* and *Polynesian Researches, during a Residence of Nearly Six Years in the South Sea Islands* after visiting the Islands in 1822 and again in 1823. When living in Huahine, Tahiti Ellis studied the Tahitian language which enabled him to communicate well with Hawaiians in their own language. His many notes provided one of the most complete records of early Hawaiian life, including extensive descriptions of Hawaiian history and culture.

1832—The Hawaiian translation of the *New Testament* is published and presented by missionary Hiram Bingham to Ka'ahumanu shortly before her death. Also published in 1832 is the Hawaiian translation of the standard New England elementary arithmetic text *He Helu Kamalii,* and a geography text, *He Hoikehonua.*

1834—The Honolulu newspaper *Kumu Hawaii* begins publication along with the Hawaiian language newspaper Kekumu.

1834—Lahainaluna Press publishes *Ke Anahonua,* which includes sections on mathematics, navigation and land surveying.

1834—The Mission Press publishes the first *Hawaiian Almanac.*

1834, February 14—Lahainaluna Seminary begins publication of a four-page Hawaiian language weekly, *Ka Lama Hawaii* (*The Hawaiian Luminary*)—the first periodical printed in the North Pacific region (west of the Rockies). Edited by Reverend Lorrin Andrews, the periodical includes woodcut illustrations and Lahaina ship arrivals.

1836—Reverend Lorrin Andrews (1795-1868), head of the Lahainaluna Seminary, publishes the first significant Hawaiian-English dictionary, *Vocabulary of Words in the Hawaiian Language,* that includes 5,700 words.

1836, July 30—Nelson Hall and S. D. MacIntosh begin publication of Hawai'i's first English-language newspaper, the four-page weekly *Sandwich Island Gazette* and *Journal of Commerce* which continues publication until July of 1839.

1837—The *Honolulu Spectator* begins publication and includes regular weather record reports written by Dr. Thomas Charles Byde Rooke.

1838—Reverend Sheldon Dibble (1809-1845) publishes *Ka Moolele Hawaii* (Mo'o 'ōlelo means "story" or "history."), a history of the Hawaiian Islands written in Hawaiian. The book is translated into English a few years later and then published in the *Hawaiian Spectator* newspaper.

1838, January—Missionaries begin printing the quarterly *Hawaiian Spectator,* the North Pacific region's first literary journal.

1839—Dibble publishes *A History and General Views of the Sandwich Islands Mission,* and then in 1843, *History of the Sandwich Islands.* Dibble's histories are developed with the assistance of two particularly prolific Lahainaluna students, David Malo (c.1793-1853) and Samuel Mānaiakalani Kamakau (1815-1876) who collected and documented many legends, genealogies and chants as well as specific details of pre-contact historical events. Malo and Kamakau's extensive writings were originally published in Hawaiian language newspapers in the 1860s and 1870s. Malo's writings dated around 1840 were not published in English until Nathaniel Emerson's translation entitled *Hawaiian Antiquities* (*Ka Moolele Hawaii*) is published by the Hawaiian Gazette Company in 1903.

1839, May 10—The first complete translation of the Bible into the Hawaiian language is completed. Entitled *Ka Palapala Hemolele,* it is published in three volumes and totals 2,331 pages.

1843—Reverend S. C. Damon starts *The Friend,* a monthly journal that continues publication for more than 100 years.

David Malo. [Hawai'i State Archives]

1845—The Lahainaluna Seminary Press publishes the first English-Hawaiian Dictionary, *He Hoakakaolelo no na Hualelo Beritania* (A Dictionary of English Words), edited by Artemas Bishop (1795-1872) and J. S. Emerson (1800-1867). In 1865, Andrews publishes a Hawaiian-English Dictionary containing about 15,000 words.

Mid-1800s—Zephyrin Kepelino (c.1830-1876), a descendant of the famous Tahitian priest Pā'ao, writes at least six Hawaiian language books. The most notable of these is Kepelino's *Traditions of Hawaii*, published in 1932 by Bernice Pauahi Bishop Museum.

1851—Kamakau serves in Hawai'i's Legislature until his death in 1876.

1852—John Papa 'Ī'ī helps draft the Hawai'i Constitution of 1852 and serves as a justice on Hawai'i's Supreme Court from 1852 to 1864. Previously he was a language advisor to missionary Hiram Bingham (1789-1869) and had been appointed to the House of Nobles and Privy Council under Kamehameha III. In 1959 Pūku'i's translation of 'Ī'ī's writings, entitled *Fragments of Hawaiian History,* is published by Bishop Museum Press.

1856—*The Pacific Commercial Advertiser* starts as a weekly newspaper becoming a daily in 1882, and is later known as the *Honolulu Advertiser.*

1861—The influential Hawaiian language newspaper *Ka Nupepa Kuokoa* begins publication and continues until 1927, making it the longest running Hawaiian language paper.

1864—Abraham Fornander (1812-1887), born in Sweden, becomes a Circuit Judge. He is a member of the King's Privy Council under Kamehameha IV and later conducts extensive interviews with Kepelino and Kamakau. With the help of assistants he arranges interviews with many Hawaiians. Collectively, this information becomes the basis of his *An Account of the Polynesian Race.* After his death, Fornander's *Collection of Hawaiian Antiquities and Folklore* is published by Thomas G. Thrum. Volume II of *An Account of the Polynesian Race* is republished as *Ancient History of the Hawaiian People to the Times of Kamehameha I* (Mutual Publishing: 1996).

John Papa 'Ī'ī. [Hawai'i State Archives]

1864—*Ka Hoku O Ka Pakipika (The Star of the Pacific)* is the first independently owned newspaper produced by Hawaiians.

1866, September 4—*The Hawaiian Herald* becomes Hawai'i's first daily newspaper. The publication is short-lived, however, ending on December 21, 1866.

1866-1870—Mary Kawena Pūku'i translates articles written by John Papa 'Ī'ī (c.1800-1870) for the newspaper *Kuokoa.* In 1961 she translates Kamakau's *Ruling Chiefs of Hawai'i* for publication by Kamehameha Schools Press. A second volume of Kamakau's writings, entitled *The People of Old,* is translated by Pūku'i and published by Bishop Museum Press in 1964.

1869—Sanford Dole writes *Synopsis of the Birds of the Hawaiian Islands.*

1873, January 15—Scottish author Isabella Bird Bishop (1832-1904) begins her travels around the Hawaiian Islands, resulting in *The Hawaiian Archipelago: Six Months Among the Palm Groves, Coral Reefs, and Volcanoes of the Sandwich Islands.*

1875—The first *Hawaiian Almanac and Annual* is published by Thomas Thrum.

1888—*Paradise of the Pacific* magazine later known as *Honolulu Magazine* begins publication.

1893—The afternoon newspaper *Hawaiian Star* begins publication.

1900—*The New China Daily Press* becomes Hawai'i's first Chinese newspaper.

1905—The Methodist Church of Honolulu begins publishing *Hanin Sisa (Korean News).*

1912—Frederick Makino starts the Japanese language newspaper *Hawaii Hochi.*

1913—The *Honolulu Star-Bulletin* is formed when the *Evening Bulletin* merges with the *Hawaiian Star.*

1928—The weekly Hawaiian language paper *Ke Alakai o Hawaii (Hawai'i Guide)* begins publication.

A new edition of the earlier 1839 and 1868 printings of the Hawaiian Bible was published in 2012. It is the first time that the Hawaiian language Bible has been formatted and printed with contemporary orthography using the kahakō and 'okina so that it may continue to play a major role as a linguistic, cultural, and spiritual resource. [*Ka Baibala Hemolele,* Mutual Publishing]

THE PLANTATION ERA

1802—Sugarcane is first processed and refined by a Chinese man on Lāna'i who set up boilers and a stone sugar mill shipped from China.

1813—Spaniard Francisco de Paula Marín (1774-1837), a physician and adviser of Kamehameha I, plants the first pineapples in the Islands.

1819—Spaniard Francisco de Paula Marín, a physician and adviser of King Kamehameha I, manufactures sugar.

A Chinese family in front of their plantation house. The Chinese were among the early foreign settlers to make Hawai'i their home. As early as 1787, Chinese were coming to Hawai'i on foreign ships, sometimes as cooks or seamen. Some Chinese merchants established small businesses in Island ports, while others developed rice or coffee farms in Waipi'o Valley or Kona. They also freely intermarried with Hawaiian women, thus establishing many Chinese-Hawaiian dynasties that have survived until today. Date unknown. [Lyman House Memorial Museum]

1835—Kōloa Sugar Plantation is established for the American firm Ladd & Co. in Kōloa, Kaua'i under the direction of William Hooper. It is Hawai'i's first successful commercial sugar plantation and the first to export the product.

1850—Hawai'i's legislature passes the Masters and Servants Act, establishing a contract labor system that begins the mass importation of workers for the Islands' sugar plantations. The Act allows persons over twenty years of age to sign a contract binding them to an employer for up to five years.

1851—David M. Weston of the East Maui Plantation invents a centrifugal machine that separates sugar from molasses, speeding up the drying process.

1851—The *Thetis* arrives from China with 195 men and 20 boys. Average pay is $3 per month plus room and board.

1853—Hawai'i's first steam-operated sugar mill opens in Līhu'e, Kaua'i.

1854—Kamehameha IV encourages the development of plantation agriculture as the main force of Hawai'i's economy.

1856—A 10-mile-long irrigation ditch is dug on Kaua'i to supply water for the production of sugarcane at Līhu'e Plantation operated by William Harrison Rice. Irrigation to grow sugarcane soon leads to a massive expansion of sugarcane production as a commercial crop.

1859—South Sea Islanders begin arriving.

1861—The United States' Civil War causes the price of sugar to rise.

1861—The vacuum pan, which increases productivity by allowing boiling of sugar at lower temperatures, is invented.

1864—George N. Wilcox (1893-1933) leases Grove Farm sugar plantation in Līhu'e, Kaua'i and begins using irrigation methods pioneered by William Harrison Rice.

1867—A trade agreement between the United States and Hawai'i makes it easier to sell Hawaiian sugar in the U.S.

1868—The first mass emigration of Japanese workers includes 142 men and six women who arrive aboard the *Scioto.* These initial migrants, mostly tradesmen and craftsmen without contracts or government permission are called gannen mono ("first year men") referring to the first year of Japan's Meiji era.

1875—Kalākaua negotiates the Reciprocity Treaty passed by the U.S. Congress on September 17, 1876, allowing Hawaiian products into the United States without customs or duties. In return, the United States is allowed to use Pearl Harbor as a naval base.

1877—The firm of Alexander & Baldwin completes the construction of the 17-mile-long Hāmākua irrigation ditch from Haleakalā to East Maui.

Young Japanese women, cane workers, with their cane knives. As thousands of "picture brides" immigrated to Hawai'i from Japan and Okinawa between 1900 and 1924, the number of women employed on the plantation steadily grew. By 1915, women were 38 percent of the total Japanese sugar plantation workforce. The women also made extra money doing laundry for single men [Lyman House Memorial Museum]

A Korean family dressed up for a visit to the photographer's studio. While the father wears American clothing, the more tradition-minded wife clings to her native Korean style of dress. [Hawai'i State Archives]

1878—Claus Spreckels helps secure and develop some 18,000 acres of leased Crown lands on Maui, leading to the establishment of the Hawaiian Commercial & Sugar Co.

1878—Spreckels begins constructing the 30-mile-long Ha'ikū Ditch, completed in 1880, to carry 50 million gallons of water daily to sugarcane fields in Pu'unēnē and Spreckelsville. He becomes known as the "Sugar King of Hawai'i" and is later accused of corruption involving secret deals with Kalākaua.

1878—Portuguese workers from the Madeira Islands arrive aboard the *Priscilla* beginning an influx of laborers from that region that totals 20,000 by 1913. Considered Europeans, the Portuguese are given land and citizenship (after 1898). Unlike Asian workers, some are hired as lunas (overseers), supervising Asians for the Caucasian plantation owners. Virtually all Catholics, the Portuguese strengthen Catholicism in the Islands.

1879—More than 3,500 workers arrive from China.

1879, July 1—James Ashley bores Hawai'i's first artesian well for James Campbell near Campbell's ranch in Honouliuli, Ewa, O'ahu. More wells are soon bored to provide water for the cultivation of sugarcane on thousands of acres.

1880—The "Big Five" companies—Theo H. Davies; American Factors (Amfac); C. Brewer & Co.; Alexander & Baldwin; and Castle & Cooke, operate all 63 Hawai'i sugar plantations.

1881—Norwegian and German workers begin arriving.

1881, March—Kalākaua visits Japan and asks Emperor Meiji to allow workers to come to Hawai'i where there is now a shortage of plantation workers.

1885—Captain John Kidwell introduces the Cayenne pineapple in Mānoa, and it becomes the main variety grown.

1885—Japan and the Kingdom of Hawai'i sign a treaty permitting large-scale immigration.

1885, February 8—The first official (government sponsored) Japanese contract workers arrive in Honolulu on the *City of Tokio* —676 men and 158 women.

1886—Chinese worker immigration is halted by the passage of the Hawaiian Kingdom Chinese Exclusion Act.

1888—The first diffusion process plant for manufacturing sugar is introduced by Colonel Zephaniah Swift Spalding of Kaua'i's Makee Sugar Plantation.

1890—The McKinley Tariff eliminates the advantages of Hawai'i's sugar producers over foreign producers.

1898—Alfred W. Eames cultivates and sells fresh pineapple. His company later becomes Del Monte Fresh Produce Inc.

1898—Plantation workers total 25,881.

1898—Hawai'i's annexation to the United States (via the Newlands Resolution) ends Chinese immigration.

1900—The S.S. *China* arrives with the first Okinawan workers.

1900—Construction of 22 steel cargo vessels for transporting sugar is begun by the American-Hawaiian Steamship Company.

1900—Up from just 30,000 acres in 1880, 68,500 acres of land are now sugar fields.

1900s—At least 100 sugar mills are operated by 51 companies.

1900, June 14—The Organic Act goes into effect and contract labor is no longer legal. Within one month 8,000 laborers go on strike demanding higher wages, better working conditions, and the hiring of Japanese lunas.

1900, December 23—The S.S. *City of Rio de Janeiro* arrives with 56 Puerto Rican laborers. Thousands more will arrive during the next two decades.

1901, December 4—James Drummond Dole (1877-1958) forms the Hawaiian Pineapple Company and grows the fruit on 60 acres in Wahiawā, O'ahu.

1902—Japanese workers arriving over the previous two decades now total over 31,000.

1903—Dole's first harvest results in the canning of 1,893 cases.

1903, January 13—The first Korean contract laborers arrive aboard the *Gaelic,* and by the end of 1905 more than 7,500 Korean workers will have arrived.

1905—The Kohala Ditch, completed on Hawai'i Island after 18 months of construction, taps the streams of the Kohala mountains to irrigate the region's sugar plantations. Designed by the well-known hydraulic engineer M. M. O'Shaughnessy, it is an engineering feat that included flumes and tunnels spanning 17 miles. A long and difficult construction process, it claimed 17 lives.

1905—Dole's harvest reaches 125,000 cases.

A Filipino family awaits their father's return from the fields at the door of their tiny plantation-town house. [Hawai'i State Archives]

1906—Dole constructs a pineapple cannery in O'ahu's Iwilei district, the world's largest fruit factory at the time.

1906, December 20—The first fifteen Filipino farm workers known as sakada arrive on the *Doric.*

1907— The first Spanish workers arrive from Malaga, Spain.

1909—Honolulu journalists and merchants form the Higher Wages Association and make pro-labor demands on the Hawaiian Sugar Planters Association. The rejection of these demands leads to a strike.

1909, May 9—Japanese workers on O'ahu's 'Aiea Plantation strike, followed by other plantation workers totaling 7,000 strikers in less than one month. The island-wide strike lasts until August, 1909, costing the sugar industry millions of dollars.

1910—Seventy five percent of the annual sugar crop is controlled by Hawai'i's "Big Five" companies: Theo H. Davies; American Factors (Amfac); C. Brewer & Co.; Alexander & Baldwin; and Castle & Cooke. Living conditions on plantations are exceedingly harsh. Workers have little recourse against extremely powerful plantation owners. Significant labor unrest leads to many strikes and protests.

1911—The processes of shelling and coring pineapples is mechanized with the invention of the Ginaca machine patented by Dole employee Henry Ginaca.

1914—Libby, McNeille & Libby open a pineapple cannery in Kalihi.

1916—More than 18,000 Filipino workers have arrived and by 1931 will increase to 120,000 as they become the majority of plantation workers.

1916—A power plant is built to replace steam with electricity for milling sugar by Hawaiian Commercial & Sugar Company.

1916—The completed Waiāhole tunnel brings water through the Ko'olau mountains to central O'ahu.

In December 1900, the first group of Puerto Rican laborers arrived in Hawai'i. By 1910, there were about five thousand men, women and children who sought better opportunities in the Islands following devastating hurricanes in their homeland [Hawai'i State Archives]

1919—Labor leader Pablo Manlapit establishes the Filipino Labor Union to improve working conditions and demand higher wages.

1920s—The mechanical sugarcane planter is developed.

1920—The Japanese comprise more than 40 percent of Hawai'i's total population when the Japanese Labor Federation is established to negotiate for better working conditions. Manlapit along with Japanese labor leaders lead the Higher Wages Movement, but the Hawaiian Sugar Planters Association continues to reject their demands.

1920—Separate strikes by Japanese and Filipino workers are unsuccessful and more than 12,000 workers are evicted from their plantation homes.

1922—Dole purchases 98 percent of the island of Lāna'i for $1,100,000, and soon has 19,000 acres of pineapples planted producing almost one-third of the world's pineapple crop. He becomes known as the "Pineapple King" and the industry dominates Lāna'i for the next 65 years producing as many as 250 million pineapples annually.

1924—Immigration from Japan is prohibited when the U.S. Congress passes the Federal Immigration Act. At this time, Japanese immigrant arrival totals 200,000 since 1885.

1924, September 9—On Kaua'i, sixteen Filipino workers and four Hanapēpē police officers die in a brutal suppression of an eight-month strike. Sixty Filipinos are imprisoned for four years. The event, which becomes known as the Hanapēpē Massacre, begins when police attempt to rescue workers that are kidnapped by the strikers.

1930—Filipinos comprise 70 percent of Hawai'i's plantation work force, up from 19 percent in 1917.

1930—Eight canneries pack nine million cases of pineapple.

Hawai'i's sugar industry made some men (and families) wealthy. By the first decade of the twentieth century, the sugar barons began to build "beach homes" in Waikīkī which in size, opulence, and grandeur were unparalleled in the Islands. One of the most beautiful homes was Kainalu, the mansion of James B. Castle built in 1899 on the beach near Diamond Head. Designed by Oliver P. Traphagen, the architect of the Moana and Haleiwa Hotels, Kainalu included Tiffany stained-glass windows, stair railings of highly polished koa wood, a breakfast room made of dark koa wood, a rooftop garden, and a lānai that jutted over the water supported by beams. Circa 1905. [Bishop Museum]

1932—Manlapit revitalizes the Filipino Labor Federation and renames it Vibora Luviminda.

1933—Manlapit forms the Hawai'i Labor Association.

1933—Sugar land in Hawai'i reaches a peak of more than 250,000 acres, with the "Big Five" companies controlling 96 percent of the crop.

1935—The U.S. Congress passes the National Labor Relations Act, opening the way for the systematic organization of unions.

1935—The first union newspaper—*Voice of Labor*—is published. A local branch of the ILA, an international longshore union, instigates a Hilo dock strike that leads to the reinstatement of some workers. The International Longshoremen's & Warehousemen's Union (ILWU) eventually becomes a major political and labor influence.

1937—A strike in Pu'unēnē, Maui wins Filipino workers significant benefits, but those responsible for organizing the strike are arrested and Manlapit is permanently deported.

1938, August 1—The Hilo Longshoremen's Association strikes against the Inter-Island Steamship Navigation Company. After marching down Kūhiō Road, about 250 workers and their supporters stage a peaceful sit-in at the Hilo wharf where the Inter-Island Steamship Company vessel Waialeale is arriving from Honolulu with armed strikebreakers on board. When the ship arrives, police and strikebreakers attack the striking workers with bayonets, tear gas, fire hoses, guns, buck shot, and bird shot injuring 51 people. The event comes to be known as the "Hilo Massacre" and "Bloody Monday." The incident spurs a two year period of strikes and violence that leads to the shutdown of the docks of the Inter-Island Steamship Company. On the 50th anniversary of the event, a monument is placed at the Hilo dock.

1940—A strike by longshore plantation workers at Kaua'i's Ahukini port lasts 298 days, the longest to date in the Islands. By this time the ILWU has become a formidable union under the leadership of regional director Jack Hall.

1940—A federal sugar act eliminates restrictions on U.S. sales of Hawai'i-refined sugar.

1940—The Islands lead the world in pineapple production.

1945—Passage of the Hawai'i Employment Relations Act empowers

Plantation work was arduous. Here, a planter directs field workers loading cut cane onto flatcars. [Hawai'i State Archives]

agricultural workers and allows the ILWU to begin organizing pineapple and sugar workers.

1946—Pineapple becomes Hawai'i's second largest industry with products valued at $75 million annually. Nine pineapple companies operate nine canneries and 13 plantations on 60,000 acres employing up to 20,000 people.

1946, September 1—Over 28,000 workers from 33 sugar plantations strike statewide against the Hawai'i Employers Council. Represented by the ILWU it becomes known as the Great Hawai'i Sugar Strike and lasts 79 days. The union is victorious, with ILWU national chief Harry Bridges stating that Hawai'i is no longer a feudal colony.

1949, May 1—The ILWU, led by Jack Hall, goes on strike against Hawai'i's "Big Five" companies. The strike shuts down the docks as the union demands wage parity with mainland workers. The strike lasting 157 days and known as the Great Hawaiian Dock Strike cripples the flow of goods to the Islands, almost totally dependent upon shipping. It results in statewide food shortages and the bankruptcy of many small businesses. Labor organizers are accused of participation in a Communist plot (this is during the McCarthy era).

1950, April 1—The House Un-American Activities Committee holds hearings at 'Iolani Palace in Honolulu to investigate alleged Communist infiltration of Hawai'i's labor movement, issuing subpoenas to 70 people including Honolulu ILWU leader Jack Kawano. When Kawano and 38 others refuse to testify, the "Reluctant 39" are charged with contempt of Congress. The U.S. Supreme Court later throws out the charges.

1951, August 28—Seven union organizers, including Jack Hall, the ILWU's regional Hawai'i director, are indicted for violating the Smith Act (advocating the use of force or violence to overthrow the U.S. government).

1952-1953—The seven are convicted after a seven-month trial leading to an all-Islands walkout of union members.

The Kohala Sugar Company operated from 1863 to 1973. The mill's ruins can be seen near the Kauhola Point Lighthouse. Only the foundations are left. [Bishop Museum]

The Hakalau Sugar Mill on the Big Island was built right at the water's edge flume. [Hawaii State Archives]

1955—Pineapple acreage peaks at 76,700.

1955—The AFL and CIO merge into one union.

1957—Annual worker productivity on Hawai'i's sugar plantations is the world's best reaching 65 tons per worker.

1958—After repeated appeals, and then a 1957 U.S. Supreme Court ruling that the teaching of Communism is not illegal, the "Hawai'i Seven" verdict is overturned by the 9th U.S. Circuit Court of Appeals.

1960—For the first time total revenue from tourism exceeds that of the sugarcane industry.

1963—*The Honolulu Advertiser* and the *Honolulu Star-Bulletin* are shut down by a 44-day strike.

1966—Raw sugar production in Hawai'i peaks at 1,234,121 tons.

1967, March 1—Transit workers of the Honolulu Rapid Transit company (a private company) begin a 67-day strike, Hawai'i's longest transit worker strike.

Teamsters Local 996 represent the workers.

1968—Hawai'i Democrats establish the nation's first right to strike law for public-employee unions, strengthening a powerful union lobby that begins to significantly influence political change.

1970—The Hawai'i Public Employment Relations Act is passed allowing County and State workers to join unions, file grievances, and bargain for better wages and working conditions.

1970, October 9—A strike lasting 75 days of two thousand hotel workers represented by the ILWU becomes Hawai'i's largest hotel worker's strike.

1971, January 1—Transit workers represented by Hawai'i Teamsters Local 996 go on strike against Honolulu Rapid Transit, a private company owned by Harry Weinberg. The strike lasts for two months, inconveniencing some 70,000 commuters and leading to the creation of a city transportation system by Mayor Frank Fasi.

1971, July 1—A strike by West Coast and Hawai'i dockworkers begins, with about 15,000 members stopping work until October of 1971 when President Nixon halts the strike for 90 days. The strike resumes the day after Christmas and continues until February, lasting 134 days in all.

1973—A landmark ruling by Judge William S. Richardson in *McBryde Sugar Company v. Robinson* declares that water supplies must remain within their originating watershed. Richardson's term in the court was notable for expanding native Hawaiian rights and providing greater access to beaches and the waters around the Islands. Richardson was criticized by the legal profession and others, but championed by the public and native Hawaiians.

1975—The U.S. Sugar Act expires and leads to the end of quotas and tariffs that had maintained prices.

1982—Alexander & Baldwin closes six plantations shutting down half of Hawai'i's sugar industry.

1985—Businessman David H. Murdock purchases 98 percent of the island of Lāna'i and initiates the construction of expensive townhouses and two hotels; the Mānele Bay and the Lodge at Kō'ele.

1992—The last major commercial pineapple harvest on Lāna'i takes place, though some "show fields" still adorn the landscape. High U.S. labor and land costs are blamed for the decline of Hawai'i's pineapple industry.

2001, April 5—Public education in the state is shut down by two major strikes involving 3,000 University of Hawai'i faculty and 10,000 public school teachers, the state's first combined upper and lower education strike.

2005—Only two sugar mills remain operating in the Hawaiian Islands, Alexander & Baldwin's Cane & Sugar on Maui and Gay & Robinson's Olokele Plantation on Kaua'i.

2008—Fresh Del Monte Produce, Inc. ends its pineapple-growing operations in Hawai'i after 90 years leaving only the Dole Plantation on O'ahu and Maui Pineapple Co. growing pineapple.

2008, Sept. 10—Gay & Robinson announces that it will stop planting on Kaua'i and will exit the sugar industry completing their final harvest in 2010 ending 120 years of growing sugar in Hawai'i. Hawaiian Commercial and Sugar Company (HC&S) currently produces at about 200,000 tons of cane annually, benefitting from federal government investments in biofuel research. On a much smaller scale, Koloa Rum planted a crop of sugarcane in Koloa in August, 2012.

2009, November—Mau'i Land & Pineapple announces its Mau'i Pineapple Co. subsidiary will stop planting pineapple after 97 years. The last harvest takes place on Dec. 23 and the Kahului-based company restructures its two operating companies, Mau'i Pineapple Co. and Kapalua Land Co. to focus on Kapalua Resort.

2010, January—A consortium of Mau'i-based investors announces the formation of Haliimaile Pineapple Co. Ltd to continue growing pineapple on Maui Pineapple Co. land. The new company, Maui Gold Pineapple, will continue to sell whole pineapple under Mau'i Pineapple's well-known Maui Gold brand.

Hawai'i's sugar industry wound down by the closing of mills and ending cultivation in the cane fields. Here hula dancers volunteer to dance as a gesture of aloha and farewell to a way of Island life. [David Weiss/Final Harvest]

THE U.S. MILITARY IN HAWAI'I

1887—Kalākaua leases Pearl Harbor to the United States for eight years as part of a reciprocity treaty with the U.S.

1898, August 12—The U.S. ratifies the treaty annexing Hawai'i.

1898, August 16—Camp McKinley, a tent encampment of United States infantry and engineers, is set up at Waikīkī's Kapi'olani Park, the first United States Army camp in the Islands and home to the First New York Volunteer Infantry Regiment.

1903—U.S. warships carrying 3,000 men dock at Honolulu Harbor to take on supplies. They include: the cruisers *New Orleans, Albany, Cincinnati,* and *Raleigh;* the battleships *Wisconsin* and *Oregon;* and the flagship *Kentucky.*

1905—Kahauiki Military Reservation is established in Honolulu becoming Hawai'i's first permanent United States Army post. In 1907, the post is renamed Shafter Military Reservation in honor of Civil War Medal of Honor winner, Major General William R. Shafter (1835-1906).

1906—Fort Ruger Military Reservation is established at Diamond Head. The Reservation is named in honor of Major General Thomas H. Ruger, who served from 1871 to 1876 as the superintendent of the United States Military Academy at West Point. A network of tunnels is carved into the mountain, and cannon emplacements are placed atop the crater rim along with observation posts and bunkers.

1907—Fort Armstrong is built on Honolulu's Ka'akaukukui Reef near Kalehuawehe, a place once known for its healing power. It is named after Brigadier General Samuel C. Armstrong (1839-1893), the son of Reverend Richard Armstrong (1805-1860) who arrived as a missionary in 1832.

1907—Fort Kamehameha Military Reservation is established at the entrance to Pearl Harbor (now Hickam Air Force Base) becoming the only U.S. fort to be named after a foreign king. Soon after a series of coastal artillery batteries, a "Ring of Steel" is constructed including long-range guns and mortars to fortify O'ahu's harbors.

1908—Pearl Harbor naval facilities begin construction.

1909—Schofield Barracks Military Reservation is established on 14,000 acres in Wahiawā, O'ahu, eventually becoming the biggest permanent United States Army post. It is named for President Andrew Johnson's Secretary of War, Lieutenant General John M. Schofield (1831-1906).

1915—Fort DeRussy is constructed to protect Pearl Harbor and Honolulu. Two battery locations within the fort hold large cannons which are later replaced with anti-aircraft guns. The fort is disbanded on June 28, 1950, the guns removed, and the site designated an Armed Forces Recreation Area. In the 1970s, the fort's Battery Randolph becomes home to the U.S. Army Museum of Hawai'i.

1915, March 25—The Navy submarine *Skate (F-4),* one of four based in the Islands, explodes sinking 306 feet to the bottom of Honolulu Harbor three quarters of a mile offshore and killing the 21-man crew. It is the first submarine disaster in American naval history.

1916, February 4—The crews of seven interned steamships, including the German cruiser *Geier,* set their vessels on fire to prevent them from being used by the United States military. The U.S. is officially neutral until declaring war with Germany on April 6, 1917.

1917—Camp McCarthy opens on the grounds of the old state capitol as a state National Guard camp.

1917—Pearl Harbor (Ford Island) Military Reservation (Pearl Harbor Naval Base) is designed to protect Pearl Harbor. The site includes Battery Adair (1917-1925) and Battery Boyd (1917-1925).

1918—Pearl Harbor naval station is established.

1919—An Army-Navy air facility opens at Luke Field on Ford Island.

1921—Barbers Point Military Reservation is established at Barbers Point Beach and is operational from 1937-1942.

1922—Wheeler Field, now known as Wheeler Air Force Base, is established in Wahiawā, O'ahu near Schofield Barracks. It is named after Sheldon H. Wheeler, an Air Force major who died in a plane crash in 1921.

1923—The Pearl Harbor barracks become the home of the U.S. Marine Corps.

1927—The War Memorial Natatorium is built at the eastern end of Waikīkī as a memorial to the 179 men and women of the Hawaiian Islands who died in World War I.

1939—Kāne'ohe Bay is dredged by the Navy to create an air station but the unit stationed there is decommissioned in 1949 and moved to Barbers Point Naval Air Station. The Kāne'ohe Bay location reopens in 1952 as Marine Corps Air Station Kāne'ohe Bay.

1941, December 7—Japanese bombers attack Pearl Harbor, entering the United States into World War II.

1942, June 4-5—American fighter pilots and dive bombers sink four carriers of the Japanese naval fleet near Midway Atoll in the Battle of Midway securing this strategic base location and becoming a turning point of World War II.

1943, February 1—The U.S. announces the formation of the all-Nisei (second generation Japanese American) 442nd Infantry Regimental Combat Team.

About 10,000 Hawai'i Nisei volunteer within days (only 1,256 mainland Nisei volunteered) demonstrating their loyalty to the U.S. despite the harsh racism experienced in the wake of the Pearl Harbor attack.

1943, September 2—The all-Nisei 100th Infantry Battalion from Hawai'i lands in Oran, North Africa. In June of 1944 they are joined by the 442nd Infantry Regiment.

1944, February 13—The United States Navy submarine rescue vehicle U.S.S. *Macaw,* on a mission to retrieve the submarine U.S.S. *Flier,* runs aground at Midway Atoll due to bad weather. A crew mans the ship's pumps until a March storm finishes off the vessel.

1944-1946—Five thousand Italian prisoners of war captured in 1943 by the British in North Africa are held at four locations on O'ahu: Schofield, Kalihi Valley, Kāne'ohe, and Sand Island. (In all, approximately 50,000 Italian P.O.W.'s captured in North Africa are shipped to the United States.)

1945—About 250,000 U.S. Army troops and 250,000 Navy and Marine Corps members are stationed in the Hawaiian Islands. Millions of servicemen have passed through the Islands on their way to combat areas in the Pacific.

1945, August 15—Victory in Japan Day ("V-J Day") is declared after the United States drops nuclear bombs on Hiroshima (August 6) and Nagasaki (August 9).

1945, September 2—Japan officially surrenders on the deck of the battleship U.S.S. *Missouri.*

1948—Sixteen of twenty crew members of a fully loaded Superfortress are killed in a fiery crash at Hickam field.

1949, September 2—The National Memorial Cemetery of the Pacific, located in an extinct volcanic crater called Punchbowl Crater (known locally as Punchbowl), is dedicated to the men and women who served in the U.S. Armed Forces. To date over 53,000 veterans and their dependents have been interred there.

1950, June 25—North Korea invades South Korea beginning the Korean War. The American troops sent to war include an estimated 17,000 Hawaiian residents of whom 341 are killed and another 79 missing in action. The war ends on July 27, 1953.

1950—From November 27 to December 9, the United States First Marine Division, including the 32nd Infantry Regiment (named "The Queen's Own" by Lili'uokalani in 1916) engages in a fighting withdrawal from the Chosin Reservoir in North Korea. The U.S. forces face extremely low temperatures as well as ten Chinese infantry divisions.

1958—Communist North Vietnam invades South Vietnam, beginning the Vietnam War. The conflict lasts until 1975. An estimated 13,000 Hawai'i residents serve.

1957—Four Air Force members are killed when their six-jet B-47 bomber flying at 400 miles per hour crashes into a Wai'anae Range mountainside.

1959—The *Swordfish* becomes the first nuclear submarine to homeport in Pearl Harbor.

1991, January 17—Operation Desert Storm begins in the Persian Gulf in response to Iraq's invasion of Kuwait on August 2, 1989. The war eventually requires the services of more than 7,000 Kāne'ohe based troops before Iraq accepts on April 7, 1990 United Nations conditions and resolutions.

1993—A federal commission votes to close the Barbers Point site. It is returned to the state in 1999.

1993—Kaua'i's Pacific Missile Range Facility begins conducting STARS missile tests.

1994—The Korean-Vietnam War Memorial is dedicated at Hawai'i's State Capitol.

2001, Feb 9—The U.S.S. *Greeneville* submarine collides offshore of O'ahu with the *Ehime Maru,* a Japanese fishery high school training ship. The collision sinks the *Ehime Maru* killing nine of its crew members. The *Greeneville* had been performing an emergency surfacing maneuver as a demonstration for civilian visitors when the collision occurred.

2003, March 9—The U.S.S. *Cheyenne,* a Pearl Harbor-based submarine, launches the first Tomahawk missile to begin the second Iraq War. The target is a bunker believed to be the location of Iraqi President Saddam Hussein.

2004, July—The biennial Rim of the Pacific (RIMPAC) naval exercises take place in Hawaiian waters from June 29 to July 27 involving more than 35 ships, 90 aircraft, 7 submarines and 11,000 soldiers, airmen, sailors, Marines, and Coast Guard. RIMPAC began in 1971.

2012, May 11—Three thousand soldiers of the 25th Infantry Division's Third Brigade Combat Teams are welcomed home from a year-long mission in a parade at Hawai'i's Schofield Barracks. Thousands of Hawai'i troops are still stationed in Afghanistan including 1,200 Kāne'ohe-based marines and 2,000 25th Combat Aviation Brigade soldiers.

2012, May 24—The 3rd Marine Regiment at Marine Corps Base Hawai'i celebrates their homecoming from Operation Enduring Freedom and rededicates their regimental battle colors marking the end of the regiment's combat operations in Iraq and Afghanistan. Since 2004, 217 3rd Regiment Marines have died in combat.

HISTORIC WAIKĪKĪ/EARLY TOURISM

Waikīkī means "Spouting water," a reminder that in ancient times the region was more than 2,000 acres of wetlands and marshes. The entire area was a vast drainage basin for the Koʻolau Mountain Range. Early Hawaiians settlers converted the marshland into loko iʻa (fishponds), loʻi kalo (taro patches), and other agricultural uses. Fertile and productive, the lands of Waikīkī were fed by the waters of the Mānoa and Makiki Valleys.

1795—Kamehameha the Great's war canoes land at Waikīkī culminating in the Battle of Nuʻuanu.

1893—The Sans Souci Hotel opens in Waikīkī along the shoreline of Kapiʻolani Park, hosting Robert Louis Stevenson for a five week visit during which he does some of his best writing. In the hotel guest book he writes, "If anyone desires such old-fashioned things as lovely scenery, quiet, pure air, clean sea water, good food, and heavenly sunsets hung out before their eyes over the Pacific and the distant hills of Waianae, I recommend him cordially to the Sans Souci."

1901, March 11—The Moana Hotel opens becoming the tallest building in Hawaiʻi. Designed by architect Oliver Green Traphagen for Matson Navigation Company, the 75-room hotel is known as the "First Lady of Waikīkī." Fifteen years later, the hotel adds 100 more rooms as well as a seaside courtyard. In 1920 King George V of the United Kingdom and Edward Prince of Wales stay at the hotel.

The tram line and hotel construction begin the process of popularizing Waikīkī as a resort destination. Waikīkī gradually becomes a place of quiet palm-lined beaches where the wealthy built summer gingerbread-trimmed cottages. It is also home to Hawaiian royalty, and is considered a place of healing, peace, and hospitality.

1907—Plans are made to develop tourism and commercial properties in Waikīkī, including street-widening and bridge building.

This peaceful beach scene, looking toward Diamond Head, was taken long before Waikīkī became a mecca for Hawaiʻi's visitors. In simpler days it was a quiet strip of coconut palm-lined beach. Hawaiian royalty and well-to-do citizens kept beach cottages in Waikīkī as hideaways from the cares of everyday life. [Hawaiʻi State Archives]

This aerial view of Waikīkī in the 1920s shows (from left to right) the Outrigger Canoe Club, ʻĀpuakēhau Stream emptying into the sea, the Moana Hotel with its pier, and the homes of the Hustace and Steiner families. Waikīkī was still a rural district with farms and acres of tropical foliage. [Steiner Collection]

1919-1928—The Ala Wai Canal is constructed, and the marshlands of Waikīkī are drained. The project is financed with funds provided by the Waikīkī Reclamation Project. The prominent waterway runs for 25 blocks separating Waikīkī from Honolulu. Filling Waikīkī's duck ponds, taro patches, rice paddies, and marshland with coral rubble creates some of Hawaiʻi's most valuable real estate.

1926, September 25—Aloha Tower opens on the waterfront at Honolulu Harbor, becoming Hawai'i's first skyscraper and tallest building. Designed by architect Arthur Reynolds, the square-shaped tower stands 184 feet, 2 inches high with a domed cupola with balconied openings and topped with a 40-foot flagstaff and seven-ton clock. Each side of the tower has a clock face and the word "Aloha."

1927, February 1—The Royal Hawaiian Hotel opens in Waikīkī with the Royal Hawaiian Band playing for 1,200 guests. Nicknamed the "Pink Palace of the Pacific," the Moorish-style hotel begins the restructuring of Waikīkī's coastline. The hotel cost $4 million and features elegant chandeliers, high ceilings, pink stucco walls and pink turrets. Its owner, the Matson Navigation Company, also builds a $7.5-million premier cruise ship, the *Malolo,* holding up to 650 passengers to provide luxurious transportation to the fine new hotel. The opening of Aloha Tower and the Royal Hawaiian Hotel increased Waikīkī's reputation as a playground for the rich and famous.

Waikīkī supported widespread wetland agriculture. Banana, rice, and taro fileds border Waikīkī Road (presently Kalākaua Avenue) near its intersection with McCully Street. 1898. [Baker-Van Dyke Collection]

This 1929 aerial shows the Royal Hawaiian Hotel (left), and the Moana Hotel (right). Waikīkī Beach originally stretched from Hale Kai at the mauka-'ewa end of the old causeway, to what became Fort DeRussy. The causeway gradually disappeared and sea walls and groynes had to be installed to collect and hold the remaining sand. [Baker-Van Dyke Collection]

The end of the mule-drawn tramcar line, located at the expansive bridge where the present Kapahulu Avenue meets Kalākaua Avenue, late 1880s. The sign above reads, "Driving faster than a walk over the bridge will be prosecuted according to the law." [Baker-Van Dyke Collection]

The western-most end of Waikīkī Beach would be the future site of the Hilton Hawaiian Village. 1920. [Baker-Van Dyke Collection]

TSUNAMIS

1837, November 7—One of Hawai'i's first recorded tsunamis generated near Chile hits Kahului, Maui killing 15 people in Kahului and destroying one hundred houses in Hilo.

1868, April 2—Nearly every European-style home in the Ka'ū district of Hawai'i Island is destroyed when an earthquake measuring 8.0 on the Richter scale causes a mudslide and localized tsunami. The mud flow buries a village killing 40 people in all. The tsunami kills another 48 people when water surges ashore up to 60 feet high sweeping away the ancient village of 'Āpua in Puna.

1877, May 9—A large earthquake occurs near Peru resulting in a tsunami that arrives in Hilo before dawn killing 45 people and destroying 37 houses.

1901—An 8.0 earthquake on the Tonga Trench generates a four-foot high tsunami that hits Kailua-Kona, but causes only minor damage.

1918—A five-foot high tsunami arrives in Hilo doing little damage.

1923, February 23—An earthquake in the Aleutian Islands generates a tsunami that causes waves more than 20 feet high to hit the Waiākea area of Hilo and also causes significant damage in Kahului, Maui.

1946, April 1—An earthquake in the Aleutian Islands generates a tsunami that kills 159 people in Hilo and Laupāhoehoe on Hawai'i Island, and also hits Maui and Kaua'i. The tsunami destroys 500 buildings in Hilo, damages another 1,000 other structures, and kills 96 people. The third tsunami wave, the biggest of some 15 waves that sweep inland, also kills and destroys property. Water surges as high as 56 feet above sea level in some places and more than 33 feet above sea level in Hilo. The tsunami causes an estimated $26 million damage, including railroads, bridges, piers and ships. Other Hawai'i Island coastal areas are affected including Laupāhoehoe where 24 people are killed. The tsunami also kills 17 people on Kaua'i, 13 on Maui, and six on O'ahu.

1957, March 9—An earthquake in the Aleutian Islands generates a tsunami that destroys 75 homes on Kaua'i's north shore.

1960, May 22—A large earthquake generated near Chile, 6,600 miles from the Hawaiian Islands moves a piece of land the size of California 30 feet in just minutes. About 15 hours later, on the morning of May 23, Hilo is hit by at least seven significant tsunami waves over a two-hour period. The third wave is the most destructive creating a bore in Hilo Bay that rushes ashore over a four-mile section of the Hilo waterfront at a speed of more than 37 miles per hour and surging water as high as 36 feet above sea level. The tsunami kills 61 people and destroys 229 homes and 308 public buildings and businesses.

1964—One of North America's largest earthquakes ever recorded occurs in Alaska registering a magnitude of 8.4 on the Richter scale generating tsunami waves that cause flooding in Kahului, Maui, and Hilo.

1975, November 29—Two strong earthquakes shake the southeast region of Hawai'i Island, causing a small eruption of Kīlauea Volcano and generating a localized tsunami that comes ashore near the site of an old Hawaiian village, now a campground area called Halapē. The ground in the area sinks some twelve feet and rocks fall from the cliffs above. The tsunami wave sweeps campers onto a rugged lava field and washes some of them into a huge crack in the lava killing two and injuring many more.

1986—A tsunami warning in Honolulu causes massive traffic jams, but turns out to be a false alarm.

2010, February 27—An 8.8-magnitude earthquake in Chile triggers a tsunami warning for Hawai'i. The Islands report minimal resulting damage.

2011, March 10—An 8.8-magnitude earthquake near Honshu, Japan generates a tsunami that reaches Hawai'i. Kaua'i suffers significant structural damage while Japan experiences devastation including a death toll of over 10,000.

2012, October 27—A 7.7-magnitude earthquake near the Queen Charlotte Islands of British Columbia, Canada activates a tsunami warning for the Hawaiian Islands. No major damage is reported, though the tsunami evacuation halts Chinatown's annual Hallowbaloo party.

Earthquakes, landslides and volcanic eruptions all may cause tsunamis which have killed more people in Hawai'i than all other natural disasters combined. A typical tsunami has a wave length of 50 to 300 miles, with some wavelengths exceeding 465 miles. A tsunami can travel across the ocean at about 475 miles per hour—the deeper the ocean, the faster the tsunami travels. The time it takes one complete wave to pass a given point is known as the wave's period, and a typical tsunami may have a period from 9 to 30 minutes.

SELECT BIBLIOGRAPHY/FURTHER READING

Adler, Jacob and Robert M. Kamins, *The Fantastic Life of Walter Murray Gibson: Hawaii's Minister of Everything* (Honolulu: University of Hawai'i Press, 1986).

Bingham, Hiram, *Twenty-one Year Residence in the Sandwich Islands* (Rutland, Vt.: C. Tuttle Co., 1981).

Bird, Isabella, *Six Months in the Sandwich Islands* (Honolulu: Mutual Publishing, 1998).

Brown, DeSoto, *Hawaii Goes to War: Life in Hawaii from Pearl Harbor to Peace* (Honolulu: Editions Limited, 1989).

Bushnell, O.A. and Hanley, Sister Mary Laurence, *Pilgrimage and Exile: Mother Marianne of Moloka'i* (Honolulu: Mutual Publishing, 2009).

Cahill, Emmett, *The Dark Decade 1829–1839 Anti-Catholic Persecutions in Hawai'i* (Honolulu: Mutual Publishing, 2004).

Chinen, Jon J., *The Great Mahele: Hawaii's Land Division of 1848* (Honolulu: University of Hawai'i Press, 1958).

Clemens, Samuel, *Mark Twain in Hawaii* (Honolulu: Mutual Publishing, 1990).

Coffman, Tom, *Nation Within: The Story of America's Annexation of the Nation of Hawai'i* (Kāne'ohe: Tom Coffman/ Epicenter, n.d.).

Committee on the 90th Anniversary Celebration of Korean Immigration to Hawaii, *Their Footsteps: A Pictorial History of Koreans in Hawai'i Since 1903* (Honolulu: 1993).

Cordy, Ross H., *Exalted Sits the Chief: The Ancient History of Hawai'i Island* (Honolulu: Mutual Publishing, 2000).

Daws, Gavan, *Hawaii 1959–1989: The First Thirty Years of the Aloha State with Memorable Photographs from The Honolulu Advertiser* (Honolulu: Publishers' Group Hawaii, 1989).

————, *Honolulu: The First Century, the Story of the Town to 1876* (Honolulu: Mutual Publishing, 2006).

————, *Shoal of Time: A History of the Hawaiian Islands* (Honolulu: University of Hawai'i Press, 1968).

Day, A. Grove, *A Biographical Dictionary: History Makers of Hawaii* (Honolulu: Mutual Publishing, 1984).

Desha, Stephen L., translated by Frazier, Frances N., *Kamehameha and his Warrior Kekūhaupi'o.* (Honolulu: Kamehameha Schools Press, 2000).

Dukas, Neil Bernard, *A Military History of Sovereign Hawai'i* (Honolulu: Mutual Publishing, 2004).

————, *A Pocket Guide to the Battle of Nu'uanu 1796* (Honolulu: Mutual Publishing, 2010).

Ellis, William, *Polynesian Researches: Hawaii, The Journal of William Ellis* (Rutland, Vt.: C. Tuttle Co., 1984).

Feher, Joseph, *Hawaii: A Pictorial History* (Honolulu: Bishop Museum Press, 1969).

Forbes, David W., *Encounters with Paradise: Views of Hawaii and Its People, 1778–1941* (Honolulu: Honolulu Academy of Arts, 1992).

Fornander, Abraham, *Ancient History of the Hawaiian People to the Times of Kamehameha I* (Honolulu: Mutual Publishing, 1996).

Fuchs, Lawrence H., *Hawaii Pono: A Social History* (N.Y.: Harcourt, Brace and World, 1968).

Grant, Glen, Bennett Hymer, and the Bishop Museums Archives, *Hawai'i Looking Back: An Illustrated History of the Islands* (Honolulu: Mutual Publishing, 2000).

Handy, Emory, Bryan, Buck, Wise and Others, *Ancient Hawaiian Civilization: A Series of Lectures Delivered at the Kamehameha Schools.* Mutual Publishing: Honolulu, Hawai'i, 1999.

Handy, E.S. Craighill, and Elizabeth Green Handy, with the collaboration of Mary Kawena Pukui, *Native Planters in Old Hawaii: Their Life, Lore, and Environment.* (Honolulu: Bishop Museum Press, 1972).

Handy, E.S. Craighill and Mary Kawena Pukui, *The Polynesian Family System in Kau, Hawaii* (Honolulu: Mutual Publishing, 1998).

Hawai'i State Data Book (Honolulu: Mutual Publishing, 2012).

Helena, G. Allen, *The Betrayal of Liliuokalani: Last Queen of Hawai'i: 1838-1917* (Honolulu: Mutual Publishing, 1982).

Hibbard, Don and David Franzen, *The View from Diamond Head: Royal Residence to Urban Resort* (Honolulu: Editions Limited, 1986).

Holmes, Tommy, *The Hawaiian Canoe* (Honolulu: Editions Limited, 1981).

Ii, John Papa, *Fragments of Hawaiian History* (Honolulu: Bishop Museum Press, 1959).

Joesting, Edward, *Kauai: The Separate Kingdom* (Honolulu: University of Hawai'i Press and Kauai Museum Association, Limited, 1984).

Bibliography

Judd, Laura Fish, *Honolulu: Sketches of the Life, Social, Political and Religious in the Hawaiian Islands, 1828 to 1861* (Honolulu: *Honolulu Star-Bulletin*, 1928).

Judd, Walter, *Hawai'i Joins the World.* (Honolulu: Mutual Publishing, 1998).

Juvik, Sonia P. and James O. Juvik, eds., *Atlas Of Hawai'i,* 3rd edition (Honolulu: University of Hawai'i Press, 1998).

Kamakau, Samuel M., *Ka Poe Kahiko: The People of Old* (Honolulu: Bishop Museum Press, 1964).

Kanahele, George, *Hawaiian Music and Musicians: An Illustrated History* (Honolulu: University of Hawai'i Press, 1979).

Kāne, Herb Kawainui, *Ancient Hawai'i* (Captain Cook, Hawai'i: The Kawainui Press, 1997).

King, Pauline N., ed., *Journal of Stephen Reynolds, Vol. I: 1823-29* (Honolulu: Ku Pa'a Publishing, 1989).

Kirch, Patrick V., *Feathered Gods and Fishhooks: An Introduction to Hawaiian Archaeology and Prehistory* (Honolulu: University of Hawai'i Press, 1985).

Kirch, Patrick V., and Sahlins, Marshall, *Anahulu: The Anthropology of History in the Kingdom of Hawaii. Volume One: Historical Ethnography* (Chicago and London: The University of Chicago Press, 1992).

Kuykendall, Ralph S., *The Hawaiian Kingdom*, 3 vols. (Honolulu: University of Hawai'i Press, 1938-1967).

Kwiatkowski, P. F., *Na Ki'i Pohaku: A Hawaiian Petroglyph Primer* (Honolulu: Ku Pa'a Publishing, 1991).

Lili'uokalani, Queen, *Hawaii's Story by Hawaii's Queen* (Honolulu: Mutual Publishing, 1991).

Lum, Arlene, ed., *Sailing for the Sun: The Chinese in Hawaii 1789–1989* (Honolulu: University of Hawai'i Press, 1988).

Malo, David, *Hawaiian Antiquities: Mo'olelo Hawai'i.* Bernice P. Bishop Museum Special Publication 2 (Honolulu: Bishop Museum, 1951).

Odo, Franklin and Kazuko Sinoto, *A Pictorial History of the Japanese in Hawai'i 1885–1924* (Honolulu: Bishop Museum Press, 1985).

Ogawa, Dennis M. with the assistance of Glen Grant, *Kodomo No Tame Ni: The Japanese American Experience in Hawaii* (Honolulu: University of Hawai'i Press, 1978).

'Onipa'a: Five Days in the History of the Hawaiian Nation (Honolulu: Office of Hawaiian Affairs, 1994).

Peek, Jeannette Murray, *Stepping into Time: A Guide to Honolulu's Historic Landmarks* (Honolulu: Mutual Publishing, 1994).

Piercy, LaRue W., *Hawaii's Missionary Saga: Sacrifice and Godliness in Paradise* (Honolulu: Mutual Publishing, 1992).

Pukui, Mary Kawena, *'Ōlelo No'eau: Hawaiian Proverbs & Poetical Sayings* (Honolulu: Bishop Museum Press, 1983).

Pukui, Mary Kawena, Samuel Elbert and Esther T. Mo'okini, *Place Names of Hawaii* (Honolulu: University of Hawai'i Press, 1974).

Pukui, Mary Kawena and Samuel H. Elbert, *Hawaiian Dictionary: Hawaiian-English, English-Hawaiian,* rev. ed. (Honolulu: University of Hawaii Press, 1986).

Rose, Roger G., *Hawai'i: The Royal Isles* (Honolulu: Bishop Museum Press, 1980).

Sahlins, Marshall, Anahulu: T*he Anthropology of History in the Kingdom of Hawai'i* (Chicago: The University of Chicago Press, 1992).

Scott, E.B., *The Saga of the Sandwich Islands* (Lafayette: Sierra-Tahoe Publishing, 1968).

Seiden, Allan, *Hawai'i: The Royal Legacy* (Honolulu: Mutual Publishing, 1992).

Sinclair, Marjorie, *Nahi'ena'ena: Sacred Daughter of Hawai'i—A Life Ensnared* (Honolulu: Mutual Publishing, 1995).

Stannard, David, *Before the Horror: The Population of Hawaii on the Eve of Western Contact* (Honolulu: SSRI, 1989).

Takaki, Ronald, *Pau Hana: Plantation Life and Labor in Hawai'i* (Honolulu: University of Hawai'i Press, 1983).

Teodoro, Luis V. Jr., *Out of This Struggle: The Filipinos in Hawai'i* (Honolulu: University of Hawai'i Press, 1981).

United States Army, Assistant Chief of Staff for Military Intelligence, *Digest of Information: The Hawaiian Department and the Territory of Hawaii* (January 1, 1930).

Webb, Nancy, & Webb, Jean Francis, *Kaiulani: Crown Princess of Hawai'i* (Honolulu: Mutual Publishing, 1998).

Wichman, Frederick B., *Kaua'i—Ancient Place Names and Their Stories* (Honolulu: University of Hawai'i Press, 1998).

For more detailed information, refer to our Hawaiian Encyclopedia.

http://www.hawaiianencyclopedia.com/chapter-11.asp
http://www.hawaiianencyclopedia.com/chapter-12.asp
http://www.hawaiianencyclopedia.com/chapter-13.asp

INDEX

Red bolded page numbers indicate photo.

Index

Index

Index